Gower
Handbook
of Library and
Information Management

GOWER HANDBOOK OF LIBRARY AND INFORMATION MANAGEMENT

edited by Ray Prytherch

Gower

Published by
Gower Publishing Company Limited
Gower House
Croft Road
Aldershot
Hants GU11 3HR
England

Gower
Old Post Road
Brookfield
Vermont 05036
USA

British Library Cataloguing in Publication Data
Gower handbook of library and information management
    1. Library administration – Handbooks, manuals, etc.
    2. Information services – Management – Problems, exercises, etc.
I. Prytherch, Ray II. Handbook of library and information management
025.1

ISBN 0–566–08052–4

Library of Congress Cataloguing-in-Publication Data
Gower handbook of library and information management / edited by Raymond John Prytherch.
      p.   cm.
    Includes index.
    ISBN 0-566-08052-4
    1. Library administration – Great Britain.   2. Information services – Great Britain – Management.   I. Prytherch, Raymond John.
    Z678.8.G7G8   1998
    025.1–dc21   98-7776
                                                   CIP

Typeset in Sheffield by Peter Stubley and printed in Great Britain by MPG Books Ltd, Bodmin, Cornwall

Contents

List of figures

Notes on contributors

Terry Beck (*The technological future – an overview*) works for EARL, concentrating on the Familia directory on the World Wide Web, after several years teaching at the University of North London where he had developed his interest in information storage, delivery and access in the digital environment. He also works as a trainer and consultant. He is a Chartered Librarian and a member of the British Computer Society.

Jo Bryson (*Financial planning*) has held senior management positions in the library, information and information technology sector at local, state and international government levels. She has lectured in library and information centre management, information use and information technology, and has presented papers at national and international conferences. She is Assistant Secretary, Strategic Directions Group, Department of Communications and Advanced Technology, Northern Territory Government, Australia. She has also been a Councillor for her local government authority and when not writing information and management textbooks, enjoys artistic pursuits, travelling and meeting people of different cultures in her spare time. Her latest book *Managing information services: an integrated approach* has recently been published by Gower.

Graham Cornish (*Copyright and related issues*) studied theology and history at Durham and library and information science in Liverpool before joining the (now) British Library in 1969. He has held a variety of posts in different parts of the Library ranging from storage and retrieval to administration and research. Since 1983 he has been responsible for copyright issues within the BL and since 1986 has managed much of the BL involvement in IFLA for whom he acts as Director of the Universal Availability of Publications Programme. He is a member of the UK Library Association Council and Chair of the International Sub-Committee. He has been elected a Fellow of both the Library Association and the Institute of Information Scientists. He has published numerous journal articles and nine monographs, especially on copyright, document supply, audio-visual materials, services to the visually impaired and national libraries. He is closely involved in several EU projects on electronic copyright management and advises some EC departments on copyright issues.

Feona Hamilton (*Information auditing* and *The intranet as an information management tool*) is a freelance consultant and writer, and an expert in electronic publishing and knowledge management. She is the author of four books and many articles and has also designed and run training courses on these and related subjects. She is a Director of the Electronic Information Publishers Group and a member of the Society of Authors.

John Pluse (*Human resource management*) is a freelance Training and Organizational Development Adviser, researcher, writer and editor; he was formerly Assistant City Librarian of Bradford, UK. He is Chair of the Library Association Personnel, Training and Education Group, and editor of its journal, *Personnel, training and education*. He has written and given conference papers on a wide range of human resource topics, and clients for his consultancy services have included the public libraries of Cumbria, Herefordshire, Powys, Renfrew and Shropshire, local authorities in Middlesbrough, Newham and Wolverhampton, and a number of health authorities.

Ray Prytherch (*An introduction: definition and trends, Scanning the environment: trends and pressures, Strategic planning: the key to managing change, Research: the infrastructure for improvement and change* and *Strategic management*) is an Information Consultant specializing in Information Management, editorial and bibliographic services, and training. He is the editor of the monthly newsletter *Information management report*, and has been responsible for several titles published by Gower: *Harrod's librarians' glossary* (8th ed.; 1995 – 9th ed. to be published 1999), *Information management and library science: a guide to the literature, Handbook of library co-operation,* and the two-volume *Handbook of library training practice*. He was co-author of the British Library Research and Innovation Report *Research in public libraries* (1996).

Priscilla Schlicke (*Preservation, access and integrity, Disasters: prevention, rescue and recovery* and *Electronic publishing*) is an independent information consultant, and concentrates on training, database management and research. She has written extensively on electronic publishing and preservation issues. After an early career in the United States, she later became Senior Lecturer in the School of Information and Media at the Robert Gordon University, Aberdeen, and was Course Leader for the honours degree in Publishing Studies.

Colin Steele (*New paradigms in access and delivery*) is University Librarian at the Australian National University in Canberra, a position he has held since 1980. Prior to that date he was Deputy Librarian of the Australian National University from 1976–1980 and Assistant Librarian at the Bodleian Library, Oxford 1967–1976. He is the author/editor of a number of books including *English interpreters of the Iberian New World, Major libraries of the world* (1976) and *Changes in scholarly communication patterns* with Professor D. J. Mulvaney (1993) and over three hundred articles and reviews. He is on the Board of a number of international journals, including *The electronic library* and *The journal of librarianship and information science*. He has been an invited *xv* speaker at a number of major library and IT conferences in the USA, UK, South Africa and China and in 1995 he gave the Follett Lectures in the UK, the first Australian speaker to deliver this prestigious series.

Peter Stubley (*Customer care for libraries: accident or design?* and *Closing the information net: gateways, brokers and Z39.50*) is Sub-Librarian with responsibility for management of St George's Library, one of the major branch libraries of Sheffield University Library, which offers services to the Faculty of Engineering and the Management School. In addition to the development of library services to this client group, his main professional interests include library building design – St George's Library was opened in January 1992 as a showpiece building – and research into multimedia applications and the use of Z39.50. He is currently involved in the EU UNIverse project and the JISC-funded RIDING project which, over the next two years, will be building a Z39.50 gateway to Yorkshire libraries. He has written two books and contributed widely to the journal and conference literature.

Lawraine Wood (*Performance measurement and evaluation*) has had over 18 years of professional experience which includes work in the public, academic and special library fields. She is a self-employed trainer and consultant in information management, and immediately prior to that was a lecturer at the Robert Gordon University in Aberdeen. During 1989–91 she was a Library Association Councillor and at the same time was a member of the LA Employment Committee and the Special Libraries Sub-Committee. In 1991–92 she was the Newsletter Editor of ADLG News, and then the Chairman of the Aerospace and Defence Librarian's Group. She has published in the professional press, undertaken editorial work and spoken at conferences. Whilst at the Robert Gordon University, she taught ILS management and developed a particular interest in performance measurement in libraries and information services.

Part I
THE CONTEXT

An introduction: definition and trends

Ray Prytherch

This Handbook is devoted to Library and Information Management: this we define as the set of processes and behaviours that make up the effective production, co-ordination, storage, retrieval, analysis, evaluation, dissemination and use of information. The sources of information depend on the context of the information service: public and academic libraries are one contextual domain, commercial and corporate services represent another.

The role of information may be supportive of a learning or teaching process, or may be the raw material from which researchers synthesize advanced work; in the commercial context, the role may feature added-value components that feed into the management of the company or organization. The 'output' of various kinds of information management processes may be a library service, a knowledge management methodology, a learning resource base, a bureau offering database access, an Internet-based information resource – the imagination is the only limit to what can be done with information and expertise.

The 'products' of information management may be online databases, push-technology services, advice and support services, or even a library with a bookstock for self-service. Everyone in the information professions uses similar sets of skills; complexity varies, customers are different, purposes may vary, constraints will apply, finance must be managed, staff must be trained and developed – but the skills are set on the same basis, and they are:

- generation of information: where does it come from, how to collect it, how to organize it, how to structure it, how to make it accessible
- management and use of information: planning, marketing, evaluation, needs assessment
- systems and communications: how technology supports activities, and the problems and opportunities
- analysis of the environment: professional, legal, governmental policies, international developments, technology trends
- management skills: human resources, finance, statistics, project management, training, formation of strategic partnerships.

Garai (1997) identifies six roles for the information manager:

- the prospector
- the refiner
- the processor
- the cleanser
- the transporter
- the communicator.

Everything the information manager does is governed by questions of purpose, of accessibility, of evaluation, and of communication.

Several buzzwords are prevalent, and they matter because the image of the information profession is tarnished by lack of finesse and lack of promotional skills; the buzzwords are the jargon terms of the media and we can exploit our skills in these new fields. Networks – particularly of course the Internet – multimedia, privacy, piracy, security, cost, convergence are all information-related buzzwords that we would be wrong to ignore.

In the UK, activity in recent years shows us where the emphasis of the new reality lies; Phillips (1997) draws up a shopping list of areas needing attention as the Information Society approaches:

- universal access
- retrieval and navigation software
- security
- verification
- copyright
- information quality
- undesirable material
- legal responsibilities of online suppliers
- payment.

In the UK, the Follett Report (Joint Funding Councils, 1993) gave a huge impetus to the academic library sector; the Electronic Libraries Programme (eLib) – established by the Joint Information Systems Committee as a response to Follett and engaging the whole higher education community – represents a massive investment in the investigation of applications of new technologies. The latest UK move has been the publication of the Library and Information Commission Report (1997) which addresses the new roles that public libraries might play in the next century.

Yet the technological future is not everything; distinguished authors with impeccable 'technical' backgrounds warn that 'virtual libraries' are not just round the corner – whatever they can offer, they are expensive and socially undesirable (Crawford and Gorman, 1995); the potential of the Internet may be vast, but so are the limitations and the drawbacks – Bosseau (1995) unveils a future which brings back master print copies to ensure that scholarship does not become lost in a flood of dross.

Commentators in the professional press may rehearse the same arguments about the future of the profession, the future role of librarians, the need to change and adapt; whilst nothing in that may be fresh, some recent evidence does show us that a new maturity is slowly evolving. Out of the apathy on one side, and the harassed scrabbling for action on the other, comes a positive sense that the information profession does have a role – the world is coming to us and we need to be ready to slot ourselves into it.   5

One attitude (change now or die) 'feeds the identity crisis, resulting in stasis'; another attitude (huge opportunities for the entrepreneur) 'tends to ignore the organizational and cultural constraints in which the individual works – constraints which can stifle initiative and promote a climate of fear, inhibiting change and growth' (Garrod, 1997).

The convergence of various 'information'-related worlds of work does indeed signal opportunity and the tables of skills that Garrod offers show the match between employer requirements and our capabilities. TFPL's survey of job advertisements (Abell, 1997) backs up this view; we have skills in presentation and communication, systems and IT; sector knowledge; creativity and innovation; research analysis; team work; training skills – just the skills that employers are looking for. But the jobs that the survey noted as being advertised were not for librarians or information managers, just information-related in some way.

Abell comments: 'arguably traditional skills are becoming more valuable than ever before as the management of information increasingly underpins organisations and society'. She notes that '*the* new skill is the understanding of how to apply them [information skills] for maximum impact'. We shall soon see how much further management experts can go along the road that leads towards 'knowledge management', and this is the direction that we should be looking if we want to be abreast of the next information development.

The 'intellectual capital' of an organization has been discussed for years, but the latest software innovations, and particularly intranets, give a real chance to share knowledge within the organization; all that holds the process back is resistant cultures. If the management pundits highlight knowledge management, then we should adapt ourselves to the new jargon; our strength is in the techniques of storage and retrieval of knowledge – and the skill of applying them for maximum impact. Maybe our low profile comes from too much emphasis on support roles, and not enough emphasis on actually using our own skills to do the job ourselves.

There are gaps in what we know, but these are not too difficult to bridge. Mount (1997) compiles relevant studies of opportunities, and one of these particularly identifies five pointers to positive personal growth:

- be alert to changing technologies
- training, education, and experience should be planned
- flexibility is crucial
- vigilance and adaptability are needed
- personal networking is essential: the best opportunities and leads come from professional contacts and chat.

We have to be confident that we can do new jobs; seeking out our own training requirements and finding our feet in the new information universe are practical actions that we can readily plan and manage for ourselves. An initial, positive step we can take is to examine our own training needs; Biddiscombe (1997) discusses how IT has changed our jobs, and outlines the essential elements that form part of current training packages. He stresses the importance of basic computing skills, e-mail familiarity, Internet searching skills, Web page creation and editing skills, experience of CD-ROM interfaces, access to online publications, and knowledge of bibliographical management packages – in addition to our interpersonal and presentational skills and an understanding of learning techniques.

'Publishing, editing, translating, database creation, computing, graphics, teaching and learning, librarianship and information science; all are being forced into new and closer relationships through technological change' (Biddiscombe). Everybody is in the same stressed condition; the key difference is that information professionals have more skills, better quality skills, and more relevant skills to sort out a role in the emerging world.

The purpose of this Handbook is to provide a link between information professionals and the new world of information-related work. Readers of the book are profiled as librarians, information industry personnel, document managers, records managers, archivists, network specialists, and others in the information chain such as publishers and information providers. The Handbook will also have a role in the teaching and learning of information management, and in the continuing professional development of personnel.

The Handbook is expected to be seen as a standard, comprehensive text, presenting a picture of good current practice – but with a regard to likely future trends. In particular, four key areas have been stressed throughout:

- customer focus
- markets for services, and marketing strategies
- quality assurance
- applications coming into use through the emerging infrastructure.

The selection of topics for coverage represents a range of concerns that are of general applicability. Not everything can be included in one volume, and our aim has been to offer a comprehensive picture without significant omissions; future editions will fill out new areas and give updated chapters. Although the Handbook is a British production, the intention is to appeal to an international readership.

The contributors have been selected for their recognized knowledge of the topic for coverage, and their background of work and location has been of secondary importance. In a professional world where globalization and collaboration are assuming crucial importance, and new ways of working will make conventional careers a thing of the past, it seemed vital to draw together experts from varied services and with different career patterns, to build a resource that would be relevant to as wide a readership as possible. Authors write in different styles, and we have not chosen to impose an artificial standard style on the contributions.

The structure of the Handbook falls into four main parts:

- strategy and planning (three chapters)
- the service infrastructure (four chapters)
- managing resources (five chapters)
- access and delivery (four chapters).

8   These are preceded by an introductory chapter that analyses the

technological future – how IT will affect management capabilities, how services will be changed, and how we as information professionals will have to adapt. In an area of such rapid progress, a commentator can write only of today's scene and suggest the ways this may develop. Whatever happens, the earlier we know the directions that are likely, the more effectively we can plan to exploit new positions.

Each of the main parts begins with a shorter introduction, fitting the chapters into a context.

A directory of organizations, a glossary, and an index conclude the volume.

REFERENCES

Abell, A. (1997), New roles? New skills? New people? *Library Association record*, vol. 99, no. 10, (October), pp. 538–539.

Biddiscombe, R. (1997), *Training for IT.* London: Library Association Publishing.

Bosseau, D. (1995), The loss of control and access to recorded history and scientific discovery in the 21st century. *Serials librarian*, vol. 26, no. 1, pp. 23–40.

Crawford, W. and Gorman, M. (1995), *Future libraries: dreams, madness, and reality.* Chicago: American Library Association.

Garai, H. (1997), *Managing information: working smarter not harder.* Aldershot: Gower.

Garrod, P. (1997), New skills for information professionals. *Information UK outlooks*, no. 22, (July).

Joint Funding Councils' Libraries Review Group (1993), *Report.* [Chairman: Sir Brian Follett.] Bristol: HEFC.

Library and Information Commission (1997), *New library: the people's network.* London: LIC. (Available at: <http://www.ukoln. ac.uk/services/lic/newlibrary>)

Mount, E. (1997), *Expanding technologies – expanding careers: librarianship in transition.* Washington, DC: Special Libraries Association.

Phillips, *Lord.* (1997), Information society: agenda for action in the UK. *Journal of information science*, vol. 23, no. 1, pp. 1–8.

1 The technological future – an overview

Terry Beck

The person who sets out to delineate future events must tread carefully. The past is littered with predictions which were proved to be incorrect by the passing of time. The problem with forecasting is that the bright beacons of existing technology tend to illuminate a linear path into the future. None of the beacons will show the sudden leaps which are a feature of technological development. Moreover, some of the beacons may turn out, when future becomes present, to have burned, like magnesium, brightly but for only a short time. It is also impossible to foresee those convergences which can markedly influence the information landscape. This is amply demonstrated by the convergence of computers and telecommunications as well as by the convergence of the Internet and hypertext to create the World Wide Web. Even linear developments are difficult to judge accurately. No-one in 1980, not even the pioneers of the new microcomputers, could have guessed their future multimedia potential. Neill (1980) was clearly thinking about text-bound computers when he said, 'I can't see any invasion of the classroom by computers in the next thirty years...'. By contrast, Rochell (1982) suggested that, by the year 2000:

> ...large commercial data bases will... threaten the existence of publishing and libraries as we know them... they may well commission material to meet the demands of their

subscribers, material that will never appear in hard copy, never be 'published' in the traditional sense. It will be available only through the data base that commissioned it.

Rochell correctly predicted the development of digitization but failed to recognize, among other things, the continuing strength of the book as a container of information, and was unable to foresee other significant and sudden developments like the massive growth of the Internet in the early 1990s.

NEW ROLES FOR LIBRARIANS AND PUBLISHERS?

In a situation where the pace of development of the technology threatens to bewilder, the consideration of their objectives by librarians and publishers can help to focus attention on what is really important. The activities of information professionals may change – indeed they have already changed – but what they are trying to achieve remains the same even though the means of achieving it may alter. Kessler (1996) points out that while 'the demand and support for traditional library warehousing activities... is (sic) diminishing quickly... the demand and support for library service activities... are soaring'.

Convergence of job skills will be familiar to academic librarians in the telematic society. The need has gradually developed for individuals possessing skills in information, computing and telecommunications. A number of universities have merged their computing and library services in recognition of the fact that it becomes progressively more difficult to isolate these activities into separate departments. But there is another convergence in progress, and one that has been going on for some time, between publishers and librarians. Neither group will take over the functions of the other but each will face an increasing need to fulfil some of the functions traditionally the sole province of the other group. Publishers, for example, will need to introduce new ways for people to access their material while librarians will find themselves having to evaluate and filter, and add value to material which may not have been through the traditional publication process. In   *11* particular, librarians will have an important role in determining the content of digital archives which will require some of the skills and knowledge of publishers.

At present, activities relating to the content of digital archives are being conducted by a relatively small number of people. Within the UK higher education community, for example, the members of the JISC's (Joint Information Systems Committee's) CEI (Committee for Electronic Information) Content Working Group are taking a leading role. As the demand for, and use of, digital archives grows, however, more librarians will find themselves engaged in this activity. In addition, many librarians already have to make judgements about sources of information on the Internet. Publishers, on the other hand, are already finding themselves having to make their services and some of their publications directly available to members of the public via the World Wide Web. A number of journal publishers deliver their publications electronically and have also established Web sites to promote their services. In addition, librarians and publishers have worked closely within the Pilot Site License Initiative (PSLI) established by the Higher Education Funding Council (HEFC) which aims to encourage the use of electronic journals in UK universities as well as reduce the expense involved in the provision of paper journals.

Fine distinctions will be drawn to create the new roles needed in an increasingly digital, telematic environment. Unproductive activities will be pared away while the activities critical to the task will be strengthened and some new responsibilities will be added. What is likely to emerge from this is a new fragmentation of the relevant professions, and librarians, for example, may never again be as homogeneous a group as they are at present. But those librarians whose role it becomes to work in a largely digital environment will quickly realize that a number of the 'traditional' skills which served them well in a hard-copy world, will also see good use in the new digital information environment. For example, as the amount of information available on the World Wide Web grows, so full text searching becomes an increasingly blunt instrument for finding precisely what is required. Indexing of documents by means of metadata would provide a far more precise means of information retrieval for Web users. And indexing is an area where librarians can claim some expertise.

CHALLENGES IN THE DIGITAL ENVIRONMENT

The World Wide Web

We might isolate as major future information activities such tasks as evaluation, quality control and filtering, selection, organization and dissemination. Each of these, of course, could be decomposed into a subset of additional functions. These activities are thrown into sharp relief by the Internet which demonstrates serious problems of both quality and control as well as of access to required information. The great freedom of the World Wide Web, for example, is that there are no publishers to assess work and no librarians to fit it neatly into a particular category or to impose a set of index terms upon it. The result is to be expected: the Web as an information resource is highly variable containing a large proportion of information of dubious quality or of limited value.

No argument is put forward here for restricting the freedom people have to provide information on Web pages. In addition, a number of excellent resources are available on the World Wide Web. But the development of the means to enable users to gain more precise access to the information they desire will require librarians to exercise their talents in the future. Although the creators and developers of the Web search tools have made great strides, the daily expansion of the World Wide Web threatens to defeat their best efforts. Many opportunities therefore present themselves including the building of directories and the creation of new gateways to information along the lines of OMNI (Organising Medical Networked Information <http://omni.ac.uk>) or SOSIG (Social Science Information Gateway <http://sosig.ac.uk>).

Library sectors

The World Wide Web does not equate to the total digital environment, however, and it is possible, and necessary, to begin to ask   *13* questions about some sacredly held views as one glimpses a future where organized digital data is a significant part of the world's information store. At present we are constrained to consider alternatives for information provision in terms of sectors, commonly the academic and public library sectors. When a need is perceived for joint endeavour, we speak of cross-sectoral agreements whereby each sector works together but retains their distinctive identity. In a situation of limited resources and space, there is an argument for restricting entry to academic libraries. But digital information, by its nature, cannot be scarce since it either exists or it does not exist. Once it exists, it can be made available as often as required to as many people as require it. Similarly, digital information occupies little space and one does not need to be in a particular location in order to be able to access it. Thus, in the context of digital data, it is difficult to see the survival of a distinction between public, academic and other publicly funded libraries.

The problem is exacerbated due to the fact that the ultimate source of money for digital stores of data may come from the public purse. To differentiate between users of publicly funded sources of digital data, therefore, when the scarcity arguments no longer apply, will appear to penalize people for not having the good fortune to belong to a university, for example. It would be as if one arrived at a museum and, on failing to produce evidence that one was a university academic, one was required to pay (or pay more) for entry. This is to oversimplify, perhaps, and there are arguments which might be applied to counter this view. If an academic library forges an agreement with a publisher for the provision of digital information to members of the university which is free at the point of use, this agreement is likely to specify that those outside universities cannot enjoy the same access. Proper authentication procedures would then need to be in place to prevent those outside the academic community from gaining access. The best known method of user authentication within the UK higher education community at present is ATHENS3, developed by NISS (National Information Services and Systems).

Similar considerations apply to the use of the high speed cables connecting academic institutions. SuperJANET protects its academic-only status by arguing that capacity is insufficient to support other users. Nevertheless, the managers of the London MAN (Metropolitan Area Network) – a very fast (155 megabits) telecommunications link connecting academic institutions within the Greater London area – are planning to test the feasibility of its use by public libraries. A small number of London public library authorities may be chosen as test beds in this exercise.

The world we are moving into is one where individuals will need to constantly update skills. People will be required to engage in a process of lifelong learning and the UK government has put its weight behind this idea with the publication of *Connecting the learning society: the National Grid for Learning* (Department for Education and Employment, 1997). Members of the public are unlikely to be clamouring to use university level material in digital stores, especially given the competing services which technology will offer. But there *will* be a need to create stores which are open to all who require access. And in cases where members of the public are the ultimate providers of the money for such stores, they might argue that they should, on request, be granted the same access as university staff and students on request.

Publishing futures

This highlights the important role which publishers will play in the future in ensuring that costs are set at a level to enable librarians, acting individually or in groups, to provide access to users without having to impose direct charges – and this means any users whether they belong to a university or not. Of course, the need for publishers to obtain a fair return for the important work that they will do in providing the material for quality digital data stores is understood. Furthermore, commercial publishers will determine the form in which much information of quality will be provided and will therefore have a strong influence on the extent to which information in digital form will grow in importance. These requirements will demand great skill and not a little marketing acumen from publishing houses which will continue to provide the stamp of authority for information sources.

15

Clearly, copyright and intellectual property rights emerge as topics of importance and these are fully discussed in chapter 8. Those involved in the production and distribution of material are entitled to expect people to pay for the right to use intellectual property. It is well known that, at present, copyright is not strictly observed and this is a problem that affects the income particularly of those publishers concerned with the production and distribution of computer software and films on videotape. The whole area of copyright and the associated matter of data piracy are the subject of intense activity and debate, and a legal framework appropriate to an increasingly digital age is being actively sought.

Digital archives

An area of concern where publishers and librarians will both have a role is in the preservation of digital data. Because of the work done by librarians in the past, historians are able to gain access to much of the material which was published in previous years. Even, for example, much grey literature can be accessed because of the strenuous efforts which have been made to collect and catalogue it. Archivists have also played an invaluable role by ensuring the survival of manuscript collections and making the information in them accessible. But the historian of the future wishing to access the digital output of the late twentieth century might not be as fortunate. Changing technology and the limited life both of magnetic storage and the software that we use, also threaten the survival of digital data. It is essential that we begin to devote resources to tackle this problem now as indicated in chapter 12.

If one considers the World Wide Web, for example, it is in a constant state of change as we find out to our cost when we receive the '404 not found' message from a particular location. There is no snapshot of the Internet taken each day and the pages which disappear may be deleted without much thought being given to their potential future value. As Rothenberg (1995) says, '...the significance of many digital documents – those we consider too unimportant to archive – may become apparent long after they become unreadable'.

THE DEVELOPMENT OF TECHNOLOGY

Computers and memory capacity

In relation to computers, the library and information professions must feel that they are standing on shifting silicon as the technology continues to develop at a relentless pace. Progress is so rapid that current microcomputers are doomed to compare very unfavourably with those which appear in the following year. We consign to museum status machines which are over two years old, even though they are perfectly capable of doing most of the work required by the average user. Software houses constantly (and rightly) produce applications for the next generation of machines, and this speeds up the process of obsolescence.

And there is no sign of any diminution in the speed of development in the foreseeable future. Moore's Law states that the number of transistors able to be placed on a chip will double every 18 months to two years and this will generally lead to a doubling in speed of the device. Microprocessors are predicted to continue to conform to Moore's Law until sometime between 2010 and 2020. Gordon Moore (1997), the creator of the Law, states: 'We can expect to see the performance of our processors double every 18 to 24 months for at least several years'. The practical effect of this is described by Patterson (1995) who pointed out that: '...one desktop computer in 2020 will be as powerful as all the computers in Silicon Valley today'. Similar developments are likely to occur with memory chips so that microcomputer RAM (Random Access Memory) might be in the gigabyte range by the second decade of the twenty-first century.

The storage capacity of magnetic hard disks has increased at an electrifying pace, and looks set to continue its present growth rate. IBM, for example, claim that they have developed the techniques to produce a hard disk offering 55 gigabytes of storage. CD-ROM capacity, however, has remained static since its inception at some 650 megabytes but a new competitor, the DVD-ROM (Digital Versatile Disk-Read Only Memory), has now entered the marketplace providing a storage capacity of from 4.7 to 17 *17* gigabytes. DVD-R (DVD-Recordable) will soon be available which will enable purchasers to create their own DVD-ROMs with a capacity of 3.95 gigabytes. Ten years after the millennium, Toshiba claim that they will be able to produce a disk which will store 1 trillion (US) bits of data or 100 gigabytes.

In relation to data transmission speed, a number of improvements have been made in the provision of high speed connectivity. In the academic arena in the UK for example, SuperJANET III was initiated in late 1997 and this will extend the provision of a high speed backbone and establish new Metropolitan Area Networks (MANs) to improve the speed of transmission between universities. The SuperJANET series seems set to continue, however, as the need for transmission capacity grows along with new users and applications. Demand has a tendency to grow rapidly and overwhelm improved transmission capacity.

Internet access

The one area where progress has been slow relates to access to the Internet (and other digital networks) from home or a small business via modem. Those unfortunate enough to access the Internet in this way are still condemned to suffer very limited speeds. Although 56k (56 kilobits per second) modems became available in 1997, research has shown that such speeds are not attainable in real world environments (see, for example, Hummel, 1997). It is likely that the experience of using the Internet via a modem will remain frustrating and tedious until these issues are resolved.

Limitations in access speed have two serious implications. The first of these is that designers have to limit the size and sophistication of World Wide Web pages thus restricting what can be achieved. The Web remains a rather limited interface partly as a result of this. Secondly, although numbers of Internet users are rising, many people will not be prepared to use a service with a poor performance profile.

It may be true that the UK has one of the most developed communications markets in the world (*Progress through*

18

partnership, 1995), but the share of the market owned by British Telecom (BT) is currently too high and it still retains too much power for a truly competitive market to develop. The UK has signed a European Telecoms Directive which makes it much easier for new companies to enter the telephone and telecommunications market. It means that BT customers will be able to use facilities offered by competing telecoms operators without first having to dial a special number. If one of BT's customers wishes to use, for example, the international facilities of another company, they merely have to inform BT who will then be required to divert the calls via the alternative provider. It is expected to increase the rate at which BT is losing its share of the UK telecommunications market. The concern about the Directive, which will come into force in the year 2000, is that telecommunications providers will not be encouraged to build their own networks because they will be able to use those owned by BT (Europe dials a phone revolution, 1997).

One alternative to modem connection to the telephone system is ISDN2e (Integrated Services Digital Network 2 euro) but even this offers only a maximum 128k throughput which is still inadequate for downloading information from a true multimedia source. It would nevertheless be a considerable improvement for many people but the cost of installation, extra technology and the quarterly rental puts it beyond the reach of most domestic users. BT, however, began trials of its Home Highway service in early 1998. This provides ISDN speeds of access to network services but is dramatically cheaper.

There are other encouraging developments which may markedly improve the price performance ratio for Internet users. Nynex CableComm and Telewest Communications are testing Motorola CyberSURFR cable modems in Manchester and Basildon (in Essex) respectively. These are welcome developments as the cable and satellite companies (in the UK, at least) have been rather slow to offer high speed Internet access to their subscribers.

Some novel options for connection to the telecommunications system are also beginning to appear. NorWeb Communications, for example, began testing high speed access to the Internet via a *19* mains electricity connection in 1998. It is claimed that this makes possible access speeds to the Internet of 1 megabit per second which exceeds ISDN speeds by a factor of almost 8. One interesting service, although it provides no fast connection to the Internet, comes from Ionica which offers a telephone service employing transmission of telephone connections by radio rather than by wires or cable. Ionica's coverage of the UK is still only partial but their network is steadily growing. The mobile telephone industry may make an important contribution in the future, especially if they provide free telephone calls at certain times of the day. The cost of mobile telephone calls in the UK remains at a high level, however, relative to most other countries (Davies, 1997).

FUTURE OF THE BOOK

Hard-copy containers are likely to survive for some considerable time yet. The demise of the book has often been forecast but it has survived all the onslaughts to its primacy thus far. Some containers are of more recent vintage, however, and are fundamentally different from the book in that they require special equipment to access them. In addition, whether you view a film on videotape or via digital television makes little difference to what you see on screen – although the digital television version may offer superior quality. The contents of a book, however, can be accessed without any special equipment other than a pair of spectacles for those who require them. A digital representation of the contents of a book will show the same words and pictures but it requires of the reader the ownership of the paraphernalia of technology and the quality of what is viewed is significantly poorer than print on paper.

For this reason, the book seems to be assured of a future and book publishers and librarians will still have to operate in a hard-copy environment despite the development of digital archives. It is not too difficult to imagine the demise of the videotape, or even the DVD or DVD-ROM, if an environment existed where media such as films, computer games and music could be delivered to television or computer at an acceptable speed. This would require a high speed telecommunications environment and, for maximum choice, connection to a cable system or to a satellite service provider.

In the case of the book, all is not entirely positive. Some types of paper manufacture have unwelcome environmental impacts and books can be heavy and unwieldy. Nevertheless, if a device were announced tomorrow which promised to provide digitally all the advantages of the book, it would still be a long time before it actually began to achieve primacy over the book. Any consideration of new technology shows that from birth to maturity takes about twenty years. It is only when looking back that this phenomenon can be more clearly observed. Even then, the spread of this hypothetical device throughout the population may only be partial and, unless one was prepared to condemn a number of people to a life without information, the book would still be required.

And what a device this replacement for the book would have to be. It would need to be light, portable, waterproof (and be able to float) and very robust. The screen resolution would need to be equal to the resolution of text or graphics on paper. The software would need to recreate the ease of use of the book so that provision would have to be made for mimicking the ability to flick backwards and forwards or to mark places using fingers and thumbs or pieces of paper. Above all, this device would need to be so cheap that purchase would not present a financial problem for any person. It might also be useful if it was an object of beauty and tactile pleasure as these qualities of the book are sometimes extolled. In addition, the device would ideally need to exist in a world of pervasive communications where content could be delivered to a user on demand from any location.

The difficulty of building a device which could challenge the book is why the latter seems likely to retain its primacy as a means of information storage and distribution. But what is already clear, and demonstrated by current trends, is that digital information, access to it, and its delivery will increase in importance. The problem for those providing access to information will be to attempt to determine the content and proportion of information which should be made available in digital form as against in the traditional form of words (and pictures) on paper.

OPPORTUNITIES

Public library roles

A spate of reports appeared in the UK in 1997 including *New library: the people's network* (Library and Information Commission, 1997), *Connecting the learning society: National Grid for Learning* (Department for Education and Employment, 1997) and *The people's lottery* (Department for Culture, Media and Sport, 1997). All of these had a relevance to public librarians in particular and heralded what might be seen as a more positive environment for librarians.

The present UK government appears to be aware of the public library's potential, due to its network of service points throughout the country, to spread an awareness of online information services, particularly the Internet, and to provide access points to online sources for those unable to afford access from their own homes. *New library: the people's network* discussed the future role which public libraries might play in a telematic society and recommended the networking of public libraries. In particular, the Report stressed the need for public libraries to provide the means of access to information via the Internet for members of the public unable or unwilling to have their own connection from home. This partly educational role leads inevitably to the need for training for all those working in public libraries and the Report rightly stressed this. Because the technology will change as the telematic society develops, new skills will constantly be needed by those who work in libraries. Training will need to be continuous, therefore, and will assume a critical position in the future.

Access to information is at the core of the activities of libraries, and decisions must be taken with this at the forefront of all planning. The increase in digital sources of information, and the development of telecommunications technology to allow access to these information sources, extends people's information horizons. The public library has the potential to become the point of departure for those wishing to use global information sources whose circumstances don't allow them access from home.

Electronic libraries

Following publication of the Follett Report (Joint Funding Councils' Libraries Review Group, 1993), the Electronic Libraries Programme, eLib, was set up by the JISC with a budget of £15 million. This money enabled academic libraries to pursue research in areas of digital and online provision. In turn, this research led to some excellent new digital and Internet-based services and accelerated the learning process for many academic librarians. Public librarians did not enjoy the benefits arising from Follett and have, as a result, begun their foray into this world rather later than their academic counterparts. Formal training programmes can help them catch up to a certain extent but academic librarians might have a role to play and could perform a useful function by developing the means whereby some of their experience can be passed on to those working in public libraries. In addition, the government might be wise to consider the possibilities of funding research in this sector. £3 million has already been made available to public libraries, some of it for expenditure on IT, by the Wolfson Foundation and the Department for Culture, Media and Sport. This represents a positive start.

It is a strange, but not unexpected, irony that public library service points have been closed, and opening hours reduced from the 1970s to the present. But *New library: the people's network* suggests that service points will need to be open for longer hours to ensure access to the Internet for members of the public. Finance must be available to enable local authorities to meet what may be enhanced budgetary requirements from the library service. These might be in the form of special grants as might the finance required by public libraries to purchase new equipment. Without extra financial support, the attempt to exploit the unique position of the public library service will fail.

In this new climate, it is important that library services, of all kinds, move forward confidently, but with careful planning and a background of knowledge, to ensure the development of a virtual or digital library without adversely affecting the traditional services which will continue to be needed. There will be a need for 23

librarians and publishers to make their voices heard by government and quasi-government organizations. Commercial publishers, because of economic imperatives, will ensure that they are represented around the decision-making table. It is essential that librarians demand a place there too: they must ensure that the vital and strategic location of libraries in the community and in academia is acknowledged and that official bodies take this into account when making their decisions or producing their reports.

CONCLUSION

In a telematic, information-rich environment, librarians, publishers and others working in the information industries are forced centre stage, and the functions they perform fall under the spotlight. This presents the respective professions with an invaluable opportunity to demonstrate their value to the community. It is quite clear, in contrast to some of the concerns expressed as the telematic society began to get under way in the 1980s, that no overall stage direction threatens to write librarians and publishers out of the script. On the contrary, the limitations and weaknesses of the Internet coupled with the inexorable growth of published material, suggest strongly that their roles will become progressively more vital.

Librarians, in particular, are involved in a myriad of significant developments aimed at easing the path into a future where information in digital form will comprise an increasing proportion of published material. As the play unfolds, it will be the decisions about the content of digital archives and the routes to the information held by them, which will become critical. Librarians and publishers must ensure not only that they have learned their lines, but also that their improvisational skills are honed and ready for use.

REFERENCES

Davies, Simon (1997), The hard cell – why do we pay so much? *Daily Telegraph Connected*, 12 December, pp. 4–5.

Department for Culture, Media and Sport (1997), *The people's lottery*. London: HMSO.

Department for Education and Employment (1997), *Connecting the learning society: National Grid for Learning, the Government's Consultation Paper*. London: DfEE.

Europe dials a phone revolution (1997), *Observer Business*, 7th December, p. 1.

Hummel, Robert L. (1997), How fast is a 56-kbps modem? *Byte*, vol. 22, no. 6, (June), pp. 137–138.

Joint Funding Councils' Libraries Review Group (1993), *Report* [Chairman: Sir Brian Follett]. Bristol: HEFCE.

Kessler, Jack (1996), *Internet digital libraries: the international dimension*. London: Artech House.

Library and Information Commission (1997), *New library: the people's network*. London: Library and Information Commission. Full text available at <http://www.ukoln.ac.uk/services/lic/newlibrary/>.

Moore, Gordon (1997), An Update on Moore's Law: Keynote. *Intel Developer Forum*, September 30, San Francisco. Full text at: <http://www.intel.com/pressroom/archive/speeches/gem93097.htm>.

Neill, S. D. (1980), *Canadian libraries in 2010*. Vancouver: Parabola Systems.

Patterson, David A. (1995), Microprocessors in 2020. *Scientific American*, vol. 273, no. 3, (September), pp. 48–51.

Progress through partnership: the report of the Technology Foresight Steering Group (1997). London: HMSO.

Rochell, Carlton (1982), Telematics – 2001 AD. *Library journal*, vol. 107, no. 17, (1st October), pp. 1, 809–10, 815.

Rothenberg, Jeff (1995), Ensuring the longevity of digital documents. *Scientific American*, vol. 272, no. 1, (January), pp. 24–29.

Part II
STRATEGY AND PLANNING

Strategy and planning

INTRODUCTION

Three topics stand out as the essential background knowledge base for information managers: environmental scanning, strategic planning and financial management.

Before we can sensibly operate as information managers, we need certain professional background knowledge. Traditionally schools and departments of librarianship or information science have educated students in the necessary topics. Today, a once-and-for-all professional grounding is inadequate: the environment of our lives changes too quickly for material we learn to be relevant for more than a few years. The importance of continuing professional development is generally accepted, both to keep us aware of change and refresh our attitudes.

Many other players in the information world are not from the 'library school' background; for information providers, for commercial database specialists, for Webmasters, for strategic planners – to take a handful of instances – the information content of their background education and training will be different in scope and emphasis from that of librarians, but they are all legitimately operating in the information industry.

We all have a need to see other viewpoints on our professional world. The chapters in this part do not represent the only topics we now 'need' to know, but they are the topics in which our expertise is most likely to be deficient: hence our placing them prominently in this Handbook.

Scanning the environment is the necessary preliminary to everything we do; whatever our individual situation we cannot ignore what goes on around us – changes in society, new ways of working, re-engineered business processes, revised organizational cultures, personal empowerment, electronic information sources, new technological applications. What other professionals are doing in the face of these changes, and how organizations can adapt and survive also need to be monitored, both for ideas we may gain and for niches we may exploit. Our own effectiveness as managers and our appreciation of the information commodity represent a third segment of the environment, and we need all the support we can get as we scan the world for new influences.

Financial planning is another priority; whatever we used to know about finance has become irrelevant. We place this chapter here because finance is now the key to everything else we do – maybe it always was, but it seemed less evident than it does now. Competition, tendering, selling, marketing, outsourcing, leasing – these are the new reality of information finance. The planning and management of finance form an imperative for survival.

Strategic planning is the crucial link from the environment to the objectives of our own organizations. Our demand for resources, and the services we provide are founded on planning – a pervasive process that we must come to terms with if we are to make headway against competitors, whether organizational or commercial.

2 Scanning the environment: trends and pressures

Ray Prytherch

> If librarians and their libraries are to benefit fully from strategic planning, they must first understand and confront the environment in which they work and in which libraries exist. Perhaps the greatest strength of strategic planning is that it provides a process whereby library administration and staff can analyse their environment and relate the results of their analysis to organizational goals, objectives, and future plans. (Butler and Davis, 1992)

To exploit the advantages of the strategic planning process, it is necessary to feed into it all relevant data that could influence the outcome. The surrounding world has a bearing on information services; maybe on the way information should be presented, maybe on the delivery mechanism, maybe on the level of analysis or interpretation required. The client community – a local authority, an educational establishment, a business – has a bearing. The internal process of management also has a bearing: the way in which work is done, and the methods and evaluative techniques employed. So, there are three strands to the environment:

- the world outside: how the 'macro' environment will influence our field; trends in society, electronic handling of information, organizational cultures

- the professional environment: the best practices and expectations of our peers
- the internal organizational environment: how our own practices influence our efficiency and competence.

With such a wide spread of factors, clearly other chapters in this Handbook contribute to our understanding of the environment. The audit of information resources, the evaluation of the services we provide, our marketing approach and other techniques will be part of our analysis of the environment and will influence in turn what data we feed into strategic planning documents.

THE TURBULENT ENVIRONMENT

This examination of the environment is based primarily on the situation in the United Kingdom, but the trends are international; readers from any background will see the relevance of the points that emerge, although the detail may vary in different contexts.

Stueart (1986) characterizes US public libraries as so overwhelmed by demands and pressures that they have developed a 'schizophrenic profile'. Barnes (1995) believes that the conflicting demands placed on librarians of all types are inducing fragmentation so severe that it is becoming difficult to see the way ahead – 'the threshold of opportunity or the brink of disaster' – and we must make vital decisions; it is up to us 'to take the lead, to marshall our arguments, to influence rather than accept'.

In a review of McKee (1987), Raddon (1988) discusses political decisions and their implications on the funding and service priorities of public facilities:

> the underpinning issues brought up in the management of political and social change are the major issues inherent in this overview. They are not, however, given sufficient importance, even in this context of limited professional input and debate. This crystallizes the problem in this area, which is the disparate philosophies which have emerged, and still are emerging, from the public sector. A range of ideologies, from far left to far right,

based on conflicting beliefs, is apparent and the profession is left without the central role it once thought it held. All these cross-currents are represented, but do not point the way forward. It is perhaps unfair or unrealistic to expect this. If we cannot produce an ethos, how can this book reflect it?

The report *Information UK 2000* (Martyn *et al.*, 1990), which at the time of its publication seemed such an important document to academic and corporate librarians, neglected the public library sector. The report was criticized as far too dependent on technological advances; it became notorious for 'foreseeing' technological progress that could scarcely be justified. The rapid transfer of information by electronic means was taken to extreme conclusions, for example that local libraries would be unnecessary for information purposes, and should only investigate roles as social and entertainment centres. Whether we agree with such a prediction is still open to argument, and it is for such points that environmental scanning is an important process.

Three features of the 'turbulent environment' are identified by Rosen (1995):

- predictability: this is dependent on the adequacy and timeliness of data, obtained perhaps by constructing alternative scenarios or by futurology
- complexity: inter-relationships and local variations in a fast-changing world; multiplicity makes strategic control of a large organization very difficult, if not impossible
- novelty: the unexpected; new markets; new electronic capabilities; the need for flexibility.

He also adds to the equation three other factors:

- the analysis of 'cross-impact', for example of one industry upon another
- the need to substitute 'strategic issue management' in place of ends/means planning; this is essential for flexibility and rapid response

- the continuing role of crisis management, to respond to unforeseen changes that will occur in spite of planning exercises.

It will be necessary to bring some order to this complex field; Bryson (1997) suggests the 'environmental domains' that impact on information services:

- economic conditions
- availability of financial resources
- geographical situation
- degree of technological integration and innovation
- the historical development and parentage of the information centre and its parent organization
- customers and markets
- demographic patterns
- labour market and industrial relations
- availability of resources
- industry strata
- cultural/social conditions
- political climate.

Bryson adds to them a set of internal characteristics of the organization that will influence outcomes:

- organizational structure
- organizational culture
- management style
- values
- communication
- use of technology.

She describes the main features of the 'strategic audit' that will underpin this second group of six points. Other points to take into consideration are noted in chapter 10 of this Handbook, where Feona Hamilton identifies as key components in the information audit process:

- people
- paper
- electronic sources
- hardware
- costs/values.

Corrall (1994) notes that 'stakeholders' will have opinions that constitute part of the environmental scanning process. The audit might therefore include a stakeholder map of the organization. This will cover 'obvious groups such as customers, library staff and top management, but also others (some of them overlapping) including funding bodies, professional associations, and local community leaders, who also have a stake in the library's future'.

Corrall continues her brief discussion with a section explaining how planning assumptions can be based on alternative scenarios; these are valuable in:

- enhancing awareness of changes
- indicating relative scale and significance
- highlighting sensitive areas
- providing early warning checkpoints
- offering a resource framework
- encouraging a positive view of uncertainties.

In building scenarios, the steps she recommends are:

- establishing the scope and timescale of the exercise
- identifying the key influences
- selecting some scenarios
- turning them into narrative
- evaluating the implications
- incorporating them into the strategic planning process.

PUBLIC LIBRARIES

Of all the variety of library and information service bases, public *35* libraries probably have the widest – possibly infinite – range of environmental factors; they are serving the community at large without focus, they are always under-funded and under-resourced, governments and local authorities want to have an element of control over them, pressures of technological change and the associated human resource implications are present as they are in every sector. This chapter therefore concentrates more on the public library sector than on other contexts, but the trends identified are simply a larger span of the same influences that all information services will face.

The report from the Office of Arts and Libraries (1991) in the UK offers a straightforward summary of the environmental factors that surround public libraries: the professional environment (new formats of information presentation, online databases, declining book issues, rising costs of acquisitions, roles of community or cultural centre, services to the housebound, day centres, roles in national co-operation and interlending), the external environment (increasing demand, demographic change, local management of schools, growth of non-institutional study for all age groups), local authority environmental factors (financial pressures, corporate systems, public perceptions, the 'enabling' local authority).

Ten factors were identified by Kinnell Evans (1991a) as major environmental concerns:

- changes in local government
- the place of public libraries in local government
- public library organizational structures
- the political environment
- central and local government relationships
- the impact of technology
- measuring performance
- financial management
- service development
- local co-operation and interdependence.

Raddon (1993) comments that 'the interlinking of politically-initiated philosophies and related management theories cross and inter-cross from the public to private sectors, and have to be survived and managed'. There is also a tension that develops from 'the interaction of private sector management techniques and public sector services staffing and ethos', and Raddon notes that within the 'themes of economic policy, party politics and strategic management... other and covert relationships also play their part. Some are unacknowledged and unidentified, but those between budget holders and service managers, between committee chairs and senior officers, all add to the picture'.

Another point is made by McKee (1989), who suggests that simulating or stimulating competition in previously non-commercial operations:

> emphasizes the convergence of management approaches in the public (non-commercial and monopolistic) and private (commercial/competitive) sectors. Efficiency ('value for money' from the resource-provider's perspective), effectiveness ('value' and satisfaction from the customer's perspective), and 'enterprise' (in seeking resources and providing services) are the focus for managers in all types of organization.

Elsewhere, McKee (1987) proposes a 'counter-culture' – a focus on information provision (rather than the meeting of needs), on information content (rather than management of physical stock), and a move to a de-institutionalized service. The result could be smaller, specialized, commercially-aware services.

Politics, demography and finance

The changing environment is mentioned by many commentators as the key factor in the turbulence surrounding public libraries at present. Kinnell Evans (1991b) expands the various points made into the following summary:

- local government structures (especially size, links within and without directorates)

- local politicization (more intense, degree of involvement, pressures on elected members, need to 'network' effectively)
- interest groups (especially Trades Unions)
- central government policies (control, funding, school libraries management patterns, tendering)
- local co-operation (co-ordinated strategies, local information plans).

Monitoring and analysing these environmental factors is of central importance in the planning culture, for the definitions of strategic management stress that it is essentially externally focused. Kinnell Evans reminds us that 'managing strategically is often about the commitment of resources over the longer term to a significant change of direction in the organization', and this is dependent on the directions that are taking place in the environment.

White (1993) also examines the changes in local government; her report summarizes these as follows:

- a leaner, streamlined, corporate centre and flatter, less hierarchical structures
- a movement from 'provision' to an 'enabling' culture
- developing partnerships in service delivery
- increased focus on responsibilities and accountability to customer, client and citizen, with a 'service' focus
- increased attention to standard setting, inspection and planning
- compulsory, competitive tendering encouraging the client/contractor split and increasing devolved responsibilities for budgets, people and other resources further down the hierarchy, through service level agreements and increasing externalization
- increasing budgetary constraints and managing with fewer resources and rising demands
- increasingly 'political' environment and a changing member/officer interface; implementation of major service changes in education, social services and housing.

These changes will mean many differences to the organizations in which librarians work; the need for cultural change will be one aspect, and another will be changing career paths with an emphasis on commercial and business skills rather than technical and professional skills. Part of this change will involve additional competence in 'the ability to undertake the development of strategic planning'.

In the New Zealand 'N Strategy', key issues that were identified by professional members of the New Zealand Library Association highlighted resource sharing strategies, funding, co-ordinated collection development, the impact of technology, and accountability to users. Users and funders identified the ownership of information, marketing, access, education, and international relations as pressures urgently in need of addressing. The N Strategy is seen as a brainstorming exercise that will lead to a culture of strategic management in New Zealand libraries (Kirkus-Lamont, 1993).

A comment in the report from Comedia (1993) makes the points that public libraries 'have suffered a loss of visibility in the political realm' and that although theatres, opera houses, concert halls and other cultural institutions were regarded as key elements in urban regeneration programmes in the 1980s, 'public libraries (usually responsible for generating more city centre activity than all the others) were excluded'. In the book that followed the report (Greenhalgh *et al.*, 1995) one chapter is devoted to the 'political invisibility' of public libraries. The report from the Audit Commission (1997) may have some effect in putting them back into view.

Whilst the national political scene is obviously relevant, so is the concept of regionalism; this is much discussed in the European context. In general, public libraries in the UK stand comparison with services in most other member states and there may be a tendency not to look overseas for ideas and trends. There are few examples of work in the European context featuring public libraries, but environmental monitoring should not overlook the challenges of the European Union. Marcella and Baxter (1996) is one example of an interesting initiative – the implementation of the Public Information Relay. In particular, the European Union has *39* been favourable to less-developed regions, and to rural areas; various papers have proposed ways in which funds could be directed. An example of rural provision in the United States is contributed by Senkevitch and Wolfram (1995), who outline the possibilities for networking in rural contexts.

The traditional view that public libraries are basically for leisure use is no longer adequate: Usherwood (1993) sees that managers will have to provide for the development of leisure services 'in economic rather than social terms'. The new role of libraries in quality culture provision is made more complex by many demographic concerns:

- the population is greying
- the extended family is declining
- care in the community has raised pressures
- multicultural provision is essential
- unemployment is at a high level
- early retirement is common
- the changing pattern of leisure activities offers numerous alternatives to libraries.

Usherwood comments that 'as a society we have not succeeded in educating people in the positive use of leisure'.

The place of public libraries in local authority directorates is controversial. This topic is explored in a thorough and positive article by Asser (1994) who favours a leisure base, but other locations are of course possible; White (1993) examines settings in education directorates, leisure directorates, arts and culture services, and independent or freestanding services.

The politicization of public libraries is increasing: McKee (1989) finds them 'caught in the crossfire between ideologies with conflicting views on the role, structure and funding of the public sector... libraries in all types of organizations are caught up in the process of institutional politics by which priorities are set and resources allocated'. Usherwood (1994) discusses this area comprehensively: 'public library managers have to be politically sensitive and have an understanding of the world of politics and politicians... the public library service is part of a complicated local government framework which is influenced by central government regulation, party politics, professional values, pressure groups and a range of other interests'.

Usherwood suggests that influences within a local authority include the party group, a joint member/senior officer elite, ward interests, inter-department relations, intra department relations, professional views, and inter-party deals; outside the council organization the influences comprise the media, public opinion, the demographic structure, the local economy, the social structure, central government, and interest groups. Although this can be lampooned as a shambles, the final question remains 'what other form of democracy do you suggest?'

The possible revision of the funding arrangements for public libraries in the United Kingdom is not yet clearly in place. A major shift has been waiting in the wings for some time; the report (KPMG and CPI, 1995) for what was then the Department of National Heritage into 'contracting-out' concluded that it would be inappropriate, but a definitive statement from the new Government is awaited at the time of writing. Whatever this might say, the strategic management process would in any event seek to investigate bases of funding, as this is a topic which is of central concern and will be raised repeatedly.

The APT Partnership (1995) notes that financial issues surround the reluctance of public libraries to promote services based on co-operation, for fear that use and therefore cost could escalate out of control. They prefer to use only their own holdings, which runs counter to the need to provide access regardless of the delivery arrangements. In reviewing the APT document, Gill (1996) observes that the Follett Report (Joint Funding Councils' Libraries Review Group, 1993) stimulated academic libraries to move further and faster towards an access perspective than public libraries have been able or willing to do.

Co-operation is one major area where the environment needs to be further explored. Rice (1995) is an excellent summary of the useful partnership that could grow between the public library business information services and the Business Link network; she *41* traces the history, cites the key reports, and outlines the benefits and problems. The need for strategic planning is stressed, and although many authorities are doing this 'the public library has frequently been reactive in this respect rather than proactive'.

New technologies

New technology offers public libraries the opportunity to provide to the public state-of-the-art access to electronic information resources, particularly access to the Internet; this opportunity will be short-lived – if it is not taken up with enthusiasm and commitment in the near future it will be seized by other organizations. Frances Hendrix is quoted (Mendelsohn, 1996) with the remark: 'we [public libraries] were late coming into it. We haven't thought it through. And we don't have a strategy. The whole thing needs a kick up the backside'. The report for the Library and Information Commission (UKOLN, 1995) surveying whether public libraries had an Internet connection, found that provision at that time was very poorly developed.

The importance to public libraries of becoming part of the network community is stressed by Dempsey (1996), but he realizes 'they don't really know what their role is in the next five, ten or fifteen years'. He also comments that his response to initiatives to provide Internet connections to all libraries was 'that all the effort had been focused on the plumbing, rather than the content'. The lack of good material on the networks is surely another opportunity to be grasped, if only we have the time and expertise. To turn our backs because the content is of uncertain standard is to ignore every sign that the Internet will be the standard delivery mechanism for information in the medium term. The APT Partnership (1995) sees that libraries will be marginalized if they do not take the opportunities now; unless there is movement libraries will be seen more as 'museums of an obsolescent culture than the core of the information system that addresses the emerging needs of the general public'. This is further emphasized by the report from the Library and Information Commission (1997) which highlights the need for libraries to be repositioned as the communications backbone of the information society in the UK, and to evolve in technological expertise.

The Cumbria Genesis Project (Cumbria Heritage Services, 1996) is a far-reaching proposal to use educational funds, business support and voluntary sector enthusiasm to form a network-based facility that would serve the needs of local people, local democracy, visitors, social and economic functions, educational challenges, and business purposes; there is a unanimous political commitment, and the system will use commercial telecommunications links including videoconferencing. In the US, initiatives are generally further advanced; in scattered communities where conventional services can only be provided with difficulty and at great cost, networks offer facilities that match those of urban areas. Recent reports highlight successes of the American Library Association's 'Fund for America's Libraries' – a foundation established in April 1995 as part of the ALA Goal 2000 programme to position libraries for the twenty-first century. As part of this programme, the 'Libraries Online!' project is administered by the Public Library Association, and the Microsoft Corporation collaborated in a $3-million initiative to research and develop innovative approaches for extending information technologies to under-served populations. In particular the project has been testing the best ways of providing public access to the Internet, multimedia, and other software applications. The targets are families, small business owners, students and others without institutional access facilities.

Waters (1994) reckons that the role for public librarians in the new technological environment will include the identification and evaluation of information resources in all formats, teaching users to evaluate resources for quality and accuracy, and the assistance of users in accessing resources.

A rather different initiative is discussed by Janes (1996), and perhaps gives a signal that public libraries could be by-passed very easily by other agents in the provision of Internet access. The Internet Public Library <http://www.ipl.org/> was founded in 1995 and is operated by graduate librarianship students at the University of Michigan. It exists only on the Internet and has been regularly accessed by users from 80 countries. It mimics a 'real' 43 public library by having departments – reference, youth, teen, conference and meeting rooms, auditorium, café – and resources are chosen in accordance with an acquisition policy; all resources are of course on the Internet and the policy covers content, authority, presentation, and currency. One of the teaching uses of the library is to answer the questions: are librarians needed on the Internet? and if the Internet Public Library is successful, will it replace or supplant other libraries?

ACADEMIC AND OTHER EDUCATIONAL LIBRARIES

Similar points relate to the academic sector; the framework outlined by Corrall (1994) for the PEST – Political, Economic, Sociological and Technological – analysis is equally relevant in the academic context. The obvious extension is the need to assess trends and developments in the provision of higher and further education, patterns of learning and teaching, and lines of research.

Corrall notes that in the academic sector, where relative standards of institutions should be closer than they might be in the public library context, comparisons with competing or peer institutions can be carried out systematically to give evidence of the need for adjustment. The example she quotes based on Aston University (UK) used only quantitative data, which seems now to produce an unhelpful mass of figures that shows very little about environmental movement; her second example, however, based on the Massachusetts Institute of Technology (MIT) used comparative data on qualitative issues, and identified several institutions that met one or more of the following criteria:

- leading other research libraries in provision of innovative IT-based services
- competing with MIT for students or staff
- supporting a similar mix of academic disciplines
- beginning to redefine the role of librarians.

MIT interviewed managers and other staff to validate their own strategies and compare their own standing; the findings were fed into the strategic planning process, and on the next review were repeated, 'confirming that environmental trends and developments were being monitored as part of the ongoing planning process'.

In very general terms, academic libraries have the advantage that in the UK context a number of key collaborative initiatives have enabled them to monitor environmental change more comprehensively than any one of them could have done alone. The Joint Funding Councils' Libraries Review Group (1993) – the Follett Report – set the scene for the increased use of technology as an information delivery mechanism, and the eLib Programme has followed up with many very important initiatives. The eLib brief (Joint Funding Councils: Joint Information Systems Committee, 1995) is to foster 'increased use of electronic library services, to allow academic libraries to cope better with growth, to explore different models of intellectual property management, and to encourage new methods of scholarly publishing'.

Since the funding was made available along with the requirement, this initiative has been generally successful. Another boost to the academic community has been the broadband network SuperJANET, which has given libraries the infrastructure on which to base essential developments, and particularly collaborative work. This is the kind of support which has enabled individual libraries to see the directions that their own institutions are taking, and join in the forward-looking planning. It has been conspicuously lacking in the public library scene, and for that sector environmental scanning has been a matter of urgent individual action. The Library and Information Commission (1997) recognizes this.

THE CORPORATE INFORMATION SERVICE

Information services outside institutional frameworks have perhaps had the hardest job of all to monitor what is going on in their surrounding environment. The factors outlined in chapter 1 of this Handbook demonstrate how extensive are the changes in information provision that we have seen in the last decade; what we have seen so far is just part of a continuing process that we *45* shall have to comprehend and manage. Colin Steele demonstrates how these changes may impact on our services in chapter 17.

Technological advances have put corporate services under huge pressure; the main message of information providers and electronic publishers has been that their products are easily handled by the end-user – intermediaries not required – and the move to Web-based products further shifts the scene to the user's desktop. In fact, we may feel that the role of the intermediary is now more important than ever, but the professional emphasis is now on choice of sources and information quality assessment.

Networking of organizations, and particularly intranets and extranets, enable individual workers to share information and search sources from the desktop, and we have seen the decline and abandonment of corporate 'library' services. Those that survive have adapted fast, by anticipative environmental scanning, and are still on the move. The virtual information service is very close in the corporate sector. Bryson (1997) points out also that many features of corporate life are changing, and the information service will survive only if it can share the creation process of a new model of business. She identifies a number of key patterns and behaviours:

- value systems of the corporate culture
- beliefs and convictions
- normal standards of behaviour
- shared meanings
- corporate rituals, such as 'rites of passage', enhancement rites, renewal processes, conflict reduction, integration
- subcultures.

As well as the technology itself, the training of personnel in its effective use is a major undertaking; this is exacerbated by the paucity of experienced trainers and the rapidity of new development. If we accept that the successful information manager needs to be 'one of the team' in the business – using the jargons and protocols of the company, and working the political system – *46* then we must see that moving fast is the only way to retain credibility. If we do not keep up, then like any other worker in the organization we shall be downgraded, or downsized.

NATIONAL INFORMATION POLICIES

Over the years, the idea of national information policies has surfaced and resurfaced. Where there have been actual examples, they have proved to be little more than a focus for controversy and argument rather than a statement of purpose and intent. We look at national information policies at this point because they are an attempt to bring order to the world about us and relate it to our activities – in other words they are intended as an environmental monitoring exercise conducted at a national level and leading into a consultative process which will in turn offer some kind of framework or guidance in the shape of a policy statement.

In the United Kingdom, the most comprehensive recent summary of work towards a national information policy has been given by Hill (1996); his concise paper reminds us that a national policy is constrained by all sorts of international considerations – directives of the European Union, initiatives of the G7 group of nations, and the activities of multinational companies. The G7 nations have begun a series of pilot projects that aim to foster the 'information society', access to networks, interoperability, and the creation of new markets. The EU has similar directives and operates a whole raft of programmes from the various directorates with an information theme.

Hill presents the background as emerging from three areas:

- economic considerations: an open economy depends on market forces which depend on the free flow of information; access to information – and the exploitation of information – are essential for the healthy economy and development of a sound infrastructure; for research and higher education similarly, free flow and easy access are pre-requisites.
- technological considerations: whilst technology generally can look after itself, policies are needed to regulate excesses (such as paedophile networks), to ensure fair play (through *47*

copyright protection for example), to support research, and to protect special needs (such as rural communities).

- employment and social factors: monitoring of change in employment patterns; the implications, opportunities and problems of the information society concept; rights to privacy; pressure for Freedom of Information legislation.

The flavour of a government's own policies obviously also impacts on a national strategy: targets for higher education, spending on research, roles of private finance or public ownership, employment policies and many other areas. Whatever the political colour of government, the principal threads that will be apparent in the short term will continue to be support for partnership ideas, pressures to modernize, constraints on public spending, moves towards more open government, and support for EU policies. Moore and Rowlands (1993) presented an overview of moves in the European Union towards an information policy; their paper is obviously now dated, but the principles they outline and the problem areas identified give us a picture of the complexity involved. The speed and pervasiveness of information issues are at the heart of the difficulties, yet make a policy even more essential as fragmentation of interests between countries and organizational agencies would work against overall harmonization and eventual integration.

The position in the United States has been overshadowed by discussion of the information infrastructure; the same areas of interest are identifiable, and the same problems. Bearman (1993) presented a picture of the developing scene, with discussion of the specific context of the US Constitution that embodies certain freedoms that relate to information. In such a diverse society, many targeted information policies are likely to emerge, rather than one over-riding 'national' policy. Many other countries are moving towards the creation of policies or national plans.

CONCLUSION

The essential points to be made should have emerged from this overview: scanning the environment is an essential component of

48

strategic planning, and if it happens at a national level as well as at an industry level and local level, so much the better. The more ideas that flow in, the more comprehensive and well-informed will be our vision of the trends and developments that are likely to affect our personal and professional lives, and the better prepared we shall be to conduct strategic planning exercises. This topic is covered in chapter 4.

REFERENCES

APT Partnership (1995), *The APT Review: a review of library and information cooperation in the UK and Republic of Ireland*. Bruton, Somerset: LINC. (BLRD Report, no. 6212)

Asser, M. (1994), The integrated management of leisure directorates in UK public libraries. *Journal of librarianship and information science*, vol. 26, no. 2, pp. 93–97.

Audit Commission (1997), *Due for renewal: a report on the Library Service*. London: Audit Commission Publications.

Barnes, M. (1995), The threshold of opportunity – or the brink of disaster? *Library Association record*, vol. 97, no. 11, pp. 594–598.

Bearman, T. C. (1993), A view of information policy in the United States. *FID news bulletin*, vol. 43, no. 9, pp. 197–203.

Bryson, J. (1997), *Managing information services: an integrated approach*. Aldershot: Gower.

Butler, M. and Davis, H. (1992), Strategic planning as a catalyst for change in the 1990s. *College and research libraries*, vol. 53, no. 5, pp. 393–403.

Comedia (1993), *Borrowed time? The future of public libraries in the UK*. Bournes Green, Stroud: Comedia.

Corrall, S. (1994), *Strategic planning for library and information services*. London: Aslib.

Cumbria Heritage Services (1996), *The Cumbria Genesis Project*. Carlisle: Cumbria Heritage Services.

Dempsey, L. (1996), From Joyce to joint systems [Interview by D. Watson.]. *Library Association record*, vol. 98, no. 2, pp. 74–75.

Gill, P. (1996), The APT review [book review]. *Public library journal*, vol. 11, no. 1. p. 29.

Greenhalgh, L. *et al.* (1995), *Libraries in a world of cultural change.* London: UCL Press.

Hill, M. (1996), National information policies. *Information UK outlooks*, no. 15.

Janes, J. (1996), The Internet Public Library. In *Proceedings of the 10th Annual Computers in Libraries International*, February 1996. Oxford: Learned Information Europe Ltd. pp. 119–126.

Joint Funding Councils: Joint Information Systems Committee (1995), *Electronic Libraries Programme.* Bristol: HEFCE.

Joint Funding Councils' Libraries Review Group (1993), *Report* [Chairman: Sir Brian Follett]. Bristol: HEFCE.

Kinnell Evans, M. (1991a), *All change? Public libraries management strategies for the 1990s.* London: Taylor Graham.

Kinnell Evans, M. (1991b), Environmental factors and strategies for managing change in the UK public library service. *International journal of information and library research*, vol. 3, no.1, pp. 41–55.

Kirkus-Lamont, J. (1993), New Zealand libraries: the N Strategy. *Wilson library bulletin*, vol. 67, no.8, pp. 52–54.

KPMG and CPI Ltd. (1995), *DNH study: contracting-out in public libraries.* London: KPMG.

Library and Information Commission (1997), *New library: the people's network.* London: Library and Information Commission. Full text available at <http://www.ukoln.ac.uk/services/lic/newlibrary/>.

McKee, R. (1989), *Planning library service.* London: Library Association Publishing.

McKee, R. (1987), *Public libraries – into the 1990s?* Newcastle-under-Lyne: Association of Assistant Librarians.

Marcella, R. and Baxter, G. (1996), European information in public libraries in the United Kingdom. *Public library journal*, vol. 11, no.1, pp. 11–12.

Martyn, J. *et al.* (1990), *Information UK 2000.* London: British Library/Bowker-Saur.

Mendelsohn, S. (1996), Building the public highway. *Library manager*, no. 15, pp. 22–24.

Moore, N. and Rowlands, I. (1993), Towards a European information policy agenda. *FID news bulletin*, vol. 43, no. 9, pp. 215–217.

Office of Arts and Libraries (1991), *Setting objectives for public library services*. London: HMSO. (Library Information Series, no.19)

Raddon, R. (1993), The public sector. In *Librarianship and information work worldwide 1992*. London: Bowker-Saur. pp. 41–55.

Raddon, R. (1988), [Review of] McKee, R: Public Libraries – into the 1990s? (AAL, 1987). *Journal of librarianship*, vol. 20, no. 3, pp. 221–222.

Rice, C. (1995), Facilitating the partnership between Business Link and public libraries. *Journal of librarianship and information science*, vol. 27, no. 3, pp. 137–148.

Rosen, R. (1995), *Strategic management*. London: Pitman.

Senkevitch, J. and Wolfram, D. (1995), *Rural libraries and internetworking: proceedings of the Internetworking Rural Libraries Institute, May 1994*. Metuchen, NJ: Scarecrow Press.

Stueart, R. D. (1986), The future isn't what it used to be: long-range planning in United States public libraries today and tomorrow. In Ernestus, H. and Weger, H-D. (eds.) *Bertelsmann Foundation Colloquium – public libraries today and tomorrow: approaches to their goals and management*. London: British Library. (Library and Information Research report, no.150)

UKOLN (1995), *Public library internet survey*. Bath: UKOLN.

Usherwood, R. (1994), Local politics and the public library service. *Journal of librarianship and information science*, vol. 26, no.3, pp. 135–240.

Usherwood, R. (1993), The Library service and leisure activities. *Information UK outlooks*, no. 2.

Waters, R. L. (1994), A global view of technology: implications for public libraries. *Public library quarterly*, vol.14, nos. 2–3, pp. 49–59.

White, J. (1993), *Frogs or chameleons: the public library service and the public librarian: a research report investigating the status of public libraries and the careers of public librarians in England*. London: Library Association. (Report to the Library Association)

3 Financial planning

Jo Bryson

Once upon a time, information professionals were taught that the golden rule in service delivery was 'the right information in the right place at the right time'. In today's global economy, this rule has been supplemented by a second golden rule that reads: 'different information being delivered by different people in different ways'.

The question might be asked, 'What has this statement to do with financial planning?' Isn't financial planning about identifying, costing and delivering information services within the confines of a lean budget? ...And yes, there's also the point about ensuring the best methods of delivering services to meet diverse customer needs. Everyone knows this, and most information professionals would correctly argue that this is what they have been achieving through sound financial management for the past 20 years. So what is different?

Two global economic issues now make financial planning very different from the past. The first is the global information economy itself. Modern technologies have created a global village in which information is now time and distance independent. This has implications for information providers and their customers. In a large number of situations proximity and hours of operation are no

longer issues in either delivering or accessing information. Given the right security clearances, customers can access information on the desktop at any time and from anywhere in the world. Furthermore, information managers are now able to support continuous or twenty-four hour operations without the need for costly work rosters and overtime schedules. They can supplement their domestic eight-hour operations by purchasing services that are supported by people and databases strategically placed on different continents and in different time zones.

The second factor is the adoption by most Western countries of a macroeconomic policy framework that is based on the structural reform of the public sector and a drive towards global competitiveness. The framework includes the requirement for public sector entities to revisit their roles in service delivery according to guidelines set down for the de-regulation of the market place, competition policy, outsourcing, and regulator/ funder, purchaser/provider models.

Working together, these two global factors both necessitate and facilitate different information being delivered by different people in different ways. This chapter considers a number of issues that affect the way in which library and information services are financed and delivered to meet the requirements of the second golden rule. These issues are:

- competition policy
- outsourcing
- tendering
- owning and leasing
- strategic marketing
- value for money
- pricing of information
- other income sources.

The background to each issue is explained and strategies are suggested for managing the implications of these in libraries and information centres.

COMPETITION POLICY

Competition policy is based upon an economic rationalism that competition frequently delivers better services for lesser costs and that market forces should prevail in the economy with a minimalist approach by government. As a result, a range of service sectors have been de-regulated, services that have traditionally been provided by the public sector have been opened up to competition, and certain protective measures which were believed to distort the market have been removed.

This has two immediate impacts on financial planning for public sector libraries and information services:

Removal of competitive advantage

As true competition cannot take place without there being a level playing field, consideration needs to be given to mechanisms that remove any net competitive advantages that may arise simply as a result of public sector ownership of the services. To overcome the argument that the market can be distorted through the fact that public sector service providers such as libraries may not pay rent, or be required to make a profit or return a shareholders' dividend, some services or programmes may need to be structured such that all overheads are allocated to the service or programme, and income from service charges or fees is returned to the treasury in lieu of a profit or dividend payment.

Removal of regulatory advantage

A second consideration is that any potential for a party to have a regulatory advantage over its existing or potential competitors should be removed. As a consequence, there needs to be a separation of:

- regulatory and commercial functions. For example, national and public libraries must separate out any standard-setting programmes and activities from their service delivery programmes and activities.

- natural monopoly and potential competitive activities. Libraries and information services should separate out those programmes and activities that should remain as a monopoly on the basis of efficiency or known lack of market competition, from those that may be tested in a competitive market.
- potentially competitive activities. Libraries and information services should identify those activities that have the potential to be carried out in one form or another by the private sector and test the market by putting these services out to tender. This includes those services deemed to be a community service obligation, but where the private sector may offer these services on a more efficient basis in an outsourced environment. In this case the role of the library or information service changes to that of a purchaser rather than a provider of services.

Determining the merits of competition policy

A number of aspects can be considered to determine the merits of introducing competition policy into libraries and information services. These include the extent to which:

- the delivery of information services could be more efficiently undertaken by the private sector
- the programmes and activities are subsidized by the public purse, for example through community service obligations, the merits of these continuing, and if so, the best means of these being funded and delivered
- the information service is enjoying an artificially induced competitive advantage in the market place, for example in not paying local authority rates on its premises
- the presence of a public sector operated library or information service limits or prevents opportunities for a more efficient provision of those services by the private sector.

The introduction of competition into public sector libraries and information services also requires consideration of:

- the most effective means of separating out the natural monopoly elements from the potential competitive elements of the information service, as well as the regulatory functions from the commercial functions. These have implications for the programme and organizational structure.
- the most effective means of implementing the changes required. This is a major change management exercise in which roles, functions, jobs and people will be affected.
- skills and training requirements. Certain skills will no longer be required, and will be replaced by the requirement for new skills and expertise, such as contract management.
- new relationships and partnerships with service provider organizations. In some areas, the service will move from a service provider role to that of a service purchaser.
- the appropriate commercial objectives of the service. There will need to be a clear definition of service objectives in order to determine what business the library or information service will remain in, what business its competitors are in, whether there are or should be any overlaps of service delivery in the new competitive environment, and what objectives are to be shared with potential partners in an outsourced environment.
- the price and service regulations to be applied.
- the appropriate financial relationship between the library or information service and government body, including the rate of return, dividends and capital structure.

The introduction of competition policy is not simple. It is a complex and time-consuming financial and management exercise. It involves changes to individual roles and organizational restructuring to accommodate the regulator, funder, purchaser and service provider model. There are extensive tendering and outsourcing activities associated with market testing, or alternatively, benchmarking services against other organizations that are known to have implemented best practice systems and procedures. Other tasks are identifying and documenting service level agreements, developing and formalizing partnership agreements, including the sharing of corporate culture and values, and continuous review and monitoring of performance. Finally, there need to be contingency plans for continuous service delivery at the completion of the contract.

OUTSOURCING

Outsourcing is the contracting out of services to a third party (the vendor or service provider) to manage on the library or information service's behalf. The selection of the vendor or service provider is usually made through a complex tender process, followed by lengthy contract negotiations and due diligence studies.

In the public sector, outsourcing is a means through which the market can be tested under competition policy in areas still deemed to be the domain of the public sector. Outsourcing is also carried out within the private sector. In both sectors the drivers for outsourcing can be to reduce overhead costs, improve service levels, to gain access to know-how, or to take advantage of new technology directions.

Scope of outsourcing

Outsourcing can be applied to any service, from window cleaning in the library to security services. The outsourcing of information-related technology has increased dramatically over the last few years as organizations restructure and concentrate their activities on their core business.

Within the functions of archives, records management and library services, outsourcing can be considered for the storage and retrieval of records and archives, delivery of specialized information services, and the processing of journals and other stock (including accessioning, assigning the bibliographic description, binding, attachment of bar codes and security tags). *57*

Whilst the provision of information services can be outsourced, accountability for service levels and strategic decisions relating to service provision cannot. The fundamental responsibility and accountability for the quality of the end product or service still rests with management.

From a financial planning perspective, outsourcing is a relatively long-term proposition. The length of the contract is usually between three and ten years. This is for two reasons: the service provider needs to be assured of a long-term contract in order to achieve a return on investment for the infrastructure they provide. Secondly, the initial expenses of hand-over and change mean that the cost savings for the organization are not realized until the third or fourth year of the contract.

Viability for outsourcing

Outsourcing is a viable consideration where the goods or services can be provided more efficiently or effectively by an experienced third party. The outsourcing of information-related technologies or the storage of corporate records to a specialist in the field allows the information service and its parent organization to refocus upon its core business. From a financial planning aspect, outsourcing can also assist the library or information service to reduce costs by cutting capital investment in equipment and staff, and:

- acquire a higher level and greater range of expertise, skills and knowledge transfer than they could afford themselves
- undertake technology development and acquisition without a major up-front capital outlay
- migrate to new platforms and infrastructure without a drain on resources or capital outlay
- divest itself of legacy systems at a least cost
- lessen its overheads associated with storage
- expand the delivery of specialized services within a confined budget
- obtain access to new markets and services.

An inhibiting factor to the success of outsourcing is that organizations frequently do not take the time to determine their objectives for outsourcing and develop a strategy to match. Each objective will require different outsourcing mix, strategy, contract and management mechanisms. For example, an outsourcing strategy that is based on allowing the library or information service to focus on its core business will require a totally different partnership arrangement to one that is based on reducing the cost of migration to a new technology platform.

The information services that have been the most successful at outsourcing are those that have invested their time and energies into making a thorough examination of their options for outsourcing. The decision as to what to outsource should be based on a number of financial, technology and management issues. These will include criticality of the service to the business needs of the information service, an assessment of in-house capabilities and available skills and expertise, financial situation, market opportunities, business and technology direction, the rate of change and complexity in the external environment, risk factors and benefits. The benefits should be assessed according to the business need of the information service and its parent organization.

Risks in outsourcing

The major reasons that are given for not outsourcing are:

- a fear of loss of control
- the lack of ability to trust another party with a strategic investment
- there is not a strong business case
- the cost and effort of contractual negotiations give little return on the investment in time and legal representation
- it results in constraints on flexibility
- concerns over vendor capabilities.

The risks associated with outsourcing include the loss of expertise, key competences and skills of staff within the information service   *59* which may have long-term financial implications. It may be that costs are not actually reduced, they are only deferred. The internal changes within the organization that are required as part of the transition process may be higher than expected, or the time spent in negotiating the contract may negate any financial gain in the outsourced agreement. Additionally, there may be a lack of contract negotiation and continued contract management skills within the organization. The purchasing of these skills may be an additional overhead for the information service. Another risk is incorrectly specified service delivery outcomes: this can result in incompatible or inappropriate services being offered, leading to loss of clients and a loss of return on investment. Vendor selection may be poor; this can occur either because the vendor or service provider is less competent than believed, or the co-ordination requirements are higher than expected. The vendor should be financially stable and knowledgeable about the services offered. Other problems include inadequate or unclear contracts leading to costly litigation; problems of getting different contractors and vendors to work together (especially in areas where the integration of systems is managed by different parties – the result being an increase in the overhead costs of the outsourcing project). Vendors may lack flexibility and responsiveness to the client that could result in little value for money; thus outsourcing worsens rather than fixes existing problems. Problems remain unsolved – only the responsibility for them has changed.

Selection of the vendor

Issues to consider in the selection of the vendor should include:

- the vendor's credibility and capability to provide the services being outsourced
- size and shape, including whether the vendor is able to concentrate on the information service's needs or whether it has other business interests to attend to
- financial strength to remain in business for the life of the partnership (and longer)

- proven technical and service capability and performance in similar information related environments
- that the variety of platforms or services offered support the requirements of the information service and its clients
- their ability to be controlled in terms of future direction, so that the information service shapes its future needs rather than being manipulated by the vendor
- security and risk management issues
- tender conformance
- the full cost of the proposal
- the vendor's strategic perspective
- the vendor's understanding and ability to contribute to the information service's business
- the vendor's compatibility with the information service's corporate culture.

The contract should meet all of the information service's business needs and objectives. A detailed specification for the outsourcing contract should be drawn up with legal advice.

The relationship between the information service and the vendor must be a partnership of goodwill, the structure of which will be dependent upon the objective of the outsourcing exercise. There needs to be a high level of trust between the partners and a cultural fit between the organization and the service provider. Each party should be very clear about the objective and purpose of the outsourcing exercise, their role in the partnership arrangement, and the library's or information service's business and corporate culture. The distribution of risk between the parties and the ownership of the assets should be clearly defined. The required outcomes and outputs and the roles of any third parties to the agreement should also be clarified.

It is very important for the transition to be managed well and for thought to also be given to managing the transition period at the end of the contract. The agreement should provide that on termination the service provider or vendor would assist the information service in taking back control of the service or in handing over the service to another vendor.

TENDERING

Tendering is a mechanism through which potential suppliers of services and goods can be identified and invited to bid for the provision of the services or goods in a manner that is fair and equal. Tendering is usually employed in situations where the value of the service(s) or good(s) is high and where it is known that there will be a competitive field.

Whilst the tendering system facilitates public confidence in propriety and accountability for the expenditure of public monies, it does not necessarily guarantee the best outcome in terms of lowest price, best suppliers or the best product. The tender process is often a guessing game for the competitors, as all bids are considered in equal terms and their competitors' bids are only known after the closure of the tender. Differentiation in terms of customer service quality, ease of location or familiarity with the way in which the library or information service conducts its business, which may normally influence the selection process, are often not specified in a tender process.

Managing the tender process

There is usually a threshold expenditure figure that is set by the contracts management area, above which the library or information service must call tenders when purchasing goods or services. It is important that the specification is as complete as possible as there is no provision to amend the description once the tender process is underway. The specifications are used to ensure that there is objective comparability, so the description of what is specified will be what is provided.

Information about the prospective competitors and their bids is kept secret as the tender documents are kept unopened until the tender closes. This includes bids lodged under an electronic lodgment scheme. Once the tender has closed the bids are opened together, usually in public. Fundamental information such as business names and tender prices are then made publicly available through the tender register. Late tenders and bids that do not address the specifications should be rejected, even though they may contain the best bid. The reason for this is that the tender system is one based on propriety and equity for all competitors.

To overcome the fact that the tender process provides little room for innovative solutions, tenders may be preceded by a call for registrations of interest. This additional stage allows the library or information service to enter into discussion with likely suppliers about different ways in which solutions can be presented prior to the tender process. Suitable applicants are short-listed and then invited to prepare and submit tenders.

OWNING AND LEASING

The leasing rather than owning of equipment is another mechanism by which the library or information service can divest itself of capital costs in new projects or buildings, or undertake technology development and acquisition without a major up-front capital outlay. Leasing is also suggested if there is uncertainty about the length of time for which the asset is required, which makes it attractive to undertake a short-term agreement that may be cancelled. Similarly, if the asset is only required for a short time relative to its economic life.

Leasing is distinguished from other forms of financing by the fact that the financier (the lessor) is the legal owner of the leased asset. The asset user (the lessee) obtains the right to possess and use the asset in return for periodic payments (lease rentals) to the lessor; see, for example, Pierson *et al.* (1990). Leasing is often used as a method of financing assets such as motor vehicles, computer equipment and buildings. The more specialized the asset or the more critical it is to strategic business of the service, the more likely the asset will be owned rather than leased.

The advantages of leasing are that:

- the library or information service does not have to initially fund or outlay the purchase price as the costs are spread over the life of the lease

- in the case of commercial information services, the lease rentals are tax deductible, generating annual tax savings for the parent company
- quantity discounts often apply to lessors that are unlikely to apply to the buyer of a single item.

The advantages of owning are that:

- the library or information service owns a tangible asset, which in the commercial environment can be used as security
- in the case of commercial information services, the asset can be depreciated, generating annual tax savings for the parent company
- the long-term costs may be lower under ownership compared with leasing arrangements.

Lease arrangements

The most common lease arrangements are:

Operating leases

These may be rental agreements for computers and telephones. The advantage of an operating lease is that it can be cancelled at little or no cost, provided that an agreed notice of cancellation is given. Under an operating lease, the lessor is responsible for all insurance, repairs and maintenance and taxes.

Financial leases

These types of leases are often used by financial institutions to fund the purchase of motor vehicles. There is an effective transfer from the lessor to the lessee of all of the benefits and risks of ownership of the leased asset. The lease is non-cancellable.

Sale and lease-back arrangements

64   In these arrangements, the owner of the asset, for example a

building, sells the asset to the financial institution for the current market value and then immediately leases the asset back from the institution. The title to the property is relinquished to the financial institution in return for cash. Periodic lease payments are then made to the financial institution. The lessee is also liable for maintenance costs, insurance, taxes and all other costs of occupancy. This method of lease arrangement is often used to provide a cash flow to either leverage further investment or retire public debt.

STRATEGIC MARKETING

Economic constraint, competition policy and other financial and management considerations mean that priorities have to be set in information service delivery. Libraries and information services can no longer afford to duplicate services offered elsewhere, to offer services that have little demand or are not part of their core business.

Strategic marketing can assist libraries and information services in deciding which services they should offer. Strategic marketing has been defined by Kotler *et al.* (1980) as:

> A managerial process of analysing market opportunities and choosing market positions, programmes and controls that create and support viable businesses that serve the organization's purposes and objectives.

From the aspect of financial planning, strategic marketing involves consideration of those service opportunities that return the best value for money whilst meeting customer needs. In short, this means concentrating on a few core functions that meet market needs or fill niche market gaps not serviced by others. By identifying the following, the information service manager will be in a better position to determine the market segments to focus on:

- the primary market for the information service
- the major market segments in this market

- the needs of each market segment
- opportunities to increase resources
- major competitors and the information products and services that they offer
- the competitive benefits that can be offered to the chosen target market through market positioning.

An information product or service can be financially attractive if:

- it is of a good size; for example, if many people use it
- it has the potential for growth
- it is cost beneficial on both a long- and short-term basis
- there are adequate financial and technical resources and a competent and trained staff to support its requirements
- there are low exit barriers if the product or service has to be withdrawn at any future point in time
- the product or service is in line with the library or information service's mission and core functions.

By integrating strategic marketing activities with financial planning activities a more appropriate mix of services can be chosen to meet customer needs.

VALUE FOR MONEY

An important aspect of financial planning today is in ensuring that customers are receiving value for their money, be this indirectly through rates or taxes or directly through fees or charges under the 'user pays' system. As different people have different ideas about value, there are often difficulties in determining how to measure the value of information and information services in monetary returns.

Customer perceptions and value

The provision of consistently higher quality services or products than those of competitors is an excellent way to differentiate the library or information service. Customers must also place a greater value on the library's or information service's products or services (or see them as being more important) than others which they may receive from competing sources. Like beauty, quality is in the eye of the beholder. Customer expectations and perceptions of quality and value often vary as these are based upon the judgements of individuals. There are also cultural differences in customer expectations and perceptions of quality and value that impact on the service delivery.

The information services manager needs to target customer requirements in terms of:

- achieving value for money in their information products and services
- knowing what distinguishes their products and services from others
- setting realistic expectations of services at levels that can be achieved.

Gaps in service delivery can influence the perception of the level of quality offered in products or services. Customers also judge quality according to certain determinants of service quality. Generally customers are seeking an information service or product that:

- is timely in its delivery, such as in promptly responding to requests for information or help desk enquiries
- meets their needs and is superior to others offered in the marketplace
- is easy to understand and use
- cannot be obtained cheaper elsewhere
- is delivered by courteous and knowledgeable staff.

In the drive for efficiency, there is often the temptation to put the quality specifications in second place. This is false economy. However, in considering value for money, one should ask can the service be carried out more efficiently and can the outcome be better achieved more cost effectively through other means?

Measuring value for money

One of the problems that information services managers have is in proving their worth or value in quantitative and qualitative terms. Bryson (1997) identifies four separate value areas associated with information services. These are:

- assisting an organization in increasing or maintaining its competitiveness by adding value to the quality of knowledge within the organization. For example, by acquiring, organizing and disseminating accurate and timely information to assist new product development and to make it successful against its competitors.
- contributing to a social value, democracy and the quality of life. For example, public libraries provide life-long educational, informational, recreational and cultural services to the community.
- valuing information as a commodity or resource. Information utilities and information providers add value to and create new information products and services by manipulating, merging and redistributing information to meet customer and prospective customer needs.
- recognizing that information has different values to different people in different situations and at different times. Information has unique economic properties that can affect its value at any one time. It can be stored and used at the same time. It can be re-used without diminishing in value or, in the case of competitive information, its value lies in no-one else having access.

The ultimate criterion for assessing the quality of a service is its capability for meeting the customer needs it is intending to serve, and the value of a service must ultimately be judged in terms of the beneficial effects accruing from its use as viewed by those who sustain the costs.

Performance and value of information

Information by itself is not necessarily useful. If it is not used, for example it sits unused on an information system because people do not know of its existence, or because it does not meet their business needs, then it has no value to the organization. Burk and Horton (1988) have suggested five ways in which the performance and value of information may be measured:

- quality of the information itself, for example, accuracy, comprehensiveness, credibility and currency.
- quality of the information holdings, for example, accessibility, adaptability, ease of use, format.
- impact upon productivity, for example, the extent to which the information assists the organization to achieve greater returns on investment, improvement in decision-making, or more efficient operations.
- impact on organizational effectiveness, for example, the extent to which the information contributes to the identification of new markets, improved customer satisfaction, or the meeting of goals and objectives.
- impact on financial position, for example, the extent to which the information assists in cost savings, the creation of new assets, or the improvement of profits.

They also go on to rank or rate the information resource according to its:

- effectiveness in supporting the activity it was designed to support
- strategic importance of the information resource (or service) to the activities of the parent organization
- strategic importance of the activities being supported to the parent organization.

By adopting some or all of these generic measurements of performance and value, and applying them to the information 69 resource and the performance of the individual programmes or activities within the information service, as well as to the information service as a whole, a true picture of value for money can be achieved.

PRICING OF INFORMATION

The 'user pays' environment and the recognition of the business value of information has created the need to consider the cost of information and how to apply a charge or price to information when it is transferred to another party in the form of an information product or service.

Pricing of information products and services is linked to issues such as equity, the opportunity presented to do something with the information, the economic properties of information, value to the customer and willingness to pay. Sometimes avoidance costs are taken into consideration, where the cost of not having the information is factored into the equation. An example of this is the public utility 'Dial before you Dig' programmes where information about the location of water pipes, energy pipelines or communications cables are provided free of charge, on the basis of this being more cost-effective than the cost of repairs in the event of accidental severance.

Pricing according to the value chain

Recently the concept of the value chain is being used to price information products and services. This pricing concept reflects an incremental growth in the value of the information at each stage of the value chain – the value chain being a series of activities, where each activity in the chain adds value and builds upon the previous activity. For example, raw data is provided at the rate of cost of transfer to a third party. The third party may add value to the raw data by either combining the data with other data or by reproducing it in another format. This creates a new value-added product that, because it has a greater value to the market than the original raw data, can now demand a higher price. If this product is

70

further distinguished in the value chain by, for example, being updated hourly, an even higher price can be charged.

There are several ways in which value can be added during the value chain. The following outline some of the ways in which value can be added, and consequently the price of information can be increased, through the value chain concept:

Intensity of detail or labour intensity

An information product that provides a greater level of detail in its content, or a service that is more labour intensive in its provision, has potentially greater value and can attract a higher price than one that contains less detail or is less labour intensive to produce.

Frequency of update

Information products derived from dynamic data that must be continually updated, or services that are provided on a daily basis, can have greater value and can therefore attract higher prices than those that comprise more static data or are provided less frequently.

Guarantee of accuracy and quality

Services that provide a guarantee as to their accuracy, such as a land title search, give greater value in the form of security and can therefore attract a higher price than those that do not.

Supply time

'Fast track' information services that guarantee the provision of information within a shorter timeframe than is normally expected can be attractive to those whose time is of value, and so there is a willingness to pay a higher pricing structure than that normally offered.

Scarcity

Information that is provided as a public good or in the public domain, whilst being valuable to some, attracts little or no charges for its provision as it is generally found to reside at the beginning of the value chain. Conversely, information that is restricted in its circulation may be of more commercial value and can then attract a higher charge.

Quantity

The economies of scale in providing information in bulk form, such as the downloading of a complete database, may be passed onto the customer. The fee for the provision of discrete information or an extraction may be higher per data item than for the bulk purchase of data because it represents a more refined stage in the value chain.

Increasingly information services are pricing their competitive services through an up-front annual subscription fee, with additional charges being levied according to the type and number of activities performed in the value chain.

OTHER INCOME SOURCES

In times of economic restraint, it is often necessary to identify innovative ways of fostering additional sources of income. Tendering to provide services to others and identifying grants that may be used to achieve a specific outcome are two ways of obtaining external funding to support library and information services.

By-products of collection and services

Not all information products and services are immediately obvious contenders to produce income for the library or information service. Sometimes lateral thinking is required. An outcome of restructuring and competition policy is that the library or information service may move into a position where it can competitively offer or tender its in-house services to other public or private sector entities that are testing the market. These services can be a source of external funds. In-house costs may also be lowered if further economies of scale can be achieved. Services such as journal processing, records storage, bibliographic or information services are some in-house services that can be offered to others.

Grants

Alternative sources of funding for library and information services can also be found through external grants. These include:

- specific or tied government grants related to initiatives that may appeal to the community, for example, the provision of money to purchase a terminal for Internet services in a public library.
- employment grants that are used to stimulate the economy or create employment opportunities in regional areas affected by a down-turn in growth; these grants may be in the form of a subsidy for on-the-job training schemes, or may cover the employment expenses of an individual for a specific time period.
- community grants that may be funded out of a national lottery; the library or information service may be eligible to apply for a grant that either covers a specific service or subsidizes a new or existing service.

Caution is required when considering any application for a grant as they rarely cover the total cost or last forever. There may be high exit costs in terms of customer expectations if the service were to be discontinued through the expiry of the grant. Grants should be considered to be 'windfalls' rather than a source of long-term funding for core services.

REFERENCES

Bryson, Jo (1997), *Managing information services: an integrated approach.* Aldershot: Gower.

Burk, C. F. and Horton, F. W. (1988), *InfoMap: a complete guide to discovering corporate resources.* New Jersey: Prentice Hall.

Kotler, P., FitzRoy, P. and Shaw, R. (1980), *Australian marketing management.* Sydney: Prentice Hall.

Pierson, Graham *et al.* (1990), *Business finance*, 5th ed. Roseville: McGraw Hill.

FURTHER READING

Costs and pricing of library and information services in transition (1996), *Journal of the American Society for Information Science*, vol. 47, no. 3, (March), pp. 208–234.

Dinerman, G. (1997), The angst of outsourcing. *Information outlook*, vol. 1, no. 4, (April), pp. 21–24.

Fong, Y. S. (1996), The value of interlibrary loan: an analysis of customer satisfaction survey comments. *Journal of library administration*, vol. 23, no. 1/2, pp. 43–54.

Getz, M. (1995), Resource sharing and prices. *Journal of library administration*, vol. 21, no. 1/2, pp. 77–108.

Grupe, F. H. (1997), Outsourcing the help desk function. *Information systems management*, vol. 14, no. 2, (Spring), pp. 15–22.

Halvey, J. K. and Melby, B. M. (1996), *Information technology outsourcing transactions: process, strategies and contracts.* London: Wiley.

Hernon, P. and Calvert, P. J. (1996), Methods for measuring service quality in university libraries in New Zealand. *Journal of academic librarianship*, vol. 22, no. 5, (September), pp. 387–391.

Homes, P., Kempton, J. and McGowan, F. (1996), International competition policy and telecommunications: lessons from the EU and prospects for the WTO. *Telecommunications policy*, vol. 20, no. 10 (December), pp. 755–767.

Jones, W. (1997), Outsourcing basics. *Information systems management*, vol. 14, no. 1, (Winter), pp. 66–69.

Ketterman, K. (1996), Marketing to libraries. *Against the grain*, vol. 8, no. 6, (December/January), pp. 49, 52–3, 69.

Lemon, N. (1996), Climbing the value chain: a case study in rethinking the corporate library function. *Online*, vol. 20, no. 6, (Nov/Dec), pp. 50–55.

Love, L. (1995), Pricing government information. *Journal of government information*, vol. 22, no. 5, (September/October), pp. 363–387.

Perry, W. and Devinney, S. (1997), Achieving quality outsourcing. *Information systems management*, vol. 14, no. 2, (Spring), pp. 23–26.

Pettit, J. (1996), Optimizing your assets. *PC week*, 5 November, pp. 24–25.

Rowley, J. (1997), Focusing on customers. *Library review*, vol. 46, no. 1/2, pp. 81–89.

Rowley, J. (1997), Knowing your customers. *Aslib proceedings*, vol. 49, no. 3, (March), pp. 64–66.

Rowley, J. (1997), Principles of price and pricing policy for the information marketplace. *Library review*, vol. 46, no. 3/4, pp. 179–189.

Shenker, S. *et al.* (1996), Pricing in computer networks: reshaping the research agenda. *Telecommunications policy*, vol. 20, no. 3, (April), pp. 183–201.

Snyder, H. and Davenport, E. (1997), *Costing and pricing in the digital age: a practical guide for information services*. London: Library Association Publishing.

Van Goethem, J. (1995), Buying, leasing and connecting to electronic information: the changing scene in library acquisitions. *Acquisitions librarian*, no. 13/14, pp. 165–174.

Woodsworth, A. and Williams, J. F. (1993), *Managing the economics of owning, leasing and contracting out information services*. Aldershot: Gower.

Yesulatitis, J. A. (1997), Outsourcing for new technology adoption. *Information systems management*, vol. 14, no. 2, (Spring), pp. 80–82.

4 Strategic planning: the key to managing change

Ray Prytherch

This chapter focuses on strategic planning, about which there is a greater quantity of literature than there is about strategic management (chapter 9); maybe 'planning' is an indefinite term used for many activities that have little strategic significance, and the addition of the adjective does not necessarily imply a shift in quality. Planning seems to be regarded sometimes as an 'add-on' activity that can be carried out as and when there is an opportunity, and its results noted or ignored as convenient. This misunderstands fundamentally the nature of strategic work, and may be why so much planning seems to have so little effect.

It is important to realize the extent to which various aspects of strategy overlap. This chapter cannot be read in isolation: *Scanning the environment* (chapter 2), *Customer care* (chapter 5), *Performance measurement and evaluation* (chapter 6), and of course *Strategic management* (chapter 9) are all very relevant to strategic planning and policy-making. Every activity in the organization needs to be examined in the strategic context; every activity should be planned – customized to respond to environmental pressures, tailored for the specific market, shaped for the customers' preference, assessed for effectiveness, and managed for efficiency and cost economy – and thus the central theme of this chapter is that its message is relevant to all other areas that we may examine.

SOME DEFINITIONS

Sheldon (1989) states that strategic planning implies creativity, innovation, and intuition; leadership is vital. The following six points are noted as the essential characteristics of the process:

- awareness of the importance of needs assessment and SWOT analysis
- good participation in needs assessment by client group representatives
- skill in developing mission, goal and objective statements
- resourcefulness in choosing strategies for implementing objectives
- strong participation by library directors and organizational leaders
- new understanding of qualitative and quantitative methods of measuring effectiveness.

Resources must be matched, and strategic planning is the discipline to identify and drop functions if they have become obsolete or irrelevant. Sutton (1993) summarizes:

> long-range or strategic planning is a mechanism by which an organization collects and evaluates information about its own operations and its relationship to its environment, generates projections about future changes in that environment, and sets organizational goals based on those projections, which then serve as both a blueprint for change and a measure of progress.

Corrall (1994), in an excellent, brief, summary of the topic, lists her choice of the essential features: co-ordination; control; commitment; collaboration; consultation; consensus; consistency; change; choice; clarity; creativity. She sees strategic planning as a continuous process combining projects into a coherent framework with a common purpose, and links it with marketing strategy – considerations of opportunities, targets, design, price, place, and promotion – in a strategic focus on missions, visions, and values. She also emphasizes that strategic planning is an 'iterative and interactive team process'. She offers a good overall definition:

> in general terms strategic planning fulfils the dual role of relating an organization and its people to the environment and providing unity and direction to its activities. The days of static, long-term strategies are over. Timescales for strategic plans may be as short as three years, and are typically no more than five years, although a longer-term perspective is often sought at a more general level. Responsiveness is the key quality: organizations need to anticipate the long-term future, but be flexible enough to respond to the deviations that will inevitably occur.

Vincent (1988) enquires whether the strategic planning model fits into library thinking; she quotes a 'normative model' of strategic planning that comprises six characteristics:

- examination of the environment as a source of constraints, pressures and opportunities
- future-orientation (either descriptive or normative – attempting to create and control)
- change-orientation
- view of the organization as a single system
- consideration of alternative goals and objectives
- formal and documented procedures.

The aim of strategic planning is seen by Armstrong (1990) as the creation of 'a viable link between the organization's objectives and resources and its environmental opportunities'. He notes that the essential steps are the expression of purpose (mission), articulation of value systems (what the organization sees as important), policies (statements of principles), and objectives. Emphasis on the formulation of a broad mission statement is generally agreed; Riggs (1987) sees that the mission statement, goals, and objectives form the template in which the strategic planning and entrepreneurial activities are established and implemented. Asantewa (1992) describes the strategic path as consisting of a mission statement, situational analysis, goals, objectives, policies, and rules or procedures. These phases are further discussed below as part of the implementation of strategic planning.

MAIN BENEFITS OF STRATEGIC PLANNING

Corrall (1994) identifies five principal purposes:

- to clarify purpose and objectives
- to determine directions and priorities
- to provide a framework for policy and decisions
- to aid effective allocation and use of resources
- to note critical issues and constraints.

These lead to a number of potential benefits through improvements in decision-making, greater managerial effectiveness, enhanced standing for the organization, and better understanding of its work. In particular Corrall suggests several positive outcomes:

- more confidence in the information service from its controlling body
- better financial prospects when funding can be shown to be targeted strategically
- improved morale and motivation of staff
- improved working relations and team spirit
- greater job satisfaction
- improved customer satisfaction
- better public/customer relations
- development of critical skills, creative thinking, effective presentation
- more relevant and effective services
- higher profile for the information service and its staff.

Change is regarded by many as unwelcome; it is however utterly unavoidable, and it is possible to work towards the idea of making change palatable and beneficial. Environmental pressures, such as technological advances, can exert an influence on the progress of the organization and thus alter its direction. Such an alteration would be undesirable – one external factor producing a shift in direction that has not been considered and planned and will in itself not be necessarily in the interests of the organization or its customers: 'Management action is one of the forces needed to move an organization from its straight line. There are other, external forces that will change the organization's direction, often undesirably. Without management applying a corrective force, the business will set off in a new but unwanted direction' (Wilson, 1997).

The advantage of strategic planning should be that, as a participative process, it is open to everybody in the organization to contribute. Top-down plans find little favour with those providing direct customer service as they tend to overlook day-to-day concerns, and equally plans conceived at a departmental level tend to ignore overall strategy. The role and benefit of the strategic plan is to merge ideas from all departments at all levels to produce a scheme that fits into overall organizational needs but also gives sufficient detail for employees to see their own role in its achievement. All planning is therefore about producing change – desirable and agreed change – before change is forced onto the organization by uncontrolled, external influences.

The Audit Commission (1997) sets great store by the need to plan; a previous UK government document (Department of National Heritage, 1997) announced that each library authority should publish an annual plan to set out 'the kind of library service the authority will provide. It will cover policies, services, targets and standards and explain how they will be achieved. It will also review the previous year's achievement against targets'. The Audit Commission notes that individual authorities have discretion on the setting of objectives and how to meet them, but 'this discretion can lead to efficient and effective service provision only if decisions are addressed systematically and coherently through the service planning process'. Such a process will enable an authority to make a success of change, by integrating aspects of service provision and demanding attention at all levels of service provision. 'It is not just another time pressure, but the means of keeping all the other pressures under control.' Another important benefit noted is that planning involves a mechanism to integrate work with that of other parts of the authority and outside agencies – 'making explicit the implications of partnership for the library service'.

The Commission report lists the beneficial features that can be expected to emerge from rigorous service planning:

- explicit links between the library's planning and the authority's corporate processes and policies
- specific aims that the authority wishes to see its library service pursue
- priorities among those aims to inform choice of services and activities
- gathering of user and non-user views, and their application in objective setting and operational decisions
- overall targets for achievement in the light of budgetary and other constraints
- specific targets for each part of the organization
- public awareness of expected stock range and services
- equal weight given to new work and continuing activities
- coherence among the various parts of the planning process
- clarity, so that staff know what they are required to do and why the planning process is relevant to them
- monitoring of achievement as a regular part of the process.

Planning on these lines gives an authority a basis for taking difficult or controversial decisions, as the coherent process stands up to examination and can be seen to be based on fair judgement after due consideration of options.

In the academic library context one advantage of the process is that participation in planning allows the institution to demonstrate that all shades of opinion have been consulted in operational decisions; assessment exercises of courses and teaching *81* departments require that all support sections of the institution should be able to prove that they are well managed. The importance of research as a funding criterion is a particularly crucial point: research is 'best' in those contexts where researchers have excellent access to information. In the organization committed to strategic planning, the needs of all users including researchers can be seen to have been taken into account and can be compared to similar processes carried out in competitor institutions.

INFORMATION STRATEGIES

Formulation of policies on information is becoming fashionable in many contexts, and further confusion is apparent between the concept of a strategy for the management of information services (which is what we are considering here), and the information strategy concept which Allen (1996) outlines. He refers to information strategy as a 'set of attitudes rather than a report', but in the same paragraph says that this represents a shift of policy 'away from the traditional product of strategic planning... – the strategy document – to the strategic planning process'.

We need to be clear that information is a resource and not a subject in its own right; the input that a library service might make to an organization's information strategy might be based on sound knowledge, but would not be different in kind from that contributed by other departments. With careful control of course, the information specialist should have an advantage over others in contributing value to the organization's thinking. Kennedy (1996) outlines the opportunities that might be taken.

Allen's definition of 'information strategy' does not tally with that of the Chair of the UK Society of Public Information Networks: Hardwick (1996) describes it as 'a strategy which:

(a) addresses how the information flows and transactions are managed within an area
(b) establishes relationships and partnerships between information providers; and

(c) makes effective use of technology, but does not concentrate exclusively on the technology'.

It seems very important to distinguish between these corporate information strategies, and our present concern – policies on the strategic management of information services and libraries.

ROLE OF MANAGEMENT

Clearly, the important role of senior management in strategic planning needs to be recognized; Riggs (1987) notes:

> the library manager is the linchpin in the strategic planning process. No other person in the library construct has the responsibility or influence held by the library director in strategic planning. This responsibility and influence cannot be delegated. If a true strategic planning system is to exist in the library, then the director must be the chief strategist. Strategic planning is indeed a 'top-down' process.

In the same paper, though, Riggs notes that wide participation should be encouraged. Birdsall and Hensley (1994) advocate a planning model that embraces many participants; their paper lays stress on a delegation system that carefully considers 'positioning the architects', as the choice of the 'best people' is vital for the success of the process. 'Strategic planning requires acceptance of the agenda by partners and constituencies. Acceptance depends on informing stakeholders about what is being planned and how their own goals are advanced by it.' They quote the Hensley-Schoppmeyer Strategic Planning Model used previously (Hensley, 1992) in which the strategic planning process is seen as comprising six activities:

- positioning the architects
- scanning the environment
- analysing strategic options
- designing unit plans

- accepting the agenda
- adopting the plan.

Wilson (1997), writing in a general context, concentrates on the role of management in establishing and using a permanent 'cycle of control' – a never-ending loop of planning, performance, monitoring and action to apply feedback to the plan. The lazy way out is to adapt the plan to the performance! Obviously, action should concentrate on changing performance in any of its aspects so that the plan is better fulfilled. This action stage will also take account of new environmental factors that need incorporation into the scheme. A coarse system of 'vital signs' monitoring is outlined that will allow the manager to notice the significant messages of the monitoring process that require action, but enable circumvention of bureaucracy and avoidance of information overload.

INHERENT PROBLEMS

White (1993) comments sharply:

> library cultures have not encouraged risk or experimentation. Dealing with people has not yet moved away much from the traditional model of the expert professional and dependent client. As external pressures escalate, the rationale for current internal practices and procedures comes under increasing scrutiny. It is no longer sufficient to take as constants existing resources and programmes, policy guidelines, aims, or objectives. Critical re-examination will be needed of the appropriateness of staff, buildings, equipment and stock, as well as organizational structures, staff training and attitudes to the customer.

Strategic planning, it was noted by Hayes (1989), was one of the areas that participants in the advanced management seminar (following the model of the UCLA Senior Fellows Program) rated as most important – indeed it was top of the list of key topics, ahead of value-added services, marketing, interpersonal communication, and general management skills; his appreciation of the need for tools and skills that will enable library managers to deal with the institutional environment, the political context, as well as the 'bottom-line' approach, is tempered by the realization that adaptation to change, uncertainty, and ambiguity are crucial parts of the concept of strategic planning. Frustration, relationships in a competitive context, and the 'murky, uncertain decision context' are recognized as uncomfortable parts of the package as well.

Other elements that are mentioned by commentators as areas where problems may occur include the updating of a plan, and the 'completion' of the process. Riggs (1987) explains: 'strategic planning is a process that requires regular updating and refining. The plan generated from the process is at best a static photograph of a dynamic scene'. 'Completion' of a strategic plan means far more than just finishing it – we should understand that its ongoing nature implies that it is never finished in that simple sense. The 'completion' phase may be scheduled at intervals and consists of the moving of the plan into implementation. Birdsall and Hensley (1994) see the process as reversing at this stage: instead of searching for information, planners 'begin to affirm goals, prioritize plans and seek endorsements from their partners'.

Needs must be transposed into problems; it is therefore not adequate to aim to turn illiteracy into literacy, for example. It will be necessary to formulate precise problems – steps on the way – that can realistically be alleviated. Sheldon (1989) quotes Drucker who wrote of 'clear, simple, common objectives that translate into particular actions'.

Sutton (1993) lists the drawbacks associated with planning:

- inflexibility (rigidity could be encouraged; timetable could be restricting; no opportunity for expedient change)
- consumption of resources (time; work; meetings)
- irrelevance (focus too wide or too narrow; unrealistic expectations; too theoretical; outdated)
- conflict (friction between departments or divisions; lack of agreement; minorities disregarded; political infighting)

- lack of funds (budgetary cutbacks)
- failure to meet goals (too ambitious; timetable too optimistic)
- neglected operations (distracting from day-to-day management).

Contributing to a journal issue devoted entirely to strategic planning, Broadbent (1995) makes six propositions that challenge the value of strategic planning:

- it is often a hindrance to strategic thinking (over-bureaucratized; unproductive of time and effort)
- alignment with stakeholders' strategies is critical for service components such as libraries (base strategic planning on the plans of host organizations, local authority and similar)
- non-alignment is more natural (contexts change rapidly and the library's plan must adapt faster than it may be able – a point also noted by Riggs (1987) who talks of the 'instability' of the environment)
- it is the role of leaders to lead the planning process (risk of 'slow strangulation' from unguided consensus procedures)
- late followers of trends should learn for themselves (just to follow the trend of planning without the rigour of thinking why and how is less valuable to the organization)
- library closures [in Australia] are a failure of understanding the strategic context (staff need to communicate their perception of service value).

It was noted by Favret (1995) that earlier attempts at strategic planning [in local authorities] failed because of over-enthusiasm (lack of sympathy for local conditions), loss of strategic view as documents became too detailed, lack of commitment, and because it was a process more suited to a growth environment than to a period of constraint.

Another issue is identified by Raber (1995), who dwells on the problems of cultural acceptance; he sees a conflict between organizational culture and the culture of planning, conflict with tradition, ideological conflict over values, conflict over strategies, and questions over the identity of the profession. Full and detailed participation of all staff is his solution to avoid failure caused by these conflicts. It would be easy to assume acquiescence where there is actually resentment. The idea of 'risk' is also of course not a comfortable concept for many services to encounter.

IMPLEMENTATION

Why do strategic change initiatives often fail to deliver? Corrall (1996) begins the discussion:

> the grand plan is only the start. More effort needs to be directed to managing the process of implementation. A common failing is to stop short and not follow through from strategy to action... The classic dilemma of balancing the new and improved against 'business as usual' is not easily resolved.

We saw above that several steps are needed to ensure that a plan becomes reality; Armstrong (1990), Riggs (1987) and Asantewa (1992) envisage various planning templates consisting of a mission statement, articulation of value systems, statement of principles, situational analysis, goals, and objectives. This author's outline of a simple template is reproduced as Figure 4.1.

Successful implementation may best be achieved if the following factors are in place (Rosen, 1995):

- a manager with clear responsibilty for the process of implementation
- a culture that motivates people to participate and co-operate
- a clear understanding of the proposed strategy at every level
- a reporting structure to monitor the progress of change
- information and control systems that enable timely decisions to be made and communicated
- reward systems to provide incentives for the achievement of milestones along the way.

87

Rosen comments that these points must be decided in advance of implementation and 'the resources – including budgets – and time-scale implications fully appreciated'. He summarizes the essential steps in a series of templates which inter-relate in various ways between stages to feed a continuous process; the basic stages are:

- agreement of a mission statement
- agreement of objectives
- environmental audit
- internal audit
- SWOT analysis
- discussion of strategic options
- criteria (based on input from *mission, objectives, internal* and *environmental audits*)
- strategic choice
- implementation.

This outline is very similar to the template drawn by the present author on the following page (Figure 4.1).

The individual, detailed unit plans that are produced from the overall plan will be aligned with other strategic data to ensure coherence. Birdsall and Hensley (1994) suggest that such other data might consist of:

- library development targets
- funding, structures, and staffing of development activity
- articulation of needs demonstrated by enhanced revenues
- library goals aligned with those of University and major partners
- ongoing planning, review, and evaluation.

They envisage the plan being accepted, adopted and implemented in the following stages:

- 'architecture' (planners project their vision to the organization's constituents)
- advocacy (plans are championed)

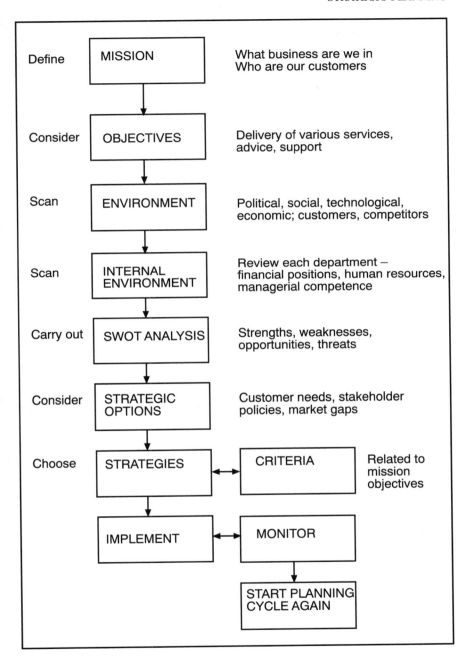

Figure 4.1 Sample planning template

- awareness (ensuring that the benefits and consequences are understood and felt to be attainable)
- acceptance (stakeholders give approval to a schedule of implementation)
- adoption (principals support detailed objectives and contribute the resources for achievement).

Examples of mission statements, vision statements, value statements, and statements of aims, goals, and objectives are quoted by Corrall (1994). She also summarizes identification of key result areas, critical success factors, and the criteria for formulating goals.

A crucial part of implementation is taken to be the co-operation of employees; it is strange that few commentators add to their lists of steps that are necessary the observation that employees must be trained to use new systems and methods. Hipsman (1996) is an exception; her emphasis maybe stems from the technical nature of the strategic change she is discussing, but her comment 'strategic plans must include training as one of the strategies of implementation' must surely be correct. She notes that strategic planning provides the opportunity to analyse staffing levels and responsibilities, and check that current requirements are matched to documented specifications; irrelevant and antiquated tasks are often enshrined in old documents and can be kept alive indefinitely unless the planning process questions them.

CONCLUSION

Clearly, as various technological skills become necessary for librarians, they will face the additional hurdle of having to develop those skills in their clientèle. Many commentators focus on infrastructure needs of the networked society and gloss over the skills crisis that is arising in the information professions. Strategic planning gives us the framework to examine the whole of our services; from this point we can set out to do certain things that we judge to be essential, put aside other things that we judge to be non-essential, and pinpoint the bottle-necks that will get in our way.

The Audit Commission (1997) feels that 'effective service planning does not require adherence to any specific model as long as the process is coherent'; but it is 'vital as a way of balancing pressures and priorities and ensuring effectiveness and efficiency'. It would be difficult but to agree.

REFERENCES

Allen, D. K. (1996), Information strategies. *Library and information briefings*, no.64.

Armstrong, M. (1990), *Management processes and functions.* London: Institute of Personnel Management.

Asantewa, D. (1992), *Strategic planning basics for special libraries.* Washington, DC: Special Libraries Association.

Audit Commission (1997), *Due for renewal: a report on the library service.* London: Audit Commission Publications.

Birdsall, D. G. and Hensley, O. D. (1994), A new strategic planning model for academic libraries. *College and research libraries*, vol. 55, no. 2, pp. 149–159.

Broadbent, M. (1995), Strategic context and information service investments: some thoughts from a hybrid. *Australian library review*, vol. 12, no. 1, pp. 4–9.

Corrall, S. (1994), *Strategic planning for library and information services.* London: Aslib.

Corrall, S. (1996), Balancing the business. *Library manager*, vol. 15, p. 14.

Department of National Heritage (1997), *Reading the future: public libraries review.* London: Department of National Heritage.

Favret, L. (1995), Local government change and strategic management: an historical perspective. *Public library journal*, vol. 10, no. 4, pp. 95–101.

Hardwick, D. (1996), Information strategies. *EPI today*, Feb/March, p. 21.

Hayes, R. M. (1989), *A long view of a broad scene: means to prepare for strategic management of a modern large library.* London: British Library. (BLRD Report no. 6049)

Hensley, O. D. (1992), *Strategic planning for university research.* Lubbock, TX: Texas Technical University Press.

Hipsman, J. L. (1996), Strategic planning for academic libraries. *Technical services quarterly.* vol. 13, no. 3/4, pp. 85–104.

Kennedy, M. L. (1996), Positioning strategic information: partnering for the information advantage. *Special libraries,* Spring, pp. 120–127.

Raber, D. (1995), A conflict of cultures: planning vs. tradition in public libraries. *RQ,* vol. 35, no. 1, pp. 50–63.

Riggs, D. E. (1987), Entrepreneurial spirit in strategic planning. *Journal of library administration,* vol. 8, no. 10, pp. 41–52.

Rosen, R. (1995), *Strategic management: an introduction.* London: Pitman Publishing.

Sheldon, B. E. (1989), Strategic planning for public library services in the twenty-first century. *Journal of library administration,* vol. 11, no. 1–2, pp. 198–208.

Sutton, B. (1993), Long-range planning in public libraries: staff perspectives. *Library and information science research,* vol. 15, no. 4, pp. 299–323.

Vincent, I. (1988), Strategic planning and libraries: does the model fit? *Journal of library administration,* vol. 9, no. 3, pp. 35–47.

White, J. (1993), *Frogs or chameleons: the public library service and the public librarian: a research report investigating the status of public libraries and the careers of public librarians in England.* London: Library Association. (Report to the Library Association)

Wilson, M. (1997), *The Information edge.* London: Pitman Publishing.

Part III
THE SERVICE INFRASTRUCTURE

The service infrastructure

INTRODUCTION

The customer is the focus of our business. This has always been true, but in recent years the idea of 'serving' the public, the students, the company executives or whomever, has moved from being an unspoken feeling to being a significant concept in our professional thinking. The 'user' was invented many years ago, and had to be investigated. User studies became a popular idea in professional education.

But now it is the 'customer' that drives the information business. New relationships are expected, competition is entering every sector – if we cannot provide what is needed by the customer, somebody else will. *Customer care* is an important chapter that shows us that our relationships can be developed. It also introduces various controls by which we can assess whether the customer is receiving careful service. These controls are based on ideas of performance measurement and quality assurance; these topics are closely related to the customer focus.

Quality is a pervasive issue; the tools that we use, whether printed sources, electronic databases, Internet Web sites, must be judged for relevance (that is to say their adequacy to meet customer needs), for currency, lack of bias, and reliability. All our services have to be good and to be seen to be good; if we cannot prove that they are, we carry no weight. Our credibility would be in doubt. *Performance measurement and evaluation* are important concerns at every stage in every project.

Both these chapters depend on concepts that derive from marketing. In a larger context, we could say that we have a product (information) and we have customers; marketing is the process of putting these two components together in the best way. The pre-marketplace days of information provision are gone, and we accept that everything has a price and everything has to be paid for.

Weingand (1995) points out that marketing is a process of exchange, a trading partnership: there are two parties, and each party has something that might be of value to the other. Crucially she takes this notion further: 'one of the essential components to the overall marketing process is planning... either of these two processes, while having intrinsic value, is incomplete without the other'.

The data that we need for strategic planning is the same data that we can use for marketing; it involves assessing performance, it involves a judgement on service quality, it is customer focused. Marketing is not an abstract idea, but very real and very close to everything we do professionally.

In the marketing cycle, we analyse market opportunities, we choose market positions and we relate these to our organization's purpose and objectives. We are examining ourselves, we are assessing our good points, and we are making strategic decisions about future actions. Later in the cycle we look at our success; we examine how costly we have been, and we look at usage – 'it is in the usage, and the growth of that usage, that the information unit's value will be assessed' (St.Clair, 1993).

We then relate performance to marketing opportunities: 'success of a service organization such as an academic library depends upon the organization's ability to adjust its products and services to correspond to user needs' (Millson-Martula and Menon, 1995). Everything hangs together around the idea of marketing: customer focus and quality of service are the two features that have been selected for scrutiny here. They embody the concepts central to the new service paradigm.

In the service infrastructure are other essentials; much of what we think and do as professionals is governed by our perceptions of the services in which we work, and the chapter on *Research* urges that feelings and perceptions – unsupported by evidence – lead to poor arguments for resources to develop services and respond to change. Research is under a cloud in some circles; development of information services needs an investigative base to carry weight and convince financial providers that we know what we are talking about when we link resources, performance and customer demand.

The final chapter in this part is devoted to *Copyright*. This is a rapidly growing area of concern and it is probably true to say that most of us break some regulation knowingly or unknowingly on a fairly regular basis. Electronic information provision opens the field to a bewildering array of issues, and in a cut-throat market to be under-informed is no defence.

REFERENCES

Millson-Martula, C. and Menon, V. (1995), Customer expectations: concepts and reality for academic library services. *College and research libraries*, vol. 56, no. 1, pp. 33–47.

St.Clair, G. (1993), *Customer service in the information environment.* East Grinstead: Bowker Saur.

Weingand, D. E. (1995), Preparing for the new millennium: the case for using marketing strategies. *Library trends,* vol. 43, no. 3, pp. 295–317.

5 Customer care for libraries: accident or design?

Peter Stubley

The adage that people become librarians because they like books (or are shy and retiring types) hopefully sank without trace decades ago. The profession is populated by staff enthused by, and steeped in, the service ethic: the idea of caring for library users – or in 1990s parlance, our customers – is second nature. So, on its most basic level, customer care is the practice of interpersonal skills, ensuring that all users are treated with respect and courtesy in their use of the library and that, as far as possible, they leave satisfied in their information needs. But customer care should not end with transactions that take place across our counters, whether issue desk or enquiry point, and in fact in its current incarnation, the term is more far-reaching than this. It encompasses the library and information centre environment (physical and electronic) and modes of communication and marketing. Furthermore, built into this are a set of consultative mechanisms and evaluation and information-gathering procedures from which the library can gain an understanding of the needs of customers. And whereby the library can respond to the requirements of its governing body. Theis (1996) correctly warns that definitions of customer care can become so broad as to be meaningless or misleading but a study of the current use of the topic suggests that in fact it permeates most aspects of librarianship and information management. For example, Pinder and Melling (1996) cover issues relating to quality, promotion and marketing, user empowerment, staff training, the particular needs of the IT user, as well as looking into the future.

In an environment in which resources are forever in short supply and governments of whatever hue are committed to reducing monies available from the public purse while insisting on accountability and value for money, libraries can no longer offer services in a vacuum simply because they are 'a good thing'. And accountability is a force acting in two directions: from above in the shape of governing bodies and local and national government; and from below in the form of reactions from library users. In pre-Thatcherite days there was perhaps a tendency to justify the non-accountable service using soft statements about the public good but in these harder times a more quantifiable approach is required to guarantee funding. This is usually tied up with government-speak ribbons emphasizing accountable services through charters or other policy documents. Irrespective of its feelings about the true usefulness of these indicators, a library service can no longer ignore the pressures from government and it must respond by making the right noises if it is to continue to be taken seriously. In this scenario, customer care means not only keeping the library users happy but making publicly available statements about the levels of service that can be expected.

In the UK there are over 4,700 libraries used by over 60 per cent of the adult population. Libraries whose services range from lending the latest best seller at one extreme to providing mediated access to electronic material on the Internet at the other. The task of service provision would be considerably easier if some of the traditional, paper-based elements just fell away leaving us to concentrate on the really interesting developments in C&IT (Communications and Information Technology). But of course, the real world isn't like that. Or is it? Meikle (1997) reported that the loan of books in England and Wales had fallen by 20 per cent in the ten years leading up to 1997 and that opening hours had been cut by 6 per cent over the same period. Even so, there is evidence that traditional services are still in demand while expectations are high for the implementation of new, electronic delivery mechanisms. One of the key challenges in library and information science is to be able to respond to these changing services in the ways required by both our users and our overseers while at the same time encouraging the take-up of new services by the less advantaged and the technophobic cynics. Customer care, like a ball bearing, falls resoundingly into this heady, mixed broth.

HARDCORE CUSTOMER CARE

The Citizen's Charter

In the UK, while many changes in the funding, organization and perception of public services originated with the Thatcher administration, it was John Major's Tory government that introduced the concept of the Citizen's Charter in 1991. This government introduced the Charter as part of its continuing attempts at transformation of the public sector, ostensibly showing the electorate that they were getting value for money by making services more quantifiable. While one does not wish to suggest that public services were beyond reproach and that shake-ups were in some instances not long overdue, it was somehow typical of the simple-minded approach of this particular government that charters were introduced as a smokescreen for reducing funding.

On one hand the surprise was the way in which such simplistic politicizing was taken up by the services concerned (an extensive list of Charters was at one time available at <http://www.open. gov.uk/charter/list.htm>). But of course the government holds the purse strings and therefore calls the shots, the implication presumably being: no Citizen's Charter, (even) less resources.

In spite of this expressed cynicism, there is no doubt that, with all its limitations, the Citizen's Charter has moved customer care from the soft focus of 'keep the customer satisfied' towards a hardcore approach which insists on a written statement of agreement between the service provider and the end-user. Whereas in the past many public services had an understanding of their service provision varying from the woolly to the well-defined, the introduction of the Charter made them consider these in a revised light, consult with customers, make their aims explicit and back these up with practical targets related to service delivery. This was the big difference.

So, what is included in Library Charters? Broadly, they seek to provide clear and accurate guidelines on the standards of service that customers can expect. The University of London Library's *Customer Charter*, for example, is divided into six sections dealing with service delivery and customer care; quality; collections; information technology; the working environment; and complaints procedures. Specific quantitative information is sparse and indicators are provided to this rather than being made explicit. For example, under 'Quality' the following paragraphs are included:

We recognize that customers will require demonstration of efficiency, effectiveness and value for money. This will be provided by:

The establishment of appropriate and measurable indicators which will enable us to monitor our own performance on a regular basis and to compare it with that of other libraries.

Charters should not, of course, be read in isolation without some understanding of the service that the library offers. For example, the University of London Library (ULL) is a second-tier research library with no directly registered users. It has no captive academic community and primary provision is the responsibility of the College where the student is registered. Thus, the ULL differentiates between core and value added services which would not be appropriate in many other academic libraries.

The *Library Service Charter* of the University of Sheffield, developed as a component of the University's Student Charter, is of slightly different structure to ULL's. Comprising three main sections, the first of these sets out in eleven bullet points the main services provided, followed by ten bullets listing the library's service standards. For example:

- to aim to reshelve returned Main Collection books within 24 hours and Short Loan Collection items within 8 hours

101

- to satisfy or report on Inter-Library Loan requests within 2 working weeks of submission.

Importantly, and in common with a number of library charters, there is a section devoted to the behaviour of students in relation to the library, stressing observation of the Library Regulations, the need to treat library staff and other users courteously, and the prompt payment of fines. This is followed by an information section explaining 'How the Library works with students and academic departments' – through Senate Library Committee, Faculty Library Committees and other means – and concludes with statements on 'Complaints procedure'. The full text of the *Library Service Charter* of the University of Sheffield is presented as an Appendix to this chapter.

The Charter Mark

Arising directly out of the Citizen's Charter came the Charter Mark. Introduced in January 1992 this is an award to organizations that provide excellent service to the public, those that put its users first. In his excellent chapter on Charters and Service Level Agreements, Payne (1996) indicates that at its launch the Charter Mark espoused six principles; by 1997 these had been extended to nine, as outlined in the *Charter Mark awards 1997*:

1. **Performance standards:** setting, monitoring and publication of explicit standards for the services that individual users can reasonably expect.
2. **Information and openness:** available in plain language about how public services are run, what they cost, how well they perform, who is in charge.
3. **Consultation and choice:** the public sector should provide choice wherever practicable. There should be regular and systematic consultation with those who use services. Users' views about services... should be taken into account.
4. **Courtesy and helpfulness:** courteous and helpful service from public servants who will normally wear name badges.

5. **Putting things right:** if things go wrong, an apology, a full explanation and a swift and effective remedy. Well publicized and easy to use complaints procedures.
6. **Value for money:** efficient and economical delivery of public services within the resources the nation can afford.
7. **User satisfaction:** need to show that users are satisfied with the quality of service they are receiving.
8. **Improvements in service quality:** measurable or demonstrable improvements in quality of service over the last two or three years.
9. **Planned improvements and innovations:** new initiatives to be introduced after the deadline for submission of applications.

The Charter Mark is awarded for three years, when organizations must re-apply. At this time there is a tenth principle:

10. **Your performance since you won your Charter Mark.**

A number of libraries and library authorities have been awarded Charter Marks at the time of writing: the London Boroughs of Brent, Croydon, Hounslow, Southwark, and Sutton; Newcastle University Library; Kent; Merthyr Tydfil; and Northamptonshire.

While the two are closely related, there is a substantial difference in workload between compiling a Library Charter and applying for a Charter Mark and this is perhaps reflected in the relatively small number of libraries that have been awarded Charter Marks. This should not devalue the Library Charter, a valuable document which lays down the performance targets of the library and, in some instances, what the library expects of its users. Chapter 6 includes many points relevant to this section.

Service Level Agreements

Of a similar nature to Charters, Service Level Agreements (SLAs) have grown out of the cost-centred approach to public services, whereby one department or section provides services at an agreed   *103* and documented level to its internal customer, generally another department. As noted by Payne (1996),

> Whilst chartism has been concerned with placing greater emphasis upon the public as customers, SLAs have developed from increasing separation of purchaser and provider roles in public services.

They are thus less aimed at end-user customers and more at institutional or departmental users. Payne goes on to point out that the main concerns of SLAs are to:

- spell out services provided
- set out standards of service to be provided
- establish mechanisms for monitoring that standard
- identify any requirements from the customer to achieve that standard
- put in place channels for reporting on performance.

Within an academic institution, a library might state the type, level, quality and quantity of services it agrees to deliver to each academic department and, as with many Charters, there will be an equivalent statement detailing the demands on the customer. The SLA of the Learning and Information Services of Leeds Metropolitan University was introduced in June 1996 and revised in November 1997; it runs to 34 pages. Not only does it list all sections of the converged service – including networking, PC installation, reprographics, and satellite recording – but for each details the responsibility of the faculty, the monitoring mechanism, the frequency of monitoring and the staff members with whom responsibility for monitoring each service resides. Sample entries (excluding the names of staff members concerned) are provided in Figure 5.1.

As indicated in the discussion on Charter Marks, the amount of work involved in the drawing up of an SLA is considerable and the significance given to it will vary from institution to institution. Where there is an emphasis on cost centres the SLA will assume greater importance and its preparation may well be inevitable.

Service to be provided	Requirement of Faculty or Unit	Monitoring mechanism	Frequency of reporting
LIS will distribute Guidelines on the production of course/module reading lists	Faculty managers will encourage academic staff to supply reading lists to the Library	Report to Schools by tutor librarians on the extent to which reading lists have been received (as part of annual review)	Annual
Books received will on average appear on the shelves within 30 days of receipt		Analysis of stock processing times	At least twice p.a.
Users of Learning Centres will receive Guidelines on Acceptable Behaviour	Faculty managers will assist in disciplinary action where students engage in behaviour which persistently disrupts other users...	Report on disciplinary action taken	Annual

Figure 5.1   **Sample entries from the SLA of Leeds Metropolitan University**

OTHER NATIONAL UK INITIATIVES

The Citizen's Charter and SLAs are two obvious ways in which the policies of national government have been reflected in public service organizations and, ultimately, in their libraries with a special focus on customer care issues. But even more recently – in 1997 – there have been three documents in particular that have similar emphasis:

- Audit Commission: *Due for renewal*
- Library and Information Commission: *New library: the people's network*

105

- Department for Education and Employment: *Connecting the learning society: National Grid for Learning.*

All three documents deal with one of the major issues facing the UK: the implementation of C&IT (Communications and Information Technology) and the ways in which this can be achieved to benefit the country as a whole, sharpening its competitive edge, through the encouragement and training of individuals and communities to the point where they become comfortable with the new technology. In particular, the Library and Information Commission report devotes a whole chapter (Chapter 2) to *Listening to the people* where it states:

> ... it is important that library users' needs and motivations are understood, and also their perceptions of IT in relation to current library services. It is also vital that we listen to people's views about our proposals to develop library services using the new technologies.

In other words, without a commitment to customer care and listening to what our users actually want and need, the library is not going to be able to satisfy the demands of its new role. While the survey carried out on behalf of the report recognized considerable goodwill towards public libraries and an understanding of their potential for furthering C&IT awareness, 'the development of IT in public libraries was considered essential if libraries are to play an integral role in the new world of networked information, knowledge and learning'. If these issues are not seized then no amount of customer care in the conventional sense of book provision will make up for this failed opportunity. Similar lessons can be gleaned from the DfEE's report on the National Grid for Learning.

KEY ISSUES IN A CUSTOMER CARE POLICY

The national imperatives outlined above must then be implemented at the local level, sometimes with the additional spin of institutional policies and politics superimposed for good measure. Ways in which this implementation is achieved will no doubt vary between institutions but the key issues to be considered in any practical policy would be:

- statements of intent
- library staff training
- library environment
- monitoring and feedback.

Statements of intent

The outline content of Library Charters and Service Level Agreements has been dealt with already and requires little further comment here – save to emphasize the public nature of these documents and the need for them to receive the widest possible circulation if they are to be viewed as serious attempts by the library to be considered as accountable by its customers. But it is also a fact that once the statement has been articulated – the Charter or the SLA written – most of the other issues should follow naturally. And, of course, the nine Charter Mark principles are an excellent starting point here, even if a formal application is not being compiled.

Library staff training

The public face of a customer care policy is manifest in two main ways: through the library environment; and in direct contact with library staff. The library environment, particularly in the electronic and broadly unmediated self-help atmosphere of the 1990s, plays an important part in leading customers quickly to their specific information requirements and is discussed briefly later in this chapter. But, important as this is, it is the library staff themselves that are in the front line, that are expected to know everything and who invariably find themselves the brunt of customers' blunt comments whether issuing books, answering queries or simply shelving returned books and journals. At these awkward times staff at all levels must know how to respond, be aware of their own *107* limitations, have an understanding of the Library Charter and recognize situations which are becoming difficult to handle and require involvement from senior staff. To achieve this requires an effective library staff training programme. In some organizations this might be an institutional programme to which library staff are invited along with personnel from other service departments, a useful combination of interests that can inform the discussions from different perspectives. Co-operative training amongst libraries in a region is another possibility. Chapter 11 is also relevant here.

From the early 1970s training sessions for library staff have used a variety of means – video, role play, seminars, group discussion, multimedia – to provide skills in handling a wide variety of situations ranging from awkward customers and difficult situations at one end to recognizing the particular requirements of international students and disabled users at the other. The centrality of library staff responses to calming or fuelling these situations is emphasized, placing particular focus on the importance of attending to customers' needs whether in answering an information enquiry or in responding to a complaint. Interpersonal skills training of this nature lies at the core of good customer care (see particularly Levy and Underwood, 1992); it can incorporate assertiveness, counselling skills, listening skills and non-verbal communication, dealing with conflict and stress, and personal awareness training. Theis (1996) utilizes the term 'attitudinal training'. Neither should the basic 'reference interview' skills of interpreting and responding to *actual* customer needs rather than to our own misinterpretation of these be either forgotten or omitted. But in common with many of the skills of librarianship and information studies, a customer care training programme that focuses solely on attitudinal training will touch only the tip – though arguably a fairly deep tip and going to the core – of the iceberg and will leave staff inadequately prepared to handle many potentially difficult situations.

A broad-based customer care training programme would include:

- interpersonal skills/attitudinal training
- reference interview training, including methods of transmitting information to customers

- functional – or operational – training
- technical – or equipment – literacy
- problem-handling procedures
- Library Charter awareness.

What are termed above functional and technical training are closely related. Staff who are unfamiliar with the capabilities of the library service or who are not conversant with all the functions of, for example, the automated circulation system, will be unable to respond to unfamiliar enquiries, risking being the focus – however unjustly – of customers' ire. The same goes for technical literacy: sending an unprepared member of staff to disentangle a reprobate photocopier from its frustrated users is not the best way to improve customer relations. One can see that in these situations all library staff should be 'fit for purpose' but, even in terms of the examples given above, this may be unrealistic and – in staffing terms – impractical. Add to this the multiplicity of services and information products now handled by libraries and it is clear that very few staff will be able to keep all the information they need at their fingertips all of the time.

The need to increase the technical competence of library staff is further highlighted in the two related UK government reports of 1997. The Library and Information Commission's 1997 report, *New library: the people's network*, emphasizes what has already been pointed out in this chapter, that 'public library staff already have many of the communication and customer care skills which underpin high-quality public service delivery'. However, in implementing the government's plan to foster a learning society, library staff will be expected to undertake the roles of net navigator; IT gatekeeper; information consultant; information manager; and educator. The report points out that:

A UK-wide training initiative must ensure that public library staff are ready to meet the challenges of their new role. In addition to anticipating and meeting the public's demand for access and interpretation of a wider variety of information material, library staff will be expected to add value and create

109

new content that will be relevant in daily living and learning. People – especially new users – will rely on library staff to support them in exploiting the potential of networks for increased community communication and for interactive links with government and public services.

Similarly, in *Connecting the learning society* (1997), the Department for Education and Employment states that 'a vital part of the programme for implementing the [National] Grid [for Learning] will be the development of teachers' and librarians' skills'.

Thus, as the complexity of the librarian's job increases and expectations of customers are raised in line with government thinking, each organization must work out for itself a pragmatic solution for operating its library service and just what 'fit for purpose' means for their library staff. A level of specialization, maybe a high level of specialization, is inevitable for some aspects of the service – not all staff will function as IT gatekeepers, for example – but this should not be seen as a disadvantage. As long as all staff are aware of the limitations of their own knowledge and responsibility, problems from customers can be passed to the next member of staff in the hierarchy when things start to become difficult. The recognition of the point at which to do this – and the realization that the act of passing on a problem does not indicate failure on the part of that member of staff – should be an integral part of attitudinal training but also be a factor that helps to bind the staff together as a team. Customers have rights as indicated in the Library Charter but so too do library staff and it is important that whatever reasonable actions are taken by counter staff in support of the library's policies, these are not undermined when complaints are made directly to library management. If clear training and awareness is provided for all staff in the implications of the Library Charter or the SLA, situations like this should not arise.

Library environment

To the librarian, a poor environment might be a reflection of the unwillingness of the overarching institution (or local authority) to fund the library service to the level required, the institution itself no doubt citing political pressures on finances among mitigating circumstances. By contrast, the reactions of customers will probably be of the 'what you see is what you get' variety and, particularly at first, are likely to be more unforgiving. While first reactions might be tempered with use – and through the dedicated implementation of the customer care policy by library staff! – the impact of the environment on the way customers use and respond to our libraries should never be underestimated or forgotten in our concentration on the more immediate issues of library charters and staff training.

Of course the real impact we can have on the physicality – the architecture – of our existing buildings is small, unless we are in the lucky position of having a new library approved and built in recent years; and there have been several of these, particularly in the higher education sector arising from contributions from Follett money. But difficulties with the physical shell should not be used as an excuse for ignoring other important environmental issues. Just as library staff should be 'fit for purpose' so should the library fabric. Clearly laid out sequences of books, journals and special collections, unambiguous and up-to-date signposting, study areas encompassing quiet study, group work and IT facilities, good quality illumination and ventilation, circulation and access space into and throughout the collections and around the circulation counter, access arrangements for disabled customers, the general level of decoration and flooring, all these need careful consideration. Much has been written on most of these topics individually but, if sound general guidance is required, an excellent starting point is Thompson (1989).

A well-laid out library with friendly well-informed staff goes a substantial way towards providing customer satisfaction but if customers cannot gain access when they need it or feel insecure in the general environment, then opportunities have been lost and the potential for complaints opens up. It does appear that there is a substantial difference in the way that public libraries and academic libraries have been able to respond to the opening hours issue, with public libraries in particular suffering from the financial *111* strictures that have been imposed on many local authorities, resulting in staff losses and in some cases severe reductions in library availability to the public. By contrast, many academic libraries open for 70 or more hours per week, a figure that generally includes part or full weekend opening. Extended opening has been a particular response to the student body, now comprising a greater number of part-time and non-traditional students who place increased demands on library and computing facilities through the needs of self-directed learning and who also have higher expectations of the services. Inevitably, whatever the opening hours, requests will be received for these to be increased still further or, alternatively, that the library be staffed with professionals who can answer any query, easy or complex, at any time, day or night.

With the increase in unsocial opening hours comes a potential security threat in some urban settings, whether in public, academic or special libraries. The preponderance in libraries of uniformed security staff, video surveillance equipment and, increasingly, access control mechanisms, shows how seriously security is now taken, though admittedly some of these facilities were initially installed to provide protection for the library stock and staff. But equipment of this nature can only provide a sense of security in the library building itself and if potential threats occur outside yet close to the library this will be bad for the morale of customers and staff alike. These are matters of customer care that need to be addressed by the institution itself, in association with the local police. If they are not handled seriously there could be repercussions on recruitment for a higher education institution.

The importance of the library *building* to the whole process of communication should never be underestimated and, as Kendall (1996) points out, buildings have a symbolic (and sometimes psychological) significance to their users that far outweighs – ironically, in spite of what was said at the beginning of this section – their physical condition. However, she also goes on to say that:

Networking through computer systems is a powerful way of sharing information, making the computer system both host and facilitator. Given that such a system is a construct which is replacing both buildings and people, little wonder that the needs met by buildings and people in the past need to be met elsewhere, perhaps, and the library/information profession needs to be rigorously redefined.

In other words, the librarian's role will develop as 'net navigator; IT gatekeeper; information consultant; information manager; and educator'. But there is another element here that relates to library environment in the widest sense and the increasing C&IT role of the librarian, particularly when coupled to the current pressures being imposed on staffing budgets which potentially leave less time to handle individual enquiries. If customer care means anything it should be able to provide customers with a degree – hopefully a strong degree – of self-sufficiency when searching information sources. In academic libraries in particular, the practice of 'user education' is long-established, the intent being to provide through a variety of means – seminars, workshops, lectures, tours – skills by which students can search out relevant information both during their course and when they leave university. This is a role that has always been difficult for public libraries to fulfil because of their much larger and more diverse constituencies, but one which has emerged yet again in the *New library: the people's network* report. And with the increasing emphasis on access to digital information in an extremely fluid environment – the Internet – the need for training in unmediated access becomes more important to give customers real control over their navigation and recovery of focused information. In this scenario the library environment takes in the universe, giving a new perspective on customer care. Furthermore, as the library catalogue receives higher use and itself acts as gateway to other information sources, it means that customer care also extends to the accuracy of individual catalogue records and the search mechanisms provided through the catalogue software.

Monitoring and feedback

The importance of monitoring and feedback at the national level formed a feature of the *New library* report. *Listening to the people* (Chapter 2) describes the findings of a survey carried out in June/July 1997 among key library user groups: mid-teens (aged fourteen/fifteen years in a deprived inner-city location); school leavers; families with a general interest in libraries; lifelong learners; and adults engaged in part-time study; their outline responses have already been discussed. The higher education eLib programme has also placed particular emphasis on evaluation, insisting that electronic developments, whether for librarians or customers, should not occur in some hermetic, isolated environment but must take account of the needs and responses of those in the real world (see, for example, Kelleher, Sommerlad and Stern, 1996). Similarly, European Union library-oriented proposals must include a well-developed impact assessment if they are to be transformed into successful projects.

How this is achieved is a matter for project managers but the lessons learnt in this way – focused so clearly on customer need – can easily be transferred to individual libraries to gather information on responses to particular services. The most obvious way of obtaining feedback is by questionnaire, though these need to be clearly focused, well designed and carefully analysed to provide acceptable results. It is also important to put questionnaires into some sort of context, for the frequency with which they are used nowadays by groups of all types, whether internally or externally, can cause them to go straight into the wastebasket; thus any co-ordinated campaign to gather information in this way may suffer if several questionnaires are directed to the same group of customers. Inclusion of a library component in a more general questionnaire – say a survey of student attitudes – is another approach, though this could reduce the depth of questions that are asked about one particular service.

An alternative to the 'traditional' approach of 'tick boxes' is that of 'Sequential Paired Analysis' developed by the company Priority Search. The librarians' version of this software is called Libra and entails initial identification of key issues – preferably by focus groups – and then the coupling of each issue with one other until the full list of 'sequential pairs' has been created. One issue lies to the left of a horizontal line on the page and the coupled, comparative, issue lies on the right of this line. Users must place a mark at a point on the horizontal line which indicates the importance they attach to one issue over the other, a mark at the mid-way point signifying equal importance between the two. A graphics tablet is used to input the data to a computer and the Libra software then produces output ranking the key issues in order of importance. Once the raw data has been input it is very easy to obtain not only a global analysis but breakdowns by particular interest groups, thus being able to compare, for example, one department's responses with those of another. While the results of this approach can be extremely useful it is not always popular with customers who can find it a little confusing and somewhat frustrating to complete.

Whereas questionnaires can be considered impersonal – and be prone to frivolous remarks and responses – semi-structured interviews will provide in-depth feedback, though with the particular overhead of significant staff resources: each interview can take anything from 20 to 45 minutes and will involve explanations and, no doubt, detours to discuss related services. Questionnaire and semi-structured interview can, of course, be combined and may be a way of improving response rates. For example, a survey of library use where customers are actually approached by an interviewer and encouraged to complete a questionnaire immediately, together with supplying opinions, will produce higher response rates and hopefully more accurate results, than a similar questionnaire distributed via global mailout. A further method of obtaining feedback is by the use of focus groups though, as with questionnaires, these require care in setting up to ensure that the facilitator does not unduly influence the contributions of the participants. Of course, the more usual forums such as user groups, faculty library committees, and suggestions boxes should not be ignored when gathering feedback from customers.

CONCLUSION

Marketing: different term, similar issues?

In his influential – and thoroughly entertaining – paper dating from 1960 (reprinted 1981), Levitt suggests corrections for the 'marketing myopia' suffered by many companies:

> ... the entire corporation must be viewed as a customer-creating and customer-satisfying organism. Management must think of itself not as producing products but as providing customer-creating value satisfactions. It must push this idea (and everything it means and requires) into every nook and cranny of the organization.

Sentiments that – hopefully – have formed the core of this chapter. For many years associated with 'the hard sell', marketing has for almost three decades now been showing its softer side and indicating how its principles can be adapted to service organizations which had previously considered themselves above mere consumerism. As early as 1969, Kotler and Levy (reprinted 1981) were stressing that:

> Customer communication is an essential activity of all organizations.

In the literature much is made of the 'marketing mix', those primary elements of which we should all be aware and that have a particular impact on the interaction between customer and provider . Four elements of this mix are generally identified:

- **product design:** the products and services offered by the library, including the consideration of new information resources and the availability of new media
- **pricing:** particularly when compared to services being offered directly to customers, by-passing the library but also, in higher education, linked to the demand for increased value for money as students pay their own way

- **distribution:** considerations of spatial, temporal and perceptual barriers to information and, increasingly, the networked environment that provides access to the wide range of information resources through C&IT
- **communication:** advertising, publicity, personal contact and 'atmospherics' – the library environment and its staff.

In structuring this chapter it was not the intention to provide a convenient mapping of the marketing mix onto the key issues of customer care. However, the overlap between the two lists indicates a clear synergy, though the marketing literature for librarianship has yet to catch up on a consideration of charters and SLAs. But one is tempted to suggest that any library seriously persuing an active marketing policy will almost certainly be one that has customer care close to its heart.

The final word repeats what was said at the beginning of this chapter, and is left to Kotler and Levy (1981):

> ... everything about an organization talks. Customers form impressions of an organization from its physical facilities, employees, officers, stationery, and a hundred other company surrogates.

REFERENCES

Audit Commission (1997), *Due for renewal: a report on the Library Service*. London: Audit Commission Publications.

Charter Mark awards 1997: guide for applicants. London: Citizen's Charter Unit. 56 pp.

The Citizen's Charter: raising the standard (1991). Presented to Parliament by the Prime Minister, Cmnd. 1599. HMSO.

Department for Education and Employment (1997), *Connecting the learning society: National Grid for Learning, the Government's Consultation Paper*. London: DfEE.

Kelleher, J., Sommerlad, E. and Stern, E. (1996), *Evaluation of the Electronic Libraries Programme: Guidelines for eLib project evaluation*. London: Tavistock Institute. <http:// www.ukoln.ac.uk/ services/elib/papers/tavistock/evaluation-guide/intro.html>

Kendall, R. (1996), The meaning of buildings in library and information work. In Rosemary Raddon, *Information dynamics*. Aldershot: Gower. pp. 69–84.

Kotler, P. and Levy, S. J. (1981), Broadening the concept of marketing. In Blaise Cronin *The marketing of library and information services*. London: Aslib (Aslib Reader Series volume 4). pp. 20–25.

Leeds Metropolitan University (1997), *LIS/University service level agreement, 1st revision*. 34 pp.

Levitt, T. (1981), Marketing myopia. In Blaise Cronin *The marketing of library and information services*. London: Aslib. (Aslib Reader Series volume 4). pp. 8–19.

Levy, P. and Underwood, B. (1992), *People skills: interpersonal skills training for library and information work*. London: The British Library. (Library and Information Research Report no. 88)

Library and Information Commission (1997), *New library: the people's network*. London: Library and Information Commission. Full text available at <http://www.ukoln.ac.uk/services/lic/ newlibrary/>.

Meikle, J. (1997), Libraries being left out in IT changes. *The Guardian*, September 24, p. 12.

Payne, P. (1996), User empowerment: striking back for the customers of academic libraries. In Chris Pinder and Maxine Melling *Providing customer-oriented services in academic libraries*. London: Library Association Publishing. pp. 59–86.

Pinder, C. and Melling, M. (1996), *Providing customer-oriented services in academic libraries*. London: Library Association Publishing.

Theis, K. (1996), Staff training: developing a customer care culture. In Chris Pinder and Maxine Melling *Providing customer-oriented services in academic libraries*. London: Library Association Publishing. pp. 123–139.

Thompson, Godfrey (1989), *Planning and design of library buildings*. 3rd edition. London: Butterworth Architecture.

University of London Library. *Customer Charter*. 4 pp.

APPENDIX

THE LIBRARY SERVICE CHARTER OF THE UNIVERSITY OF SHEFFIELD (AUGUST 1997)

Introduction

This Library Service Charter, developed as a component of the University's Students' Charter, aims to provide a clear and accurate statement of the Library's policies and service commitments in meeting the needs of all the University's students. It also details the rights, expectations and responsibilities of students in using the Library.

The Library Service Charter was developed by the University Librarian and his staff, in close consultation with the President of the Union of Students and the Senate Library Committee.

As with the Students' Charter, the Library Service Charter '...does not detract from or qualify the formal legal relationship between the University and students expressed in the Charter, Statutes and Regulations'.

The Library Regulations appear in the University Calendar and are prominently displayed in all branches of the Library. Copies of the full Regulations and of an abbreviated summary are available at all service points.

Some services may not be available to students who live at some distance from the Library. A guide to services for distance learning and part-time students is available from the Library.

The Library Service Charter will be reviewed annually, as part of our quality assurance procedures.

University Librarian	President, Union of Students	Pro-Vice-Chancellor Chairman, Senate Library Committee

The Library will:

provide comprehensive and high quality services, within the resources available and consistent with the principles of *General* and *Local Collection Development Policies**, to enable all the University's students to fulfil the requirements of their course or research. Library staff will be appropriately trained and provide courteous and helpful service to users.

Library services will include:

- provision of appropriate collections and information resources
- extended opening and service hours
- a network of Libraries on campus providing a welcoming, comfortable and safe study environment
- access to essential materials not held locally
- a range of appropriate loan periods, with reservation and recall facilities for most items
- photocopying facilities
- guidance in the use of Library and information resources
- a comprehensive, networked catalogue of Library collections and materials
- access to the campus network from within the Library
- a comprehensive reference and information service
- a written suggestions scheme

*   The *Collection Development Policy* states that: 'Feedback from students via the Senate Library Committee, Faculty Library Committees, Staff/Student Committees, together with suggestions from individual students and surveys of user needs, will play an important role in ensuring that Collection Development reflects students' needs'.

The Library will meet the following Service Standards:

- to provide, as available, at least one copy of all items prescribed for student reading
- to aim to reshelve returned Main Collection books within 24 hours and Short Loan Collection items within 8 hours
- to satisfy or report on Interlibrary Loan requests within 2 working weeks of submission
- to provide a regular free bus service to the British Library at Boston Spa in Semester
- to provide photocopier availability for 95% of posted hours
- to provide online catalogue availability for 95% of scheduled hours
- to offer introductory guidance on the use of Library and information resources to all new students within their first Semester
- to maintain opening hours and services, as advertised, in the Main Library and St George's Library for 70 hours per week in Semester
- to achieve 95% of posted opening hours at all major branches
- to respond to written suggestions and complaints within 5 working days

Students will:

- read and observe the Library Regulations
- take advantage of opportunities to learn about Library services and facilities
- treat Library staff and other users courteously
- not eat, drink, smoke, use personal stereos or mobile phones, or otherwise disturb other Library users
- take care of Library books, other materials and equipment, and return borrowed items on time
- within the resources available to them, purchase copies of essential texts as recommended by their academic departments

- take personal responsibility for the content, quality and prompt submission of work assignments, without undue reliance upon assistance from Library staff
- pay all fines and other charges due promptly
- comply with all Copyright legislation and licensing agreements
- take advantage of opportunities to provide feedback on Library services and to influence policy through the channels available

How the Library works with students and academic departments:

- Library policy is developed by the Senate Library Committee, which includes in its membership the President of the Union of Students and a representative of the Union's Postgraduate Committee, together with academic staff representing each Faculty, and representatives of the University Library
- Faculty Library Committees, which include student representatives, provide a forum for academic departments within each Faculty to discuss Library matters and to make recommendations to the Senate Library Committee
- Staff/Student Committees provide an opportunity for discussion of Library issues within academic departments
- for each academic department the Library designates a *Faculty Librarian*; each department designates a member of academic staff as its *Departmental Library Representative*
- the Library is responsible, with academic departments, for maintaining their current *Local Collection Development Policies*
- academic departments are responsible for ensuring that accurate, complete and up-to-date reading lists for each module or course are made available both to students and to the Library at the appropriate time
- academic departments are responsible for ensuring that an appropriate number of Interlibrary Loan vouchers from

departmental allocations are made available to students free of charge, on a fair and equitable basis
- the Library operates a written Suggestion Scheme in the major branches; students are also welcome to discuss Library matters informally with staff at service points

Complaints Procedure:

- If you have a complaint about any aspect of Library services, please discuss it in the first instance with the service point supervisor.
- If you are still not satisfied with how the matter has been resolved, then you may seek to take it further. In that case you should make a written complaint to the University Librarian. You can expect a written response to a formal complaint within 10 working days of it being submitted.
- If your complaint relates to a fine, charge or other penalty, and you are still not satisfied, you may appeal to the Chairman of Library Committee for the case to be reviewed. Details of this procedure are provided in section 25 of the Library Regulations.

Contact the Library for further information and advice:

Further information and advice about issues covered in the Library Service Charter may be obtained from the Main Library (details below) or from one of the branch libraries.

Address: Main Library, Western Bank
Tel (internal ext.): 22 27200
Fax: 273 9826
Email: library@sheffield.ac.uk
Web page: http://www.shef.ac.uk/~lib

August 1997

6 Performance measurement and evaluation

Lawraine Wood

Evaluation is an essential and on-going process for managers. It is achieved by collecting data (measures of performance) on the demand for and level of use of the service, the actual response of the service to the demands placed on it, and the views of the users regarding its value to them. So data is collected that *describes* the service. We can indicate to others, our users and funders, what our priorities are by the choices we make about what we collect.

SOME DEFINITIONS

Evaluation literally means working out the value, so in the library and information service (LIS) sense, it should be seen as working out the contribution that the unit makes to the work of the host organization. *Performance measurement*, on the other hand, refers to the actual processes and techniques which are employed to carry out the evaluation. Performance measurement uses *performance indicators*, which according to Abbott (1994) are 'a quantitative expression of the use or value of an aspect of library service'.

LIS professionals have argued about what constitutes 'good', but the main position seems to be that there is no concrete or objective measure. Evaluation is therefore carried out by collecting as much and as varied data as we can so that we can construct an overall picture that we can interpret.

Van House (1995) has a succinct and meaningful description of evaluation:

> Evaluation is a way of making sense of our organization and the larger context of the work that we do and involves us making value judgements regarding the measurements we take. We use evaluation internally, to see how effective we are and how we need to change what we do, but also we use it externally to let people know what we do and how well we do it, and what we need in monetary terms to achieve our goals.

There is a vast amount of literature on performance and evaluation, especially in relation to the academic sector. It is not my intention to duplicate what already exists elsewhere. Rather, this chapter is an attempt to bring together some practical strategies that can suggest a way forward for those who have wanted to get involved in evaluation, but weren't sure how. Alternatively, it can offer to those who already conduct measurements the opportunity for review, and possibly suggest a different perspective that they may not have thought of.

Concepts of performance measurement are *effectiveness*, that is the degree to which objectives are achieved (seen as doing the right things), and *efficiency*, or how well things are done (doing things right). Efficiency is often related to the economy and appropriateness of the way in which money is spent. Effectiveness can be related to cost – making sure that money is spent in an optimum fashion on satisfying identified user need. Attempts have also been made in the past to relate cost to benefit (Blagden, 1980) that is, trying to relate the benefit of a service to the cost of providing it. The difficulty here lies in trying to define what constitutes benefit. Can it be seen merely in terms such as time and effort saved, or are the benefits more intangible, such as the long-term 'good' that a public library can contribute to society? Some of these difficulties are as yet unresolved.

Hernon and Altman (1996) caution about the confusion that arises between effectiveness and efficiency: many librarians do things well (efficiency) that do not need to be done (ineffectiveness).

125

The twin concepts of effectiveness and efficiency are inextricably linked to the idea of quality in service provision. A quality management approach emphasizes the need to view service as a holistic system. Brophy (1996) suggests that information and library services should be viewed very much in terms of establishing quality in all the stages of internal processes that result in customer satisfaction. A request for a particular book may result in an order being placed by the acquisitions department with an external supplier. On arrival the book is processed by acquisitions and passed to the cataloguing department, and eventually the book is issued to the customer. At all stages of this process exist a series of internal supplier/customer interactions, as each department is a customer of the previous department. This is known as a supplier chain. As Brophy notes, 'the strength of the whole is determined by the weakest link,' so the importance of effectiveness and efficiency throughout library processes is clear.

WHY EVALUATE?

LIS managers now recognize the need to account for the money that is invested in them. Whilst there has always been some pressure towards accountability, this has increased over the last 20 years through such initiatives as the UK Government's *Citizen's Charter*, with its emphasis on standards; this is fully explored in chapter 5. Many managers of LISs now routinely build into their planning and operations some kind of measurement and evaluation of services, although the degree to which they do this varies considerably, according to the size and nature of the service offered.

Justifying our existence is not the only reason why we want to evaluate. In the public and academic sectors, external bodies such as the Audit Commission and SCONUL (Standing Conference of National and University Libraries) are now recommending a standard 'basket' of measures so that they can judge which libraries are perceived to be below par. Comparisons in the special library sector are more difficult to make meaningful due to the disparate nature of this sector, although perversely it is often those in this sector who would like to be able to use such data. Special librarians are quite used to being assessed by company accountants, so comparative data about the performance of other similar types of service, in terms of number of staff, total materials budget and so on can be useful for bargaining purposes.

One use of comparative data is to establish a benchmark, or standard, for a particular level of service. Benchmarking involves a systematic analysis of the way a particular task is performed, to establish a best way of doing something and can be used for comparing a service with 'the best' in its peer group. Academic libraries are increasingly interested in this technique, and research is being carried out at the time of writing (Evans, 1995; Town, 1995) to determine how this technique can be usefully applied to libraries.

The final purpose for an evaluation is for the manager to identify possible sources of failure and inefficiency, as we have suggested in the discussion on quality above. Many of the writers on evaluation remark on the fact that librarians often seem to forget that their service should be customer focused, often believing that users have no concept of what they want or the relative value of the service that they receive. Hernon (1996) suggests that this view misses the point. Customers *do* have a view about factors such as courtesy, clear communication and attention to the customer's request, factors which are often ignored at the expense of creating perfect systems of which the user is oblivious.

HOW DO WE EVALUATE?

Evaluation looks at what we do, how well we do it, and what our customers think of our efforts. This can be seen in terms of a model in which the inputs, processes and outputs of the information service are influenced by feedback from a combination of three key elements: outcomes; evaluation; and objectives. The outcomes look at the impact of the service – its value and benefits – which feed into the evaluation process and in turn influence the objectives. This model provides us with some clues about the What and How of evaluation.

Measurements are best done by having an overall approach related to the objectives of the organization itself. Management process models such as this have been used by a number of writers (Lancaster, 1993; Van House, 1990), and further adapted for use in different sectors of LIS work.

What can be measured?

Firstly, we need to decide what criteria we are going to use for the measurements. In LIS terms, that usually means three criteria:

- time: was the information delivered in time – also known as 'delay' (Kantor, 1984)
- quality: was it what the user wanted, was it relevant
- cost: was the cost, in terms of staff time and material costs acceptable and appropriate to the enquiry – also known as 'accessibility'. Ford (1989) suggests that it might be instructive to compare the time spent in getting a document with the time spent using it.

These three criteria can be used to judge many of the components of an information system, although other criteria become useful such as availability, that is, the proportion of expressed demand for documents that is satisfied in a given time period. We can choose to measure performance by looking at individual components, or a whole system. We can look at:

- information processes: providing specific data or information on request
- information functions: literature searching, identifying appropriate papers
- information system components which make services available: people, equipment, software, and work/study space
- products and collections: online systems and publications, their range, currency and quality
- the comprehensive information system: the whole library

128

- the information system environment: the organization/users served (Bawden, 1990).

These can be translated into measurements of specifics:

- information processes can be measured by examining the document delivery service. Did the item requested arrive in time? Was it relevant? Question answering services can also be measured more qualitatively – was the answer the right answer?
- effective literature searching depends upon the skills and expertise of the information professional. Does the person have sufficient breadth of subject knowledge and sources, know which databases are likely to produce the papers needed? Do they know what deficiencies are exhibited in the databases?
- system components. Do you have enough staff with the right kind of skills? Is there enough study space to cater for the users' requirements? (this might mean the right kind of space – for example, enough space near to a computer terminal to put paperwork). Is the computer system reliable? Does it do the job you want it to do, provide information that the managers require?
- products and services: CD-ROM services, online and Internet facilities. How well is the user knowledgeable about/able to use these services? Consistency, coverage and scope, timeliness, error rate, ease of use, integration (in harmony with other databases), output, documentation, customer support and training, value to cost ratio? Do they get what they want and if not, why not? Are current awareness bulletins timely and relevant?

Thus, the whole library is measured by combining data from the above questions. A further issue is the organizational environment where performance can be measured in relation to the amount of money that is invested.

Overall objectives

LIS managers attempting evaluation must be clear in their own minds exactly what they are trying to achieve – measurement of the whole service, or only a part – and draw up detailed objectives.

Evaluation of a whole service can be a very time-consuming and expensive process. Large LIS systems, the public and academic libraries, have found themselves in a better position than some of their smaller counterparts in the special sector to introduce and use data collection processes, simply because there are more staff. An important factor for special libraries therefore is that data collection should not interfere with the normal work of the unit, but rather proceed as part of that work.

Apparently only one attempt has been made to measure the whole range of activities, stock and services. This was carried out by McElroy (1982), at a pharmaceutical company in Edinburgh. More usually in the past there has been a tendency to look at an indicative sample of parts of the service, or evaluate just one particular function such as the value of a current awareness bulletin (Blick and Magrill, 1975).

So the initial planning of evaluation is crucial. Objectives should be related to the overall mission of the library and ultimately the host organization. While services considered for evaluation are a matter of choice, they should be related to focus on the customer through the objectives.

Aims need to state the overall intention of the evaluation exercise; to investigate the contribution of the LIS to the work of the organization, the following questions need to be asked:

- how adequate is the collection in terms of: (a) subject coverage; (b) timespan?
- what are the user expectations of the online searching and document delivery services?
- what priorities do the users attach to LIS services?
- are the services and staff expertise sufficiently well known about throughout the organization? Is the best use being made of services available?

Methodologies

Having formulated objectives, thought needs to be given to the method by which the evaluation will be carried out. Will objective data be used, using quantitative measurements such as time and cost, or will subjective measures of satisfaction rate be used, by interviewing users, and perhaps non-users if the non-users happen to be managers in your organization? As we suggested earlier, a combination of the two gives the best overall end result. It is useful also to have an idea of the timescale of your data collecting activities, so that there is an end point at which a report is compiled. The method might be as follows:

1. Collect information on how well current processes and services function, and user reaction to these.
2. Analyse the work of the LIS staff, and in comparison with the information gathered in point 1 (above), determine whether (a) staff are engaged on the right activities, and (b) money is being allocated appropriately.
3. Measure the impact of the LIS on the work of the organization by attempting to determine the use of the information provided.

Detailed objectives

When the decision is made regarding the methods to use, detailed objectives need to be drawn up. For example, if we were going to look at the adequacy of the collection, we might want to:

- find out the *amount* of use, and the *timespan* of material used, of the printed journals collection by department and grade of staff
- assess the adequacy of stock by analysing the proportion of in-house use in relation to total demand
- analyse the suitability of subject coverage by comparing holdings, books, reports and journals with the organization's business programmes.

131

Or, in assessing services, we might want to:

- quantify demand for the various services by type of user
- establish the cost-benefit of the weekly current awareness bulletin by comparing user satisfaction with production time
- identify any areas where there is un-met user demand.

It can be seen from these examples how, by proper planning at the outset, a good picture can be built up of exactly what is being attempted. Not only do these objectives tell us *what* is being done, but *how* it will be done. We must now examine more closely some of the measurements that can be taken.

GATHERING DATA

Orr (1973) was the first writer to establish methodologies for evaluation, but the writings of Cronin (1982) and particularly Lancaster (1993) brought a number of methods together. Small LISs tend to concentrate on one small area or service. Thus, a variety of methods are at our disposal:

- compiling statistics and financial data, to determine the level of use and how well money is being spent
- checking lists and bibiliographies to discover the adequacy of the collection
- obtaining user opinion to gauge customer satisfaction
- direct observation of users to discover how well your systems perform
- applying external standards to compare yourselves with others
- rating total resource adequacy in terms of what you are trying to do.

Clearly the methods used will be determined by individual circumstances and objectives. The discussion that follows suggests some of the methods that can be employed to collect this data. The suggestions are by no means exhaustive.

Services/stock

Information obtained from the users using the techniques described above can be added to statistical data to give a rounded picture. Swash (1997) notes that statistics have been kept extensively as a traditional measure of service: number of users, number of visitors, number of loans and reservations and so forth, but cautions that we should ask ourselves who wants these figures, and for what reason. Some LIS managers have kept such statistics 'just in case', without giving much thought to how useful they can be. So for example, managers of library operations will have a need for information to feedback into the service; funders of the library service will want information for planning and decision-making. Information could be collected on:

- the number of reference requests
- the number of documents supplied, and where they came from (in-house or externally)
- the number of documents supplied, broken down by staff level and/or department
- the number and age of documents supplied from external sources
- the number of literature searches carried out
- the most heavily used journals.

At this point, it is important to sound a warning for smaller LISs. Computer systems are now sufficiently advanced to provide basic statistics, and full use should be made of these. Where collection has to be performed manually, it may only be possible to record statistics for a four-week period every six months, and arrive at an annual figure by multiplying up.

In public libraries, the Audit Commission has proposed that measurements be taken by using the following mandatory indicators:

- number of items issued, books and other items
- number of libraries related to opening hours per week

133

- number of mobile libraries
- number of visits
- amount spent per head on materials
- net expenditure per head.

Public librarians are cautious about the use of these figures, which in themselves do not tell us very much – how many of the books borrowed were returned unread, how many of the visits to the library were to pick up a leaflet, pay a fine, rest tired feet during a shopping trip? Clearly without careful interpretation, the figures can be quoted out of context to negative effect.

Another reason for LIS apprehensions is that such figures do not reflect the differing 'local' factors that come into play. For example, two libraries of a similar size and function may have widely diverging material costs, due to particular specialized business interests in the user population of one where the cost of business publications might be significantly higher than average.

In recognition of the pressure from public librarians, CIPFA (Chartered Institute of Public Finance and Accountancy) proposed that a standard user survey be used in an attempt to ensure that public libraries conform to some kind of national standard. PLUS (Public Library User Surveys) aims to collect further data so that comparisons can be made within library authorities and against other library authorities, although as Swash (1997) notes, there is little commitment for such a national standard.

In academic libraries, similar initiatives have been underway. As in the public library sector, however, much development has been driven by external political pressures for accountability. The unification of the Higher Education sector in 1988 changed funding for Universities. The subsequent Follett Report (Joint Funding Councils, 1993) made it a condition of funding that universities produce information strategies, and be able to demonstrate value for money in five different areas. As a consequence, SCONUL, which had already been doing work on performance measures, published a consultative report, *The effective academic library* (HEFCE, 1995). This report adopted the framework proposed by Follett for measurement, suggesting the following criteria:

134

- integration – the extent to which library objectives were linked to institutional objectives
- user satisfaction
- effectiveness – output measures and service standards
- efficiency and value for money – the ratio of inputs to outputs
- economy – the ratio of costs to number of students or staff.

It suggested that these measurements be carried out in six different areas of academic library service provision:

- provision of stock: acquisitions, cataloguing and classification
- public services: circulation, shelving, inter-library loans, photocopying
- information services: enquiry desk, information retrieval, user education
- study facilities: study places, audio-visual facilities and other types
- other facilities: binding and conservation, special collections, photographic services
- management activities: policy making, liaison with users, staff management and development.

A great deal of developmental work on measurement has been carried out in the academic sector, where expenditure per FTE (full time equivalent) student, access to items in popular demand (short loan collections) and lengthening queues are of more immediate interest than some of the preoccupations of public librarians. They do, however, share the concern that it is important to get a measure of quality to balance the quantitative data, and this now seems to be accepted by SCONUL.

Returning to the question of stock, it is important not to neglect processing costs. A useful technique known as TSCOR (Technical Services Cost Ratio) (Wills and Oldman, 1977) is a way of balancing the cost of library materials (books, journal subscriptions, and documents) and the internal handling costs incurred by the library *135* (purchasing, indexing, retrieving, worked out in terms of the cost of information workers' time). The ratio should be as near 1:1 as possible. An unequal ratio could point to wrong procedures (staff inefficiency), wrong purchases (ineffective), too few staff or too large an acquisitions budget. The exact interpretation will depend on judgement and experience of the library staff.

Internal processes and practices in libraries are surprisingly divergent. Some are exceedingly efficient, others the opposite. A common error is to continue to do things in a certain way because they always had been done that way, with no-one ever questioning whether parts of the process are still needed. Another processing failure is cataloguing delays and backlogs which are clearly unacceptable and the TSCOR formula would be particularly appropriate in this instance as a means of focusing on where the failures lie.

The efficiency of acquisitions and even shelving processes can be gauged by constructing a systems analysis flowchart. Flow charts (Figure 6.1) allow the identification of unnecessary or redundant procedures, and provide an opportunity to review the relationship of those procedures to overall objectives of the service. Cronin (1982) suggests that if use of a particular service is low, then input effort should be restrained. For example, detailed subject indexing of books might be inappropriate for certain kinds of service. Involving all staff in systems analysis ensures their commitment to the idea of continuous improvement.

Cataloguing, classification, abstracting and indexing are more complicated since they require the input of considerable intellectual effort. They are therefore expensive activities requiring specialist staff, for which reason many larger organizations have decided to 'buy in' from an agency such as BLAISE, BLCMP, or similar. Whatever the answer, the question of quality arises, as there is known to be considerable variation in consistency and accuracy in records from some providers. Another factor is to balance the costs against the needs of the individual LIS. Are full catalogued entries necessary, or would something simpler do? In one very specialized research library, the costs of joining an agency were thought to be prohibitive, since the specialized nature of the

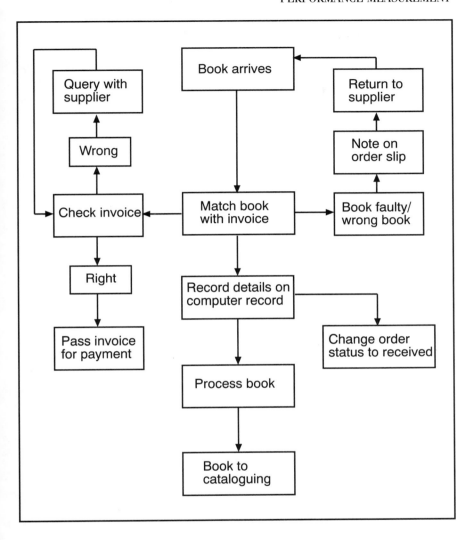

Figure 6.1   Example flowchart – process for adding new books to stock

material acquired meant that the 'hit rate' of cataloguing records from these big providers was quite low. Again, the involvement of all staff in conducting such an evaluation is desirable.

CD-ROM, online services and reference sources

Delivery of CD-ROM, online and reference sources can be measured in a number of ways at the point of delivery, such as relevance and quality of the items retrieved. But there is also an onus on the LIS staff to ensure that services available and subscribed to are the right ones for their users and to advise them accordingly.

Professional LIS staff have been trained to evaluate the quality of reference sources as a part of the selection exercise. They are used to making decisions based on such criteria as the reputation of the publisher or author, sources used in compiling entries, quality of indexing, digestibility of the text, and the opinion of reviewers.

CD-ROM can also be evaluated in this way, where it is possible to get a copy 'on approval'. But how can the quality of a database be assessed prior to purchase, when each excursion into the database is a costly exercise in itself? This is a difficult area. Database producers are not usually in the habit of publishing database specifications, which provide parameters and limitations by which the resource can be evaluated. Access to a database also includes other items which will affect the ultimate quality, such as the search software, documentation, and help-desk facilities.

Armstrong (1996) has suggested the following criteria by which an online service may be evaluated:

- consistency: of records within a database, or of authority control for main indexes
- coverage and scope: subject and geographical coverage as advertised, or gaps
- timeliness: issues of updating and currency of material
- error-rate/accuracy: source material, data errors, duplicate records, 'dirty data'
- ease of use: software facilities and access to the data
- integration/harmonization (with other like databases)
- output: formatting of records, downloading, aesthetics of delivered records
- documentation: currency, adequacy and accuracy of print and online versions

- customer support and training: includes knowledgable help desks, training and system support so that changes are not made without warning
- value to cost ratio/charging: records priced for content, good system value, fair and consistent pricing.

Clearly the experience and judgement of the staff over a long period may be the only way to tackle this particular difficulty.

Costs

Costs of providing various services can be worked out using staff salaries. In services that are sectionalized (for example, reader services; technical services) costing will be a relatively straightforward exercise but in others some kind of proportioning will be required, based on, for example, the number of items purchased; the number of inter-library loans handled. Gross cost must also, of course, take account of 'employment cost' – anything from 20 to 27 per cent of salaries – and overheads such as heating, lighting and maintenance.

What do the users think?

There are two main methods of finding out how users feel about the LIS and its services. Questionnaires allow the gathering of some basic data, but their disadvantage is always that they do not allow scope for expanding, or qualifying an answer. Also, it is human nature for people to give an answer that they think is expected, rather than what they really feel. If they like the staff of the LIS, for example, they may not want to say anything that they perceive might upset them. This difficulty is resolved by following up the questionnaires with interviews with a selected sample of individuals, or by relying solely on interviews. The interviews will follow a structured pattern of questions, similar to a questionnaire. Often in small LISs, individuals are so busy that they see making the extra time as a real obstacle to carrying out an evaluation, especially if it means leaving the library unattended. In reality, if   *139* the purpose of the evaluation is explained carefully, users can be persuaded that it is in their own best interests that the library is closed on Wednesday afternoons, for example.

Another matter for consideration is *which* users we will interview. Senior managers sometimes have a tendency to be non-users, so their views will differ from frequent users. It is appropriate therefore to have two different sets of questions to reflect the interests and concerns of each group. Examples of possible questions are given in Figures 6.2 and 6.3.

Further questions might seek to discover how individuals satisfy their information needs, reasons for non-use, something of individuals' reading habits, and responses to specific services or products, such as a current awareness bulletin. Answers should be recorded on pre-designed sheets.

Interviews with Directors, or Senior Managers will focus on some of the same concerns, but also different concerns. It would be appropriate to discover how they see the role of the LIS in terms of supporting company objectives. This may be something that they haven't really considered in detail, and the act of doing so, with some prompting from the library and information manager, can have an influence on how they regard the service. For example, they may initially think of the LIS as 'a drain on company resources', but when presented with some searching questions, they may begin to value the service more highly and appreciate its contribution. The sample questions in Figure 6.3 indicate the kind of approach that could be taken.

If a decision has been made initially to only examine the impact of selected parts of the service, users can be asked to fill in a short reply slip at the time of use. This method was used successfully by Blick (1975) at Beecham's Pharmaceuticals. A note attached to the weekly current awareness bulletin asked users to indicate what percentage of items in the bulletin they found useful; whether the items were considered to be important or urgent; and whether the bulletin supplied the information needed. This technique has also been used by librarians to measure journal usage.

In a research environment, such as in special libraries and some universities, many users will publish the results of their research.

1.   The library may be said to provide the following types of service:
  •   Making publications available
  •   Literature searching, identifying appropriate papers
  •   Providing answers to requests for information or specific questions
  •   Providing study and reading facilities
  •   Advice on keeping up-to-date; training on CD-ROM; Internet searching
  •   Adjunct services such as editing, translation, provision of photocopying facilities

      Rank these a) in order of importance from your point of view, and b) in the order that the library best provides them.

2.   What do you think the library's job is?
      What services do you think it provides?

3.   For a service to be valuable to you in your work, what should it do?
  •   Save time
  •   Avoid the need for certain work
  •   Allow decisions to be taken by staff at a lower level
  •   Provide solutions to specific, current problems

4.   Give examples, if possible, of the following events occurring as a result of information supplied by the library:
  •   Decisions taken
  •   Courses of action developed
  •   Advances made
  •   Time saved
  •   Resources saved

5.   When you visit the library, which do you most often want?
  •   Specific document
  •   List of documents on a subject
  •   Answer to a specific question
  •   Answer to a broad question/investigation of a problem area

6.   Which library services do you like/use most?

7.   What does the library not do that you would like it to do?

Figure 6.2   Example questions – topics for discussion with users

1. What expectations have you of the LIS? for example:
   - staff development
   - archiving
   - helping communication in the organization
   - prestige
   - other (specify)

2. For anything to benefit the Company/Organization/College, would you expect it to:
   - save staff time
   - reduce the need for research work
   - allow decisions to be taken at a lower level than previously
   - other (specify)

   Can you rank these in order of importance?

3. How do you *expect* the staff to use the LIS?
   - for current awareness related to business objectives
   - to solve specific problems
   - for general business and personal development
   - to maintain contact with the business community
   - other (specify)

4. Do you think they *actually* use the LIS in this way?

5. If the answer to 4 is 'no', is this because
   - LIS services are inadequate/inappropriate
   - there is no reading/study facility
   - they are too busy doing other work
   - you provide them with all the information they need to do their work

Figure 6.3   Example questions – topics for discussion with senior managers

Here, citation studies can be used to determine the appropriateness of the journal collection by analysing the citations at the end of users' publications to determine how many of the publications cited are held in stock. The result will reflect the extent to which the journal collection is meeting the users' needs.

142

McClure and Reifsnyder (1982) suggested a technique for measuring users' response to reference services, which they called 'Reference fill rate'. It was expressed as a percentage of the number of information products which met user needs divided by a sample number of information products delivered. This technique is an attempt to measure the usefulness and timeliness of information provided.

Staff

Whilst an analysis of workflows is a useful technique, the actual efficiency of staff can be studied in other ways. Asking staff to complete work diaries for a specific period of time, perhaps two to three weeks, in which they record information about the duration of some of their activities is one way. Activities can be related back to library service categories: provision of documents, advice service, and so on. Other activities, such as paperwork, telephone calls, meetings can be recorded separately. Results from such a study can be analysed to see if the ways in which staff *actually* spend their time correspond to how the users think they *ought* to spend their time.

Academic libraries in particular use another measure, that is the ratio of staff to users. In the special library field, Slater (1981) conducted a study which suggested that one member of staff per 50 on-site users might be appropriate, although by that standard, 44 per cent of the libraries she surveyed were under-staffed.

Users can also be asked about how they feel they were treated in the LIS (customer care) – are library staff seen as knowledgeable, helpful, courteous, interfering, retiring? Naturally LIS managers will want to ensure that users have a positive view of the service. This suggests that the staff should possess relevant and up-to-date skills. The introduction of staff development and appraisal schemes in most places of work is a way of ensuring this, although caution has to be used if any kind of grading criteria are applied, since the results may be highly subjective, or merely a mechanistic exercise. There are no objective measures of performance for staff. Readers interested in staff development would do well to look at   *143* the work of Corrall (1993) or Oldroyd (1996) for example, although there has been a great deal of other material published.

REPORTING

The final stage of an evaluation is an analysis of all the information that has been collected together, so that decisions can be made regarding the future objectives of the service, and any modifications that need to take place in staff effort and services provided. The results of the investigation can be written up and distributed to users as a positive marketing tool. In any event, information will have been provided which is invaluable in making recommendations for the future.

OTHER DEVELOPMENTS

Performance measurement and evaluation are really only a part of a much larger approach to providing good quality library and information services.

The Total Quality approach

Some practitioners have adopted a Total Quality approach to service provision. Usherwood (1996) has argued that Quality Management is part of the political agenda by which the government seeks to increase management control and legitimize change, suggesting that there is a need to get back to basics. However one chooses to view quality, one cannot get away from the fact that Total Quality Management (TQM) advocates a holistic approach which is, or should be, a part of the strategic planning process. TQM may be seen as the development of a systematic approach by an organization to ongoing and continuous improvement. The approach involves the development of error-free procedures and processes; it depends, through the commitment and involvement of all employees, upon the need for constant customer focus. A large strand in TQM is the need for staff training in new ways of thinking in the initial phases and later in ongoing development.

BS 5750 and ISO 9000

These are now widely used standards of quality which have been adapted for use by librarians. Ellis and Norton (1993) have suggested a practical approach to implementing the standards. The public library services of Brent (Tyreman, 1993) and Oxfordshire (Asser, 1993), and the University of Hertfordshire (Martin, 1993) are examples of implementation.

Service Level Agreements and Customer Charters

The UK Conservative government's Citizen's Charter initiative spawned a whole series of customer charters in different public sector organizations. Such agreements or charters tell the users what to expect in terms of service, and what to do if the published standard is not being met. Public libraries were encouraged to adopt a charter by The Library Association (1995), which published its model charter and standards.

This move to setting up standards for the customer has been followed by other governmental incentives to attain accreditation or a recognized level of proficiency. The main schemes have been **Investors in People** (explained in chapter 11), which ensures an organization's commitment to staff training through the establishment of proper procedures, and the **Charter Mark** (discussed in the preceding chapter), an award for all-round excellence.

CONCLUSION

This article has reviewed some of the theoretical approaches to performance measurement and evaluation. It has suggested ways in which some of the techniques might be applied in practice, at a micro level. In researching this article, the author has been struck by the number of times writers find it necessary to re-iterate that information services must be customer-focused. Could it be that there is still too much concentration on the internal processes at the expense of the customer? One is left with the thought that *145* library and information managers can no longer afford to run their services without being intensely self-critical.

REFERENCES

Abbott, C. (1994), *Performance measurement in library and information services*. London: Aslib.

Armstrong, C. J. (1996), The quality of publicly available databases: Wysiwyg or what? *BUOPOLIS 1: Routes to quality. Proceedings of a conference held at Bournemouth University, 29–31 August 1995*, edited by B. Knowles. Bournemouth: Bournemouth University Library and Information Services.

Asser, M. (1993), The demand for quality: the pressure for change on Oxfordshire's Department of Leisure and Arts. *Library management,* vol. 14, no. 4, pp. 13–16.

Bawden, D. (1990), *User-orientated evaluation of information systems and services*. Aldershot: Gower.

Blagden, J. (1980), *Do we really need libraries? An assessment of approaches to the evaluation of the performance of libraries.* London: Bingley.

Blick, A. R. and Magrill, D. S. (1975), The value of a weekly in-house current awareness bulletin in serving pharmaceutical research scientists. *The information scientist*, vol. 9, no. 1, pp. 19–28.

Brophy, Peter (1996), *Quality management for information library managers*. London: Aslib/Gower.

Corrall, S. (1993), The framework – making it work. *Personnel training and education*, vol. 10, no. 2, (June).

Cronin, B. (1982), Taking the measure of service. *Aslib proceedings*, vol. 34, no. 5, pp. 273–274.

Ellis, D. and Norton, B. (1993), *Implementing BS 5750/ISO 9000 in libraries.* London: Aslib.

Evans, M. Kinnell and Garrod, P. (1995), Benchmarking and its relevance to the library and information sector. In *1st Northumbria international conference on Performance measurement in libraries and information services*, 31 August to 4 September, Longhirst Hall, Northumberland. pp. 159–172.

146 Ford, G. (1989), Approaches to performance measurement: some observations on principles and practice. *British journal of academic librarianship*, vol. 4, no. 2, p. 79.

HEFCE (1995), *The effective academic library: a framework for evaluating the performance of UK academic libraries*. Bristol: HEFCE.

Hernon, P. and Altman, E. (1996), *Service quality in academic libraries*. Norwood: Ablex.

Joint Funding Councils' Libraries Review Group (1993), *Report* [Chairman: Sir Brian Follett]. Bristol: HEFCE.

Kantor, P. B. (1984), *Objective performance measures for academic and research libraries*. Washington, D.C.: Association of Research Libraries.

Lancaster, F. W. (1993), *If you want to evaluate your library...* 2nd edition. London: The Library Association.

Library Association (1995), *Model statement of standards*. London: The Library Association.

Martin, D. (1993), Towards Kaizen: the quest for quality improvement. *Library management,* vol. 14, no. 4, pp. 4–12.

McClure, C. R. and Reifsnyder, B. (1982), Performance measures for corporate information centres. *Special libraries*, vol. 75, no. 7, (May), pp. 249–265.

McElroy, A. R. (1982), Library-information service evaluation: a case history from pharmaceutical R&D. *Aslib proceedings*, vol. 34, no. 5, pp. 249–265.

Oldroyd, M. (1996), *Staff development in academic libraries: present practice and future development*. London: The Library Association.

Orr, R. H. (1973), Measuring the goodness of library services: a general framework for considering quantitative measures. *Journal of documentation*, vol. 29, pp. 315–332.

Slater, M. (1981), *Ratios of staff to users: implications for library/information work and the potential for automation*. London: Aslib. (Aslib Occasional Publication no. 24)

Swash, G. (1997), Measuring performance in library and information services. In *Managing user-centred library and information services*, edited by Ken Bakewell. 2nd edition. London: Mansell.

Town, J. S. (1995), Benchmarking and performance measurement. In *1st Northumbria international conference on Performance measurement in libraries and information services*, 31 August to 4 September, Longhirst Hall, Northumberland. pp. 83–88.

Tyreman, K. (1993), Quality, competition and contracting out: the Brent approach. *New library world*, vol. 94, no. 1110, pp. 5–10.

Usherwood, B. (1996), *Rediscovering public library management.* London: The Library Association.

Van House, N. A. (1990), *Measuring academic library performance: a practical approach.* Chicago: American Library Association.

Van House, N. A. (1995), Organization, politics and performance measurement. In *1st Northumbria international conference on Performance measurement in libraries and information services*, 31 August to 4 September, Longhirst Hall, Northumberland. pp. 1–10.

Wills, G. and Oldman, C. (1977), *The beneficial library: a methodological investigation to identify ways of measuring the benefits produced by libraries.* London: British Library Research and Development Department. (BLR&DD Report 5389)

7 Research: the infrastructure for improvement and change

Ray Prytherch

In-house research 'should be encouraged, even demanded, by library managements because without it there can hardly be any objective assessment of services, performance, or needs'. It is also crucial for the development of staff, and the continuing evolution of the profession. Overall, therefore, management cannot do other than support the need for research, and has a responsibility to promote it – creating the conditions, encouraging and supporting, and 'managing these activities effectively' (Allen, 1986).

Examples of the problems that are caused by the lack of fundamental research are highlighted by Edmonds (1987), who claims that 'youth services in public libraries are often based on superstition… the incorrect assignment of cause-and-effect relationships based on chance occurrences'. 'Superstition… can get in the way of effective management of libraries and it can inhibit the ability to adapt to a changing environment' – examples are quoted – and although most librarians presumably try to avoid superstitious behaviour 'the profession does not have strong theory, a large body of research, or established facts to protect it from superstition-based library management'. The point of course is that 'research is the antidote for superstition'.

Sumsion (1994) reminds us that research from the profession should be considered as not only aimed at the profession; the audience for research includes all those who have a role in the future of services – politicians at national and local level, policy makers and advisers, service heads, media, authors, as well as all levels of staff. He also identifies several other purposes for research:

- to remove common misunderstandings
- to determine underlying principles and features
- to establish trends
- to respond to new user needs and opportunities
- to discover and develop new ways of service delivery
- to apply discoveries/innovations from outside the profession
- to apply intellectual disciplines from outside the profession
- to monitor and broadcast results of local projects and enterprise
- to analyse and compare projects and enterprise undertaken in different places.

In the editorial leader of *Library and information science research* (*LISR*) (vol. 16, no. 4, (Fall), 1994) a discussion is presented on the apparent decline in the amount of research performed by librarians. Participants in the discussion – all members of the journal's editorial board – questioned whether the premise of decline was true; and what is research? who are 'librarians'?

If there is a problem, and there seems to be agreement that LIS research is not a 'growth area', then what is that problem? Suggestions put forward in *LISR* point out that we are not a social science and not a trade; what sort of research model are we likely to be able successfully to create? We have imitated others without full commitment, and the result has been a lack of work with a strong theoretical basis, which is directed at specific issues and has policy implications.

Using the extent of publication as a measure of quality is a false base; we need more useful or more effective research, not simply more research. 'So the real issue may not be the amount of research, but quality and relevance... this is cumulative.' Some early research gave the impression that LIS had a scientific basis, but now with the incorporation of technology into the profession much of the effort that went into the 'science' is channelled towards using the technology for service purposes – so the apparent decline may be a healthy sign of client-directed action rather than introspection.

The US emphasis on having a large number of researchers active to ensure plenty of papers is reflected in the *LISR* discussion: 'a field whose researchers are greatly outnumbered risks losing its standing'. Practitioners might comment that as we are asked to do more with less, research may decline not just for time reasons but because of lost confidence and questions on the direction of the profession; a 'breakdown of the historical roles within the profession' may have upset the framework where leading figures would have something worthwhile to say to colleagues – they are all now struggling with the new world.

Practitioners have too many other claims on their time, and academics are becoming overburdened by raised student ratios, administration, and increased pressure to concentrate on revenue-rich conference organization. Funding issues are not addressed in the *LISR* editorial, but may well be a constraint as funders seek to channel limited resources into priority areas rather than let researchers find their own niches.

Library and information science research has long been an uncomfortable and unsatisfactory field and there could be two major contributory factors – one is the nature of information study, a 'soft' science that defies strict analysis. Sutton (1993) summarized this in four underlying themes that encapsulate the barriers:

- contextualization (we need to understand the context, to avoid undermining the validity of observations by isolating them from the environment that gives them meaning); 'It is probably the case that all forms of observation necessarily alter that which is observed... the researcher must be cautious about prematurely imposing categories on the setting'.
- understanding (we need to move beyond the data to get some level of understanding; the constantly changing details of social reality need modelling to construct useful theoretical statements); Sutton quotes views on the structure of knowledge held by a librarian and a user 'who *151*

does not share the library profession's view of what organized knowledge is'.

- pluralism (we have to accept that uncertainty requires flexible standards); 'the results of individual studies of unique problems may not be incorporated easily within broader covering theories... contrasting research methods that come to different (or even incompatible) conclusions are equally valid'.
- expression (we have a poor history of disseminating research, and a poorer history of actually making practical use of results); research reports may need 'translating' to make them intelligible as 'times and audiences change'.

The second contributory factor is outlined in the *LISR* editorial cited above: it suggests that we have too much of three kinds of research:

- introspection, such as studies of faculty status, studies of content, authorship, reviewing practices of the literature itself, and studies of role identification, self-image of librarians
- over-energetic number crunching – taking data that could be genuinely useful and running it through 'multidimensional techniques that ultimately prove only that the author is competent in computing'
- how I did it good – the 'trade school' approach.

To these three we might add another from a more recent *LISR* editorial (vol. 18, no. 1, 1996):

- 'wash and wear' research that leads to unrealistic expectations; instead of getting the best quality, we may prefer the cheaper but superficially attractive action-based research 'frequently devoid of any theoretical context, and not always linked to decision making... [it] involves the use of pre-existing data collection forms that librarians can use without any adaptation, is easy to administer, does not

152

involve time-consuming data collection and analysis, and is easy to interpret and apply to a particular situation. Perhaps another characteristic is that the findings convince management of whatever points on which they need convincing.' Merely 'proving' how busy we are and how important we are can never be research.

WHAT ARE THE BARRIERS?

There are of course other problems besides these; logistically the barriers to research are a crucial concern. The reasons why research is not undertaken may vary from time to time but certain patterns are discernable, and pressures of everyday management are high on everyone's list of reasons why they can't pursue research. Dyer and Stern (1990) suggest barriers to research activity at the organizational level:

- lack of time
- lack of resources
- lack of supportive colleagues
- pressure of other work
- lack of feedback
- lack of blocks of time
- relatively low priority given to research
- discouragement of collaborative research
- lack of administrative support.

And at the personal level, they highlight:

- lack of confidence about ability to undertake research
- lack of skills/experience
- lack of motivation
- doubt about field of research
- publishing results
- entering new field/making new contacts
- focusing research
- over-specialization – discouraging new approaches and areas. *153*

As one would expect, it is the practitioners who suffer most from the major barriers – lack of time, and lack of experience – which lead therefore to lack of confidence.

Robbins (1992) lists some militating factors which act against collaboration between researchers and practitioners:

- researchers identify problems by talking to other researchers and ignoring practitioner views
- practitioners have difficulty identifying researchable topics
- researchers tend to use their own jargon which seems irrelevant to practitioners
- practitioners are not skilled in research processes and find difficulty in using and interpreting findings
- researchers disseminate findings in journals not read by practitioners
- practitioners fail to read research literature
- co-ordinated and accessible dissemination systems are not well developed
- practitioners and researchers fail to use the dissemination systems that are available.

Clearly there is a mismatch here, and in such a small profession – and one that makes information its business – it will be extraordinary to outsiders that both participants on one 'side' in the library world (suppliers rather than customers) have such disregard for each other.

CLIMATE AND PERCEPTIONS

The organizational climate has a great bearing on whether an individual feels that the effort of research is worthwhile. Allen (1986) stresses the place that research must have within the organization if it is to be successful. In-house research – which is noted in passing as being far more extensive than official registers suggest – 'may well be the greater part of all library research that is taking place'. Research is seen as needed to investigate a specific problem, for planning new services, for operational needs, and to improve the understanding or competence of the staff; this is essentially a pragmatic approach to research, but Allen's analysis is fuller than this synopsis would imply.

Allen outlines the responsibilities of managers in relation to in-house research: they should offer:

- facilitation (a positive climate, a policy of unambiguous support for approved projects)
- motivation (enthusiasm, encouragement, participation)
- determination (initiation and response)
- specification (consultation, approval)
- control (further consultation, support)
- realization (support, publication, implementation, recognition).

Commentators agree that practitioners must feel that they recognize the research, identify with it, accept it, feel an 'ownership' of it, otherwise its value is unappreciated and the likelihood of its implementation is low. The United States Department of Education formulated a research agenda in 1980 which met with overwhelming professional criticism but which was nonetheless pursued – inevitably with limited effect. In 1987 the same problem was repeated: a new agenda was proposed and condemned as a political document (Robbins, 1987) although it had apparently begun progress through a consultation procedure. Previous agenda-setting efforts were seen as inadequate because of their 'limitation to enumerations of issues without assessments of the current status of research, without knowledge of conclusions reached and priorities set in major reports... and without the benefit of extensive input by independent specialists'.

Robbins sets out the consultation programme and it is clear from her tone that there is too much reliance on commentators, on international experts, on representatives of funders, and on the deliberate limitation on the numbers of topics. An agenda implies pre-selected goals. Robbins' editorial received a prompt and well-argued rebuttal from an official of the Department (Matthews, 1988), but the damage was done: the practitioner community did *155* not identify with the process of agenda-setting and without their commitment the whole exercise would be flawed.

Wilson and Moore (1981) report that the main conclusion of a seminar on public library research was that there was a pressing need for improved co-ordination at both local and national levels; this led to the establishment of a body to provide a continuing link with the community to ensure relevance to the needs of practitioners. Not only was there a lack of confidence that the work done in or for public libraries was really 'research', but there was a notable shortage of people to link into joint projects and generally participate in the process of awareness and dissemination.

According to Braunstein (1989), in public library research 'the lack of theoretical underpinning often leads the results of such studies to be of questionable value to both library managers and policy makers'. Stewart (1984) similarly noted that 'almost all responses were concerned with practical problems rather than theory (notwithstanding the fact that librarianship has no recognized central theoretical base such as exists for most other disciplines'.

Stewart also detected a number of problems of attitude in the public library community. She found a tendency to use research only in cases of high uncertainty, hence the fascination of community research. There were difficulties over credibility, and over value judgements; dissemination was – and still is – a significant problem. The 'sharp-end' remains uninformed. But there is another very awkward attitudinal snag: 'to support research is to admit uncertainty about the nature of a problem and its solution'. This is one managerial hang-up that we must hope has been dispelled in more recent years!

In the report of a seminar on the general future of research in librarianship hosted in 1994 by the British Library Research and Development Department (Information UK, 1995), the discussion session threw up some salient points:

- it is difficult for practitioners to identify research that is useful and appropriate to their needs
- research appears retrospective and does not address new demands and problems

- environments are changing – libraries need information on technology and equipment, on access, on ways of working with the private sector
- there is a lot of information, and this is daunting for those in the field; better means of accessing it should be found
- where there is good research and good dissemination, the results are still not taken up by practitioners; some sectors do not turn to research results for development or to solve specific problems; research can be ignored; 'we must find ways of conditioning the community to think about research and to use the benefits of research before they rush into developing systems or services'.

EARLIER RESEARCH AGENDAS

The research needs of practitioners were summarized by Stewart (1984) as follows (in order of priority):

- resources *versus* demand for services
- new technology
- management of change
- public and political awareness of the importance of the library service
- acquiring the right calibre of staff
- decline in literacy
- staff motivation
- charging.

The summary of research activity by Moore (1987) notes a lack of coherence and unrelated studies; some work is unco-ordinated or incompatible. He concludes that projects vary widely in subject matter, scope and rigour. Positive comments were that there are some 'interesting snippets' and that there is a 'developing body of knowledge and understanding'. The pace of change, political influence, economic factors, technology, and the staffing climate are seen as the priority areas for future work.

157

Matters of research need from a government or funding authority point of view were suggested by Line (1991) to be:

- how much money is spent and where is it going?
- is the government getting value for money?
- what do libraries contribute to the economy and to society?
- how much money should be spent on libraries?
- how can effective provision be best achieved?
- what should be the balance between public and private sectors in provision?
- what roles should libraries perform in future?
- how can people develop skills in information handling?

and from the librarians' point of view:

- how should library budgets be optimally used?
- what budget should be sought?
- what will be the effects of technology?
- what functions should libraries perform?

Again in a public library context, Coleman (1991) has asked a series of questions about research that demonstrate the practitioners' suspicion of the researchers' private world:

- what is the funders' vision? Is there one?
- who makes the decisions on research? Why don't we know them?
- why are so few people involved? Why are the same names on so many committees?
- why are grant details so secret? Why are procedures so bureaucratic?
- why are grants and awards distributed to such a limited number of individuals and organizations?
- do consultants possess the necessary knowledge and skills?
- is there adequate dissemination?
- are libraries getting the research they deserve or need? 'In public libraries the answer has to be NO.'

Stewart has commented (1987) that 'information must be disseminated to the right group, at the right time and in the right form and language. Researchers' inability to do this has led practitioners to question whether some researchers have a firm grip on reality'. Current research agendas are discussed below.

ASSESSMENT ACTIVITY AS A RESEARCH TOOL

To facilitate research, certain basic data is necessary; libraries routinely collect such data – maybe for monitoring purposes, or as management information, or to provide statistical data for various authorities. Collection of such data may be unco-ordinated – formats may vary, procedures may be unreliable, innaccurate or cumbersome. However, data is the basis of research, and the collection process is probably to be encouraged in principle provided that the data has some validity so that improvements in handling can put it to some good use.

An area which has received much attention in recent years and in which data is necessary for measurement and comparison is performance assessment/appraisal/monitoring/evaluation and related processes such as quality assurance. Evaluation must have some basis on which to stand; typically this basis has been output, although there is doubt about whether this is a sound basis for libraries to use, or whether it needs to be combined with other measures, or replaced. The report from the Audit Commission (1997) notes that decisions on priorities need to be based on views of stakeholders and partners, not just on output.

Van House (1992) notes that evaluation processes can be used for purposes such as:

- attention directing
- problem solving
- scorekeeping (how are we doing? Better/worse than before?)
- conflict resolution (where activities are in competition for resources)
- complacency reduction (over-estimates of value)
- postponement of responsibility (no action during evaluation) *159*

- public relations
- fulfilling official requirements.

Data is usually collected on the basis of evidence such as:

- resources
- intensity of use (for example, circulation per volume)
- internal processes (for example, items catalogued)
- output (circulation, transactions)
- adequacy of performance (for example, user success rates)
- availability
- accessibility
- costs to library
- cost to client
- outcomes.

But Van House points out that what we really need to know is whether certain things have occurred, such as:

- are students learning more?
- are people finding jobs?
- are workers more employable?
- are people coping better with their life circumstances?
- are researchers more productive?

In the UK, the Office of Arts and Libraries (1990) has explored performance indicators in depth; their report suggests that assessment can be made at various levels – resource, activity, function, service, location, and entire library. As well as inputs, outputs, and effectiveness, the concept of overall impact is included. The development of standards in individual areas of service is important, but overall standards are harder to devise.

Work on library performance indicators has also been published by the European Commission; Ward *et al.* (1995) summarize work on indicators and other management tools in various countries. The study has been carried out under the EU Telematics
Programme by De Montfort University, LISU, and Essex Libraries in

the UK; it reveals inadequacies that could be corrected in the next stage of development. Chapter 6 of the Handbook, *Performance measurement and evaluation*, covers this topic in more depth, and its mention here is a reminder that all parts of this field overlap and are inter-connected; no aspect can be viewed simply in isolation.

NEW AGENDAS

The research agenda of the US Special Libraries Association (SLA) is outlined by Sayer (1996); this is one of the most thorough and well-reasoned accounts of future needs to have been set out recently. Sayer reminds us that research can be seen as an 'overarching perspective from which to weave these sometimes disparate threads together'. Collaborative activity appears in the SLA agenda in various ways: one particular piece of work was designed so that other librarians could augment the research by using the methodology in their own services. Replications of the work are also reported to have been funded in the UK.

The SLA's agenda is keen to emphasize its relevance and linkage to practitioners in a programme planned 'to help members take control of their futures'. One way this goal is achieved is through the reponsiveness of the research program to the dynamic environment of special libraries. The main points of the SLA agenda are:

- *Futures*
  what is the impact of the projection of futurists?
  what new technologies in development will impact on libraries?
- *Current/use issues*
  how do people decide what they need to know?
  how can artificial intelligence and expert systems facilitate access?
  what are information seeking and using behaviours of different professions or fields of work?
  what are the interface design considerations for question-answering or fact-finding online systems?
  what consumer behaviour models can be adapted to libraries?   *161*

- *Measures of productivity and value*
  what are the existing measures?
  how do clients/users value information?
  is there a difference between the cost of information and its perceived value?
  how do libraries relate to corporate success?
  how can cost/benefit methodologies be used by libraries?
- *Client/user satisfaction measures*
  how can existing measures be adapted?
  what is the role of expectations in measuring quality?
  what are client/user perceptions about the quality of information services?
  what techniques can measure value?
  what can libraries learn from other service businesses?
  what corporate marketing strategies can be adapted?
- *Staffing*
  what measures and methods can assess optimum size of staff, and organizational structures?
  what data and criteria are needed to optimize staffing?

Other plans for the future show that targeting of resources will become ever more necessary. The British Library Research and Innovation Centre in its Research Plan document for 1997–1998 has targeted two areas for action (BLRIC *Research bulletin* 17, 1997):

- Management of libraries and information services: to stimulate research on management techniques and issues of current concern, including evaluating the systems and structures used to achieve a quality service, securing more resources, and identifying and motivating an appropriate workforce to meet the new challenges
- Library co-operation: to include issues of regional co-operation and the interactions between libraries in different sectors (especially between the public and academic sectors) with emphasis on the outcomes of co-operation and how it can lead to improved access for users of services.

At the end of 1997 the Research Committee of the Library and Information Commission issued a document – *Prospects: a strategy for action*. In line with the Commission's Vision 2020, the Committee sees three core themes for research:

- connectivity: access to the information society
- content: resources for the information society
- competences: skills for the information society.

These are all underpinned by two fundamental themes for the information society:

- impact and value of library and information services
- economics of library and information services.

CONCLUSION

Research needs of the future

These recent agendas highlight one of the real problems that is coming our way – the crisis in recruitment of the workforce for libraries and the information world. As technology is now part and parcel of the librarianship scene, there is a danger that instead of quiet bookish people we shall get introverted IT buffs; as ever, the outgoing people-friendly recruits will be in short supply.

A big disparity in recruitment will be in the area of knowledge workers in commerce and industry; the growth of the concept of the 'learning organization' – the firm that values its information resources highly and seeks to exploit company knowledge to improve its competitive edge – will expand the demand for people who can manage information. The rewards should be good, and we may see the take-off of a new breed within the profession of entrepreneurial information managers who can build up a portfolio of skills and who will be head-hunted by ambitious companies. How conventional library employment will fare when the competition tries to corner the market for skilled recruits is unknown. We urgently need research into this whole question: *163* what are the skills, how are they acquired, how are people to be trained, how will new roles develop?

Also in the commercial context, the role of information needs further investigation and clarification; information helps build strategies for future business, through such activities as anticipation of new legal requirements, new design features, re-skilling of staff for new processes, but the value of information and how it works is poorly understood. Information can be used for control, for planning, and for gaining competitive edge. How can some manufacturers charge more for a product not dissimilar from a competitor's product? The answer is usually based on information, either because the premium-priced manufacturer has developed a neater way of completing the product, has researched the market more accurately, or has built up a reputation for quality and good service – features that need an information input so that they can be turned to advantage. Know-how in design, quality and finish appeal to customers better than cheapness and poor design; costs may be higher, but consumers whose choice is not limited by price will appreciate the difference and pay over the odds for it. Research is needed here to clarify what is happening and how information is creating business opportunities.

Development of an information strategy in a business environment should clarify directions, add management credibility, ensure a place in the budgeting process and enhance corporate visibility. As another resource in the company, information performance should be open to inspection for accuracy, timeliness, relevance, and cost. At present, however, there is no agreed mechanism for examining the information asset in these terms; research has failed adequately to address crucial areas and thus information management has been handicapped by poor infrastructural planning. The failure to exploit the organizational significance of information is a major obstacle to the progress of the information professions.

There is a growing emphasis on the client/user perception and expectation of service, and interestingly on how clients decide what it is that they need to know. Research will need to explore the image of information services, and plan how to avoid the furtherance of the current situation where librarians are ignored – not because their service is no good, but because they are so low-key that their service is invisible. IT staff routinely investigate new ideas on information retrieval, unaware that there is 40 years of research literature on that question, but it hides behind the label of librarianship.

Client use of information is also becoming better understood, and more work is needed here; when someone needs information, what is it that they actually think they want to find? We are gaining more expertise in realizing that information use is dependent on many subjective impressions, and success in operating an information service is determined by client satisfaction, not simply by having the correct answer.

Another problem area that – unsurprisingly – remains with us is expression: dissemination of findings in a world increasingly plagued with information overload, and persuasion of the practitioner community to take up and implement research results. In part, this is a reflection that research has not kept up with the times: old ideas and old methods have been re-used and re-used and the result is that few practitioners listen any more. 'We must move from measurement of inputs and outputs to outcomes and impacts, and better realize what the word 'research' means, and how particular circumstances affect research design.' (*LISR* editorial; vol. 18, no. 1, 1996)

Interdisciplinarity works both ways; in the same manner that we regret that others ignore our literature, so we should explore literature outside the strict subject area. Accessibility is no longer a barrier, and although overload could be a problem, the gains would outweigh the headaches. Perhaps particularly the areas of service quality and client satisfaction need wider investigation. 'Value' is a concept of the moment; Sayer (1996) refers to the 'value' of the library, 'valued' staff competences, most 'valued' service. This term can mean anything, and the last thing we need is another catch-all concept that will obsess the researchers and further alienate the practitioners. Value is important; research should tell us what it is for our clients, and how we discover if we can offer it.

Sutton (1993) reminds us that 'one of the reasons that these problems deserve our attention is precisely because, since we cannot easily resolve them, we must therefore learn to manage them'. Technology gives us the means to do more, but at present we remain limited by our own vision. The contributions to this Handbook show us some of the new directions that the profession should be urgently researching.

REFERENCES

Allen, G. G. (1986), Management and the conduct of in-house library research. *Library and information science research*, vol. 8, no. 2, pp. 155–162.

Audit Commission (1997), *Due for renewal: a report on the library service.* London: Audit Commission Publications.

Braunstein, Y. M. (1989), Library funding and economics: a framework for research. *IFLA journal*, vol. 15, no. 4, pp. 289–298.

Coleman, P. (1991), Research and the public library: are libraries getting the research they deserve? The librarian's view. In Harris, C. (ed.) *Research policy in librarianship and information science. Papers presented at a conference of the Library and Information Research Group and the Public Libraries Research Group, Salford, 1990.* London: Taylor Graham. pp. 93–98. (BLRD Report no. 6010)

Dyer, H. and Stern, R. (1990), Overcoming barriers to library and information science research. *International journal of information and library research*, vol. 2, no. 2, pp. 129–134.

Edmonds, M. L. (1987), From superstition to science: the role of research in strengthening public library service to children. *Library trends*, Winter, pp. 509–520.

Information UK (1995), The future of library and information science research in the UK. *Information UK outlooks*, no. 13. London: LITC.

Library and Information Commission: Research Committee (1997), *Prospects: a strategy for action.* London: Library and Information Commission.

Line, M. (1991), Research policy in librarianship and information science: keynote address. In Harris, C. *Research policy in librarianship and information science.* London: Taylor Graham. (BLRD Report no. 6010)

Matthews, A. J. (1988), D.O.E. responds to the 'Another research agenda' editorial. *Library and information science research,* vol. 10, no. 1, pp. 119–120.

Moore, N. (1987), *Research and practice: 21 years of library research in the UK.* London: British Library, 1987. (LIR Report no. 55)

Office of Arts and Libraries (1990), *Keys to success: performance indicators for public libraries,* [by] King Research Ltd. London: HMSO. (Library and Information Series, no. 18)

Robbins, J. (1987), Another! research agenda. *Library and information science research,* vol. 9, no. 4, pp. 141–142.

Robbins, J, (1992), Affecting librarianship in action: the dissemination and communication of research findings. In Estabrook, L. S. *Applying research to practice.* Urbana-Champaign, IL: University of Illinois GSLIS. pp. 78–88.

Sayer, L. (1996), A research agenda for special libraries. *Publishing research quarterly,* vol. 12, no. 1, pp. 20–30.

Stewart, L. (1984), *Public library research: a review of UK investigation between 1978 and 1982.* Loughborough, CLAIM. (CLAIM Report no. 35)

Stewart, L. (1987), *The dissemination of library and information research and development to the practitioner: an investigation into public libraries.* Loughborough, CLAIM. (CLAIM Report no. 61)

Sumsion, J. (1994), Strategic research areas and possible research models for UK public libraries. *Library review,* vol. 43, no.4, pp. 7–26.

Sutton, B. (1993), The rationale for qualitative research. *Library quarterly,* vol. 63, no. 4, pp. 411–430.

Van House, N. (1992), Evaluation strategies. In Estabrook, L. S. *Applying research to practice.* Urbana-Champaign, IL: University of Illinois GSLIS. pp. 52–62.

Ward, S. *et al.* (1995), *Library performance indicators and library management tools.* Report to the EC, DGXIII-E3. Luxembourg: Office for Official Publications of the EC. (EUR 16483 EN)

Wilson, A, and Moore, N. (1981), Public library research. *Journal of librarianship,* vol. 13, no. 2, pp. 63–74.

8 Copyright and related issues

Graham Cornish

This chapter seeks to examine some of the major issues in copyright law to determine where the information intermediary stands and what the challenges are in the future. Because of the national nature of copyright and related legislation no attempt will be made here to interpret the law on specific points in any particular country.

The idea behind copyright is rooted in certain fundamental ideas about creativity and possession. Basically, it springs from the idea that anything we create is an extension of 'self' and should be protected from general use by anyone else. Coupled with this is the idea that the person creating something has exclusive rights over the thing created, partly for economic reasons but also because of this extension of 'self' idea. Copyright is therefore important to ensure the continued growth of writing, performing and creating. Copyright law aims to protect this growth but, at the same time, tries to ensure that some access to copyright works is allowed as well. Without this access creators would be starved of ideas and information to create more copyright material.

Copyright divides into two main areas: economic rights and moral rights. In the Anglo-Saxon tradition the emphasis has always been on economic rights, that is, the economic benefit that rights can bring in terms of royalties, sale of all or part of copyright, licences and so on. Moral rights include the right to be named as the author, the right not to have another person named as the author instead, the right not to have works falsely attributed to oneself and the right to prevent the mutilation of the work which includes adding bits on and chopping them off, or changing the meaning of the text. Of course, copyright law abounds in myths relating to issues such as legal deposit, use of the copyright symbol and registration but these are, generally, myths; some of the more obvious ones are briefly discussed in the Appendix to this chapter.

Because copyright is such an intangible thing, there is often a temptation to ignore it. Those who take this approach forget that they, too, own copyright in their own creations and would feel quite angry if this were abused by others. Some of the restrictions placed on use by the law may seem petty or trivial but they are designed to allow some use of copyright material without unduly harming the interests of the creator or author.

The rapid growth in the dissemination of information by electronic means has had the effect of heightening awareness of the subject, making people more keen to know their rights and privileges and generally creating an atmosphere of extreme caution in case anyone puts a foot wrong and ends up in court. Whilst this is no bad thing, nobody should become too paranoid. Although there has been a recent tendency for copyright infringement cases to be heard in criminal courts, this is usually where important commercial considerations apply such as republishing or reproduction in bulk for commercial purposes. Most infringements of copyright by individuals are dealt with through the civil courts so that the rights owner must take legal proceedings if it is thought an infringement has taken place. As there are few cases recorded involving libraries as such it would be reasonable to assume that a similar route would be taken, given that libraries are not, or should not be, involved in mass reproduction for commercial gain!

INFORMATION MANAGERS AND COPYRIGHT

Libraries are in a unique position as custodians of copyright material. They have the duty to care for, and allow access to, other people's copyright works. This places special responsibilities on *169* all those working in libraries, archives and the information world generally. Librarians and information intermediaries, in the widest sense of the phrase, practise their profession by using this property so they should take all possible steps to protect it, whilst, at the same time, ensuring that the rights and privileges of users are also safeguarded.

Information managers need to be able to look in at least three directions at once to fulfil their role in relation to intellectual property. Obviously they are responsible for ensuring that the copyright and other rights vested in the material under their control is respected and the law obeyed. At the same time they need to protect the interests of their users within the context of the relevant laws, exploiting to the full any legislative rights or privileges given them. However, all information managers will also be responsible for the creation of works which are themselves protected by copyright such as bibliographies, databases, literature analyses and summaries as well as promotional material for the services offered. What is said in this chapter should be read with all three of these duties in mind and the different implications carefully drawn.

UNDERSTANDING THE LAW

As stated at the beginning of this chapter, legislation on copyright is national in character and, despite efforts by the European Union to harmonize laws within the EU, still varies considerably from one jurisdiction to another. In a number of countries it has been the subject of considerable analysis by general copyright scholars and those specializing in library and information aspects of the law. Consequently there are monographs on the subject which can be useful for library and archive staff, especially in the UK (Wall, 1993; Cornish, 1997), the USA (Brewelheide, 1995; Gasaway and Wiant, 1994), Japan (Oyama, 1991) and Australia (State Library, 1991). Every practising librarian or information worker should know what the law says (even if it is not always clear what it means!). This is important so that any privileges or rights given to users or librarians by the law can be safeguarded and upheld.

One of the great pitfalls of taking any legislation at face value, and certainly copyright law, is to assume that the words in the law mean what we think they mean. Current UK legislation, for example, abounds in words which are not defined and are therefore open to various interpretations. On the other hand some words are defined in a way that defies understanding by the normal English speaker! Examples are 'reasonable', 'substantial', 'lending' and 'librarian'. All law needs to be understood within the context of the whole legal regime of which it is part and other branches such as contracts, liability, privacy and, especially for EU countries, competition law and the relevant sections of the Treaty of Rome.

International treaties

Quite often references can be found to 'international copyright law'. Copyright law is, in fact, national in character and is framed within the general context of international conventions. There are, in effect, three of these. The first and oldest is the Berne Convention (International Convention, 1979) which requires, amongst other things, no formalities before copyright can be claimed and a minimum protection (as at December 1996) of 50 years from the end of the year in which the author dies. The Universal Copyright Convention (1971) requires a shorter period of protection and the use of the famous copyright symbol (©) in order to claim copyright protection. The third international treaty is the Agreement establishing the World Trade Organisation which requires those taking part to put in place legislation for the protection of intellectual property of which copyright forms a part. This latter has considerably increased the number of countries enjoying reciprocal copyright protection. The result of these treaties, in broad terms, is that works published in any other country which has signed them are protected in the UK as if they were UK publications, except that the length of that protection in the UK will not be longer than that granted in the country of origin.

Which works are protected

No work is protected by copyright unless it is 'original'. Originality *171* is tested in different ways by different countries. Some countries would not recognize something as commonplace as the telephone directory as being copyright whereas others see it as eligible for protection. In addition, copyright is limited by the time it lasts. Within the European Economic Area (the 15 EU members, plus Norway and Iceland), as a rule of thumb copyright lasts for 70 years from the end of the year in which the author dies or 70 years from creation or publication if there is no author (Directive 93/98). There are special rules for sound recordings, films, videos and computer-generated works as well. If the work was first published outside the European Economic Area (EEA) then copyright may last for only 50 years depending on the rules in the country of origin.

Ownership

Ownership of copyright is a complicated issue. Owners' rights extend far beyond straightforward copying and include issuing copies to the public (which itself may embrace lending, rental and electronic distribution), performing, playing or broadcasting and adapting and translating a work. These rights are exclusive to the copyright owner and, because they form a type of monopoly, have to be limited in some ways to ensure that users have access to copyright material. Although the author is usually the first owner, that ownership often passes immediately to an employer if the work is created as part of normal employment. In addition, parts of copyright can be transferred to others by sale or contract while the author retains other parts or sells them to different people. For example, an author may sell the right to publish a book for five years to one publisher, the rights to turn it into a film to someone else, the rights of translation to other languages to half-a-dozen different agencies and subsequently sell the right of publication to a different publisher for a further five years.

Those working to provide information services to clients need to examine the law in their own country carefully. Firstly because they need to ensure they understand who owns the rights in any compilation of information they provide; secondly to be properly informed about the ownership of the copyright in the material they are using. For example, the copyright in internal records in a company will almost certainly be owned by that company but this may not be true of reports commissioned from external specialists or, indeed, some elements of the company's own internal reports such as photographs or statistical tables.

Limits on owners' rights

Because copyright is a monopoly, limitations on these rights are provided by quantity, time and use. Time (duration) has already been discussed. Quantity is essentially the idea that copyright protects all or a substantial part of a work and therefore less than a substantial part can be freely copied and copyright is not infringed unless a 'substantial' part of the work is copied. This is true for most legal regimes although different terms may be used. Just what is substantial can be determined only by circumstances. One learned judge in the UK said 'If it's worth copying, it's worth protecting' (Petersen, 1916) which seems reasonably fair.

The third limitation is the use to which copies of a work may be put. Most countries permit limited copying by individuals and libraries/archives. Many also have special rules for copying by or for those with visual impairment and most countries also allow copying for the purposes of reporting current news, criticizing or reviewing works and for judicial or parliamentary purposes. Although countries with an Anglo-Saxon tradition often employ a phrase such as 'fair dealing' or 'fair use' this terminology is not found in most other legal regimes although the underlying concept often is (Hugenholtz and Visser, 1995). There are rarely any limits stated and each action of copying must be judged on its context and merits.

Where special regulations exist for libraries, these should be studied carefully for the detail set out in them. As an example, in the UK, libraries may copy one article from a single issue of any periodical title. But the definition of 'article' in UK law is 'an item of any description' so if the contents page has been copied for a user then no article from that issue can also be copied for the same person because they have already had their allowance by having the contents page (an article)!

Information managers also need to be aware of privileges enjoyed by other sectors of the information user community such as education. It may well be that a library or information service is asked to copy something for educational purposes which would not be permitted for libraries as such, but which can be done for the education sector. This is also true for such areas as judicial hearings or parliamentary business.

Lending and rental

In many countries lending and rental are not actions which are part of copyright law, neither was the Public Lending Right Scheme operated in public libraries in a number of countries. The European Union has introduced limited lending/rental rights for owners of the copyright in all kinds of work and this may well be a trend followed by other countries and regions. Rental is defined as for commercial benefit whereas lending brings no direct commercial or economic benefit. Member countries can make derogations for various types of material and lending by different kinds of institution but as these will differ from one Member State to another it will be important to study the legislation carefully.

The 'publication right'

The EU, once again, has introduced a Directive which requires legislation to allow anyone who first publishes an unpublished work which is out of copyright to have an exclusive right over that work for 25 years. This will mean that anyone who first published an unpublished manuscript which is out of copyright but kept in a library or archive, would have an exclusive right to publish or copy it for 25 years. This could be a reader who obtained a photocopy of the work and the library would lose all rights to make copies of that work even for research and private study. This could be a serious impediment to the free-flow of intellectual information. The implementation of this legislation should be monitored with care to ensure that libraries and archives do not lose their traditional role of being able to release unpublished materials to the general public.

Computer software

Computer software is treated in many ways as a literary work and protected as such. However, the very nature of computer software and the way it is used required specific legislation to be introduced. For example, it is virtually impossible to use software without copying it, yet copying is an exclusive right of the copyright owner! There are also clear problems with vulnerability and it is desirable to make a back-up copy in case a fault occurs or a virus is subsequently introduced. Again this would be an infringement of copyright. There are also problems with the fact that one piece of software may be needed to design or run a completely new application (for example, Windows-type applications). To do this requires the technician to get into the software to see how it works and make the necessary adjustments to the new application. Again, this process, known as reverse-engineering, is an infringement of copyright. An interesting feature of the legislation required by the EU and suggested by the WIPO (World Intellectual Property Organization) Treaty is that, if the copyright owner tried to introduce clauses to prohibit these actions, such clauses would be null and void.

PRESERVATION

Preservation is a major issue for all those managing information resources, as explained in chapter 12. Initially this may not be seen as a serious issue from a copyright point of view, but preservation increasingly involves reproducing a work, either in the same form (paper-to-paper) or more often, in different forms such as paper-to-microform, paper-to-electronic format (using Optical Character Recognition or more sophisticated technologies) or microform-to-electronic. There is also the immediate challenge of preserving electronic materials – how and in what format. Many countries have laws which permit libraries (often only non-commercial libraries) to make copies either for preservation purposes or, more often, to meet the needs of their activities (UNESCO, 1976). This is of little help to the records manager in a major commercial *175* organization or archivist of a private estate. Generally, copying for preservation cannot be undertaken if the work to be preserved can be purchased through the normal commercial channels of supply, otherwise the economic interests of the copyright owner would be undermined. However, there are other issues facing the information manager when considering preservation matters.

Without permission it is certainly not permitted to publish a work but publication needs careful consideration in itself. In some legislations publication specifically excludes making a work available to the public by means of an electronic retrieval system. Therefore to digitize a work and then make it available over a WAN (Wide Area Network), or perhaps even a LAN (Local Area Network), could lead to claims for damages by the copyright owner.

Ownership of the new work may also be a problem. Once a digital work has been created, and, assuming it is legal, the information manager wishes to use it in some way, it is necessary to decide who owns it.

As stated earlier, for a work to be protected by copyright law it has to be original and this is unlikely to include merely scanning a document into a computer. This is analogous to just making a photocopy and it has been demonstrated there is no copyright in a mere photocopy which is a slavish copy of the original. Another test of originality is the 'sweat of the brow' idea whereby sheer effort used to create a work may count towards claiming it is original. However, making a slavish copy using a computer system hardly involves sweat of the brow. A little perspiration on the palm might be demonstrated but it is doubtful if real labour could be shown as a prime reason for copyright in the digitized work. However, it is well-known that scanning, however sophisticated the technology is, does not produce the perfect result that is needed and all electronic documents need some editing. Here it is quite likely that copyright could be claimed in the new work because sufficient intellect and skill has been used in correcting the mistakes or gaps which the machine has left to call this a work.

But the complications of ownership do not end there. Where work is carried out by library and archive staff using their own equipment then the copyright will certainly belong to the library or archive concerned. However, if an outside contractor is used for this work, unless a clause is written into the contract specifically, it is likely that the outside contractor will own the copyright in the new work created. The contractor may well allow the library or archive to use the work for the purpose for which it was originally commissioned but might be quite able to prevent its subsequent use in such items as anthologies, publicity, multi-media materials and similar activities because the person commissioned owns the copyright not the commissioner. All contracts for this sort of work should be looked at very carefully.

SOME ELECTRONIC CHALLENGES

Information managers are in the business of providing access to materials in any form, electronic or any other format. In achieving this, they must deal with a range of issues such as privacy, data protection, liability, obscenity, libel and contractual relationships as well as copyright (Franken, 1991; Oppenheim, 1995). Such access raises the challenge of the fairly obvious one of format. The hardware and software which is now being used to create digital images will not be around in ten years, or even five years, time. There will be a need to be able to change from one format or program to another. However, libraries may not have the right to do this because of the ownership of the digital images which have been created. For example, CD-ROMs have more than one copyright element: the content will be protected as a literary or artistic work; the program used to drive the CD-ROM will be a literary work but with distinctive legislation to protect it; and the actual compilation (the disc) will also have copyright protection as a compilation. These rights may all be held by different people. In addition, CD-ROMs which are multimedia in nature may well contain performing rights as well. In order to view a CD-ROM work a copy may have to be made for viewing. Therefore, the act of viewing can be seen as a restricted act. In normal circumstances, contracts of sale will stipulate what may or may not be done and viewing is usually one of the acts permitted. A recent EU Directive should prohibit the introduction of clauses into contracts which *177* prevent lawful users of such works from being able to use them in the normal way. Copying a CD-ROM in its entirety would be an infringement of all the rights listed above. Back-up copies for preservation would also be an infringement of the content and the CD-ROM as a whole but not of the computer program used to drive the CD-ROM. Similarly it would probably not be an infringement to decompile the program to create another program to run the CD-ROM if the original program became obsolescent.

But it also has to be faced that actions which are considered normal in the paper environment are rapidly becoming viewed with great suspicion by copyright owners in the electronic world. Even viewing is seen as a potential infringement of a work because to load the documents onto the screen means making a copy of it and this is not allowed in law. Similarly, to transmit a work to somebody else would effectively make a further copy of it and this again would not be permitted by any copyright owner. This even extends to the fact that where electronic documents are sent to a remote user they are not allowed to view them before they download them. Otherwise, they might view the document and decide this is not the one they want and therefore send it back again – whatever that means in electronic terminology! – therefore a delivery would have taken place or a copy made but to no benefit to anybody who owns the copyright material. Similarly, browsing is seen by many copyright owners as a potential threat because it means that there may be multiple access to the same document whereas in the paper world browsing must be restricted to one person at a time.

Moral rights

Moral rights have been mentioned earlier. In an electronic environment these are crucial as it is so easy to infringe any or all of the actions defined as moral rights with very little detection. Authorship, provenance, content and meaning can all be changed and material added and deleted with very little difficulty. Ironically, it may well be these rights which play the most important role in the electronic world as scholars are as anxious as authors that the works which they receive are intact and their integrity has been retained. Obviously how one views a report on lung cancer from the Tobacco Research Council will be different to how one views a similar document on the same subject from the Medical Research Council. The real challenge for information managers is, firstly to establish systems which ensure reasonable integrity of the electronic documents under their control, and secondly to look at ways of validating the electronic documents which they receive to add to their collections.

Databases

Not all countries protect databases (whether electronic or otherwise) because they are not perceived as being original enough to warrant protection. Cases in the USA (Miller, 1991; VerSteeg, 1995) and Europe (Vijne, 1995) have tended to raise the threshold for eligibility for copyright protection. This has caused the EU to introduce new legislation to cover especially those which would not otherwise be protected and this, in turn, influenced WIPO to try to conclude a treaty on this subject in September 1997 (WIPO, 1997). Although this may be seen as important for users of information it also has significance for creators of information sources, many of which are constituted as lists, compilations of data which, in themselves, are not copyright. The doubt surrounding the protection given in some laws to bibliographies, lists of organizations or individuals should be clarified under this new round of legislation.

In the UK, a database is already recognized as a literary work protected by copyright but this is not the case in many countries and definitions of what is 'original' (as stated earlier) vary considerably. To try to harmonize the situation the European Commission has introduced a directive on databases which recognizes that a database, regardless of the content, shall be regarded as a copyright work provided that sufficient investment has been made in it by the creator in terms of data collection, verification or arrangement of the material to make it a new work. Thus, even if the content is not of itself copyrightable, then *179* nonetheless the database can be. An obvious example is the telephone directory where each entry is not a copyright item because it is a statement of fact but the compilation is regarded as a copyright work. In this case the Commission has given the protection of 15 years for such databases. This is called a *sui generis* right as it is not actually copyright but analogous to it. It is important to notice that the EU definition of a database is not restricted to an electronic document but can be any type of compilation (Directive 96/9). However, in the United Kingdom they are almost certainly protected under the doctrine of 'sweat of the brow' which is part of the originality test. In America, a different decision was reached when one telephone company took the entries from another telephone directory and used them as part of their own database. The American Court ruled that the mere telephone directory arranged by family name could not be a copyright work because it is the obvious way to arrange such a work. The doctrine of 'sweat of the brow' was not considered sufficient.

The important thing to note is that even where a series of documents are old and probably out of copyright, turning them into some sort of compilation, whether in paper or electronic form, will mean that the publisher of this collection has copyright in the overall total package even though not in individual items within it. This is already the case in the United Kingdom and is also linked to typographical copyright, mentioned earlier.

Protection mechanisms

Because of all these problems there is considerable research into the mechanisms for protection which look at the possible technology for controlling and managing copyrighting documents. They all revolve round the idea that 'the answer to the machine is in the machine'. Models have been developed which would enable the copyright owner to monitor, inhibit or control the use of documents and also to set royalty payments which might vary between different types of user and even within the same document. To overcome the more extreme elements of this sort of technology the European Commission have established a European Copyright User Platform (ECUP) which is trying to strike a balance between owners and users. Nevertheless we need to be aware that the documents which we create or cause to be created, may pose serious copyright problems in the future.

To deal with some of these issues the European Commission has funded a number of projects on electronic copyright management systems (ECMS). This is the catch-phrase of the moment. As far back as 1989 a major project called CITED (Copyright in Transmitted Electronic Documents) began to design a model for the management of copyright in the electronic environment (CITED, 1994). This model has subsequently been taken into other projects with such names as COPICAT, COPYSMART and COPEARMS. COPICAT (Copyright Ownership in Computer Assisted Training) has developed technology to handle copyright protection for distance learning use, while COPYSMART is working on the use of Smartcard technology to control access and collect royalties. COPEARMS (Co-ordinating Project for Electronic Authors Right Management Systems) is a European Union-wide project to develop a standardized approach to the implementation of the CITED technology. A further major EU project, IMPRIMATUR (Intellectual Multimedia Property Rights Model and Terminology for Universal Reference) is charged with the task of building a worldwide consensus on standards and methods of copyright management without indicating a specific type of software/hardware solution. The results of all these different projects is that there are embryonic systems available for dealing with many of the problems which have just been outlined. However, the interests of libraries and, indeed, academic publishers, are very small fish in a very, very large pool. In Australia, the Propagate Project is also working on these issues, whilst the Japanese COPYMART technology aims to deal with electronic payment mechanisms. The real driving force for many of these developments will be the entertainment and leisure industries such as music and video. Some of these projects do have partners from such industries but the span of interest is very wide, as demonstrated by the fact that one project focuses exclusively on the textile design industry.

LICENCES AND CONTRACTS

As copyright in many countries is increasingly viewed as a property right, it can be traded like any other property and therefore the owner can allow anything to be done under contract or licence which the owner wishes to permit and can, at the same time, agree the terms for such actions. Most electronic publications are currently supplied with a clearly defined set of parameters for what can, and cannot, be done. Such actions as downloading, retransmitting, networking, printing onto paper or incorporating into other documents, are all allowed, or not as the case may be. By agreeing to such a contract the purchaser agrees to abide by the limitations set out. These may be more or less generous than the exceptions given under national legislation but anyone subscribing to a CD-ROM or online database should always study carefully the terms of the contract under which it is supplied.

Licensing for some aspects of copyright, namely neighbouring rights, has been established for many years in the shape of the Performing Rights Society but this concept has now been extended to all forms of copyright use. Over 20 countries now have copyright collecting societies, probably the best known of which are the Copyright Clearance Center in the USA (CCC) and the Copyright Licensing Agency in the UK (CLA) which offer licences to copy a wide range of published material most often only in paper format. Licences exist for various sectors and activities and this is a constantly growing area of activity. Other agencies are playing an increasingly important role, for example in the UK, for newspapers, hymns, slides and off-air educational recording, as well as the long-established societies for performing rights and the making of sound recordings.

Where there is a need to develop services outside the exceptions, information professionals can talk to the licensing agencies and other rights owners' organizations to negotiate use of material in return for royalties. Those working in the information industries should view this as a real way forward when the law inhibits the introduction of new services without the owners' consent. Therefore, although the privileges given by the law to users and libraries should be stoutly defended, it is important not to lose sight of the exciting possibilities that may be achieved in co-operation with copyright owners.

Co-operation with rights owners

Licensing and contracts are part of a much wider issue in the use of copyright material when information managers are providing services to their clients. The information intermediary provides the interface between the publisher and the untapped, and untappable, market and therefore enables one aim of publishing – to reach the public – to be more effectively achieved. Publishers cannot hope to reach every potential outlet for their products because they do not have the direct contact with the necessary groups to achieve this. Publishers are also limited in what they can provide in terms of a repertoire which will normally be limited to their own products or those of associated companies. Libraries, however, can, and do, reach a wide audience as they have direct access to a very broadly based user community. They can also offer a much wider range of products than the publisher or even other intermediaries (booksellers, subscription agents, database hosts) as they are not motivated primarily by financial incentives, although they may need to limit the range of resources available because of financial constraints. In the case of public libraries and the majority of academic and educational libraries, this achievement is at the expense largely of the tax-payer throughout the world.

Naturally libraries, as major resources of information, and valuing their unique role to reach so many users, want and need to be able to exploit new possibilities. However, if they are no longer going to rely on a paper-based industry, the alternative will be to use materials in electronic formats of many kinds, all of which are vulnerable to a range of threats including unauthorized copying, redistribution, repackaging and even republishing under different labels.

WEB SITE LINKS AND THE WIDER DIMENSION

One of the greatest benefits of the Web site mechanisms is the   *183* creation of hypertext links to other Web sites, forming a complex and effective method of cross-referencing and information retrieval. This system, originally seen as totally harmless and of enormous benefit to the user and provider communities, is now under considerable pressure from legal questions. It may be useful to look at the various issues to see how they may affect the retrieval of information in the future.

Firstly, there is a technical question which has considerable legal implications. The perception of users is that, when they click on a link to another Web site, this provides access to that site. This is technically not the case. Rather, by clicking on the hypertext link the text sought is transmitted to the user. Therefore the user is not simply viewing something which exists but having it transmitted to their own PC. This in itself constitutes copying a work. The natural reaction to this is that, if the owner of the site to which the link has been created did not want a work copied then they should not have allowed the link to be built. However, links are not always built with the knowledge and permission of the owner of the Web site to which they are connected. This has raised the question of whether clicking on the hypertext link actually causes the material sought to be broadcast. So it could be argued that not only was the work copied by the person doing the searching but they also caused it to be broadcast which is a separate exclusive right of the copyright owner.

A further aspect of hypertext links is the question of 'passing off'. Passing off is not a direct copyright matter but more of trade. Nevertheless it often involves infringements of copyright. Hence the passing off is providing goods or services which look sufficiently like somebody else's goods or services that they may be considered as coming from the second person even though they do not and may not, on close examination, be considered as coming from that second source. However, creating something which looks very like, sounds like, or has the general appearance of another product may well lead to a charge of passing off. It is important when creating Web site links that the user is always aware of whose information is being used. If a user starts a search in a Web site and then uses a hypertext link into another Web site this may give the impression that it is the first Web site being viewed, even though it is now a different Web site being viewed. It is therefore important to make sure there are displays, borders or icons which make it quite clear whose Web site, and therefore copyright material, is being viewed and possibly downloaded or printed. A small icon which says something like 'copyright information available here' would overcome this difficulty to some extent.

This problem is linked to a related one that, when links are built from one Web site into the body of another rather than to the opening pages, then all sorts of important information is lost. The user is not aware whose information is being viewed or used, neither are they aware of ownership or any restrictions, limitations or privileges granted by virtue of using this second Web site. Therefore, it would seem a good idea that all links are built initially into the opening page of a Web site rather than into the body of the site itself.

Yet further problems are being caused for hypertext links because it is claimed that creation of the hypertext link is tantamount to publication: if a work is available on one Web site and this is then accessed through hypertext links then the work is copied and transmitted to the user. If this happens repeatedly then the work is essentially being published by repeated transmission to different people. Once again the technology and the law are at variance.

Those creating Web sites or building hypertext links also need to be aware that national legislation on these issues varies considerably. This raises the whole question of the international dimension of the Web. Copyright law is essentially national in character but the Web is international in its nature and structure. Therefore what may be legal in one country may be quite illegal in another. This is a major problem, not just for copyright, but in relation to such issues as privacy, pornographic materials and security risks. The creation, viewing and ownership of some types of material may be totally legal in one country but, as soon as they are transmitted to another, they may in fact cause the viewer to commit a criminal offence by having them in their possession. This *185* is going to be a major problem in the immediate future. Nobody owns cyberspace but everybody wants to control it.

THE FUTURE

The future of copyright is assured despite many prophets of doom and gloom who see its days as numbered. Some experts say that copyright will be replaced by contracts but there are two major difficulties to this: firstly there will always be a need to define what is protected and therefore owned and this will continue regardless of the technology; secondly there is a need to define the rights that owners have and how they need to be limited and this cannot be left to individual private contracts. An example of how the law can be used to limit rights is the Computer Programs Regulations which permit certain actions even if the copyright owner tries to impose a contract preventing them. There are also other pressures to ensure that copyright not only continues but extends its scope. Commerce and industry need a system of protection for a growing segment of their intellectual property rights as exists for inventions (patents) and indicators of quality and origin (trademarks, service marks). Paradoxically technology, seen as a threat to copyright by many, is the very reason copyright is becoming more important. On the one hand, networking and digitization present major challenges and threats to copyright material; on the other hand the same technology offers the possibility of being able to control use of material and receive payments for it. This is an attractive possibility for owners who are less concerned to prevent access than obtain payment for use. The value of much electronic information is such that investment in high technology to protect it may become worthwhile. The increasing internationalization of information also means that laws need to be harmonized to ensure that information provided in one country is protected in another and therefore offers a 'level playing field' for information providers. This is the motivation for much EU harmonization and also the increasing pressure on WIPO to amend the Berne Convention to broaden the scope of owners' rights.

CONCLUSION

Copyright was once seen as a dull and almost irrelevant area of law relating to information provision. It has now become central to all that libraries, archives and information centres wish to do. Far from being dull it has become one of the most dynamic and fast-moving areas of law. For a real intellectual challenge which will continue to affect all that information professionals want and need to do – watch this space!

REFERENCES

Brewelheide, J. H. (1995), *Copyright primer for librarians and educators*. 2nd.ed. Chicago: American Library Association.

CITED (1994), *CITED Final Report*. Boston Spa: British Library.

Cornish, G. P. (1997), *Copyright: interpreting the law for libraries, archives and information centres*. 2nd.ed. London: LA.

Directive 93/98 (29 October 1993), *Harmonizing the term of protection of copyright and certain related rights*.

Directive 96/9 (11 March 1996), *On the legal protection of databases*. Section (14) and Article (12).

Franken, H. *et al.* (1991), *Information technology and the law*. Lelystad (Netherlands): Koninklijke Verrmande.

Gasaway, L. N. and Wiant, S. K. (1994), *Libraries and copyright: a guide to copyright law in the 1990s*. Washington, DC: Special Libraries Association.

Hugenholtz, B. P. and Visser, D. (1995), *Copyright problems of electronic document delivery*. Brussels: European Commission. (EUR Report 16056)

International Convention (1979), *International Convention for the protection of literary and artistic works*. [Signed in Berne 1886; variously revised until 1979 in Paris]

Miller, P. H. (1991), Life after Feist: the First Amendment and the copyright status of automated databases. *Fordham law review*, vol. 60, no. 3, pp. 507–539.

Oppenheim, C. (1995), *Legal and regulatory environment for electronic information*. 2nd.ed. Calne: Infonortics Ltd.

Oyama, Y. (1991), *Copyright law in Japan.* Tokyo: Copyright Research Institute.

Petersen, J. (1916), *University of London Press Ltd v. University Tutorial Press Ltd.* [1916] 2 Ch 601 at 610.

State Library (1991), *Coping with copyright: a guide to using pictorial and written materials in Australian libraries and archives.* Sydney: State Library of New South Wales.

UNESCO (1976), *Tunis model law on copyright.* Paris: UNESCO/ Geneva: WIPO.

Universal Copyright (1971), *Universal Copyright Convention.* [Signed in Geneva 1952; revised Paris 1971]

VerSteeg, R. (1995), Sparks in the tinderbox: Feist 'creativity' and the legislative history of the 1976 Copyright Act. *University of Pittsburgh law review*, vol. 56, no. 3, pp. 439–538.

Vijne, T. C. (1995), The last word on Magill: the judgement of the ECJ. *European intellectual property review*, vol. 17, no. 6, pp. 297–303.

Wall, R. (1993), *Copyright made easier.* London: Aslib.

WIPO (1997), *WIPO Treaty on Databases.* Geneva: WIPO.

APPENDIX

DEMYTHOLOGIZING

Copyright is a fast-moving target. It is not surprising that copyright law abounds in myths, most of them based on a smattering of knowledge often obtained a long time ago when the law, technology and society were rather different. So, in an attempt to dispel some of those myths once and for all, the following list is provided:

Legal deposit. There is a common belief that, in order to claim copyright, a copy must be deposited with the national library or some other organization. This is essentially untrue. By the regulations of the Berne Convention (International Convention, 1979), copyright subsists whether or not a copy is deposited. In the USA this is true but if the owner wishes to bring any legal action relating to the copyright in a work, it must first be registered with the Registrar of Copyright.

Copyright symbol. This symbol has no real meaning in any country which has signed the Berne Convention. It was widely used in the USA until that country signed the Berne Convention and can still be found in a number of developing countries' publications.

Copyright registration. It should now be clear that there is no such thing as registering copyright. Patents, designs and trademarks can, and must in some cases, be registered but no such system exists for copyright.

International Standard Book Numbers and International Standard Serial Numbers (ISBNs and ISSNs). For some incomprehensible reason there is a rumour abroad that works without either of these identifiers are not copyright. These numbering systems are devices for the book trade, which have been hijacked by the library profession for its own purposes, but which have nothing whatever to do with copyright.

World Wide Web. 'If it's on the Web, it's not protected.' This is a statement of hope rather than reality. Just because a work has been mounted on the World Wide Web or any other publicly-accessible information service, this does not change its copyright status. Certainly there are many WWW sites which state that works may be freely downloaded or copied but this does not mean they are not protected by copyright and increasingly Web sites are becoming protected by passwords and other devices as the real value of the information provided through them becomes evident. One day someone is going to be too free with another person's copyright material on the Web (republishing it or retransmitting it as if it were their own) and the original owner will take action which may help dispel this myth too!

Part IV

MANAGING RESOURCES

Managing resources

INTRODUCTION

In this section we concentrate on topics that are not new in themselves, but where fresh approaches and sharp ideas are important. The central component is the good management of resources.

Strategic management builds on strategic planning in order to put into effect the results of environmental scanning, identification of constraints, drawing up of priorities, assessment of effectiveness, presentation of objectives. It subsumes other management processes, and gives us the chance to make our management style coherent and effective.

For the organization, discovery of the information resources that it possesses is the first stage towards an effective policy of information management. As information comes to be regarded as an asset with a cash value and a place on the balance sheet, *Information auditing* is a vital assessment exercise.

The skills crisis is perhaps the biggest threat to the information world; too few people are equipped with the types of ability that are now increasingly in demand. *Human resource management* is critical for the organization. New ways of working, career breaks, short-term contracts and self-employment make the individual more than ever before aware of their own responsibility for their own professional development.

The management of resources also extends to the physical state of the materials that we need as information sources. *Preservation, access and integrity* examines the need to maintain adequate storage and accommodation for all types of stock, to have in place policies to ensure good practice, and to train staff in appropriate methods and techniques. The management of digitization programmes is especially interesting and important.

And if the unthinkable happens, the organization has to have the means to survive. *Disasters: prevention, rescue and recovery* deals with the processes that will keep us afloat after a crisis – and no organization or public institution can afford to lose its trading assets or its premises. Good housekeeping requires that we know how we stand, and how we can replace our resources if an emergency happens.

9 Strategic management

Ray Prytherch

Strategic management is the key to successful development of services, in the information sector as much as in any other. Various routes may be followed, but the essentials of the investment of time and energy that strategic management requires are fixed: an understanding of the nature of the business we are in, acceptance of the nature of the world around us, and a commitment to make choices about the directions we will follow.

Scanning the environment (chapter 2) and *Strategic planning* (chapter 4) are examined elsewhere; the environment impinges on strategic management in that we need to recognize the changes in our surroundings so that we can target our business towards the real needs of the community – not an out-of-date idea that we think we are sure about; strategic planning takes the process forward so that our ideas and our analysis of the environment can be structured and applied in a purposeful way. Strategic management and strategic planning are two contiguous areas of expertise that information professionals have to use increasingly, to enhance their ability to convince senior management and funding sources that information matters – that it carries weight in business value terms.

WHAT IS STRATEGIC MANAGEMENT?

Definitions of strategic management are lacking in clarity; a specific   *195* definition may be unhelpful, as too many components might be compromised if the boundaries are drawn too closely. Probably the greatest confusion is caused by differing views on whether management is part of planning, or planning part of management. Commentators prefer one scenario or the other, but seldom explain in detail why they have a preference; it is our view that management is the overall process, and that planning is a part of that process. Hayes (1993), discussing change, states:

> it became clear that something more than 'planning' was necessary if this kind of dynamic environment was to be properly dealt with... we must concern ourselves with strategic management, within which planning may play a role, but at most only a supporting one.

This over-arching role is emphasized by Kinnell Evans (1991):

> it differs from some other aspects of management in its concern for the whole organization and the direction in which it will travel; other types of management activity are essentially concerned with the effective operation of various functions to improve efficiency. A strategic approach to management is externally focused; and internal operations are considered primarily in relation to the positioning of the organization with regard to competitors and profitability – in the case of public sector organizations, survivability and resource acquisition are of key importance. Strategic management involves analysing the current position of the organization, generating and choosing possible alternative courses of action, matching these to the resource capabilities of the organization and then planning the implementation and review of the chosen strategy.

A concise definition which will serve very well for this chapter is given by Hayes (1993):

196   strategic management is that part of the general management

of organizations that emphasizes the relationships to external environments, evaluates the current status and the effects of future changes in them, and determines the most appropriate organizational response.

He observes also that it is oriented toward long-range institutional goals and objectives and is concerned to identify these, create a political consensus on their validity, establish priorities among them, determine the necessary resources, and create the environment within which these resources can be assembled.

He also notes that the overall concerns of strategic management include 'goals and objectives, administration, constituency and market, sources and resources, competition and co-operation, politics, technologies, economics, social policy, and sources for staff'. It also revolves around new interpretations of the meaning of such concepts as 'product', 'market', 'competition', and performance criteria.

This implies a certain measure of flexibility, and although strategic management should be proactive and assertive, strongly developed and committed professionally, it is nothing if it does not accept the reality of its environments. In this regard, it is a more powerful tool than strategic planning which may be less responsive.

The key concepts in strategic management are listed by Armstrong (1990) as:

- distinctive competence (what the organization is good at and what special or unique capabilities it has)
- focus (concentration on strategic issues)
- competitive advantage (the targeting of markets where its competences give it an edge)
- synergy (the abilities and skills of people throughout the organization contribute to problem-solving and strategy development)
- environmental scanning (examination of the internal and external environment to be aware of strengths and weaknesses, threats and opportunities)

197

- resource allocation (ensuring that human, financial, plant and equipment resources are available, and that their use is optimized).

Armstrong further suggests examples of areas in which strategy could be formed – organizational growth or change, marketing, 'production' resources, research and development, personnel, finance, and data processing (management information).

Organizational planning involves the stages of setting objectives, scanning the environment, analysing existing strategies, defining strategic issues, developing new or revised strategies, deciding on critical success factors, preparing operational, resource and project plans to implement strategies, and monitoring results.

The strategic issues that Armstrong identifies in a general business context are:

- how to maintain growth in a declining market?
- how to maintain advantage and leadership in the face of competition?
- to what extent are new 'products' or markets needed?
- what proportion of resources should be allocated to R and D?
- what to do about aging plant and equipment?
- what to do about overheads?
- how to determine stock levels?
- how to finance growth?
- how to improve quality?
- how to improve customer service?
- how to find and develop the well-qualified and highly motivated staff that will be needed in the future?

Heeks and Kinnell (1992) see strategy as emerging 'from a range of complex inter-relationships and responses to environmental factors, rather than being a precisely articulated and co-ordinated process'; it may have high-risk, long-term implications for viability, but will determine survival and direction in the medium term. They identify three steps which comprise strategic management: strategic analysis, strategic choice, and strategic implementation.

Values, expectations and objectives feed into the first step; this leads to the generation of options which feeds the second step; resource planning is added to complete the process.

Four points are made by Carr (1992) in the definition of strategic management:

- identification of social, technical, economic, political, structural environments
- identification of constraints
- prioritization
- monitoring.

These could be applied in the context of customer use, definitions of products or services, skills (that is, human resource development), objectives, and resources. The outcomes foreseen could be judged by usage levels, education of users/non-users, increased value in the organization, and changed perceptions.

The key issues listed by Johnson (1994) are finance, IT, stock provision, staff, client groups and marketing; she points out that strategic issues should not be confused with goals and objectives thus causing incomplete descriptions and failures to see inter-relationships.

The identification of strategic issues is considered by Wilt and Wilt (1995); they quote a definition of a strategic issue as a 'condition or pressure' on the organization that involves outcomes that are important to overall performance, or controversial, or which have strategic consequences. Analysis of issues is followed by 'array' – the categorization and prioritiz-ation of issues – which is constantly changing; sound application of such a method would help to facilitate the next phase – crisis issue processing. An alternative handling method is strategic issue diagnosis, which allocates inputs, process characteristics, and outputs to each issue; the input stage allows the decision maker to simplify the issue, the process stage helps in the synthesis and understanding of the issue as it moves through the organization, and the output stage is the end product of the social, interactive decision process.

Strategic planning, for which the literature is much fuller, is perhaps easier to grasp as a concept; it is more of a readily-assimilated process with a start point, an action phase, and various definable outcomes. Strategic management, on the other hand, is more awkward to control because it is so pervasive; it is, however, impossible to ignore in times of structural, organizational or technological change. It can make the difference between success or mediocrity in management.

Other considerations are added to the picture by Bryson (1997): management involves a series of processes that have to be understood as individual parts and as a complex together. The parts comprise:

- understanding the role of manager
- understanding the environment
- creating the corporate environment
- managing and communicating in the corporate environment
- managing risk
- service delivery
- managing the individual
- getting things done in the corporate environment.

The particular points that she makes in addition to the ideas we have seen in other definitions centre on managing and communicating information in the corporate environment; she itemizes four principal facets:

- personal communication (individual skills, interpersonal communication, barriers)
- internal communications (services, channels, meetings, reports)
- external communications (corporate image, formal links)
- corporate information (information use, management support systems, design).

The life-cycle phases of information (planning, acquisition, maintenance, exploitation, retirement) are appended to this list as relevant to the idea of information in the corporate context. It is a 'utility' in an organization, and serves many purposes, such as:

- supporting strategic planning and policy-making
- meeting legislative and regulatory requirements
- protecting the interests of the organization and the rights of employees and customers
- supporting research and development
- supporting consistent and rapid decision-making
- enabling effective and efficient utilization of resources
- identifying and managing risk
- evaluating quality, performance, and achievements.

We need to remember that although Bryson is concentrating here on the corporate scene, libraries of all types represent 'corporate bodies' in management terms – they are organizational cultures in themselves, and form a part of a larger academic or local government organization. The commercial feel of their environment – for instance, the provision of service to a customer base, the revenue to support services – adds to the pervasiveness of Bryson's points.

In summary, strategic management can be viewed as the overall process of longer-term achievement; the organization needs to be considered as a whole – although it may be split into segments for accurate appraisal – and decisions should be made, by managers at all levels, in line with the future pattern that is agreed through the strategic process. The focus is on what the organization is aiming to achieve (its objectives), when it should achieve those objectives, and how it should achieve those objectives.

Other aspects include the position of the library or information service in the marketplace; what competition is there to our services, why should a customer use us rather than another source, how can we develop a different 'brand image' for what we do so that new customers will become aware of us? Developing our services through new 'products', new strategies, new marketing are all part of the strategic management process. Strategy is about making things happen; not by chance or good luck, but by detailed, *201* consistent analysis followed by disciplined implementation and monitoring procedures. It is deliberate, and it can be realized; flexibility is built-in so that the unexpected becomes part of the process and can be incorporated into advancing plans. The important feature is to be in control of the service or business, not to be led by the nose.

This chapter will examine the business that we are in, the inputs to the process of which we need to take account, our internal organizational culture and management styles, the options that the strategic management process gives us, the choices we have to make, and the vital phases of implementation, and of control and monitoring.

THE BUSINESS WE ARE IN

Although strategic decisions are made in order to meet targets or reach objectives, both the strategy on which they are based and the objectives themselves are tuned to the organization's mission. It is accepted generally that to define the mission is to find the answer to the question: what business are we in? To say that we are in the business of 'information' or 'libraries' does not answer the question. Our organizations, in common with most other organizations of any size or type, exist in order to satify some demand in the marketplace. The needs or wants of our customer base are the starting point for the mission; if nobody wants library services then there will be no library services. If nobody has a need for information, then we are out of a job. The mission in our field is to meet customer need for information and related services; the handling of information, the acquisition of CD-ROM databases, provision of a fiction bookstock, advice to readers – these and many others – are the jobs we do to further the mission, but they are not the business we are in.

Customer orientation is the first essential of marketing, and as marketing is basically the raising of awareness of our business, we can extend the concept to the whole organization. Although economical means of working, efficiency, effectiveness or whatever may be required to maintain an image or achieve a profit, these processes are only part of the support mechanism of the mission. Thus the mission statement stresses three components:

- the customers or clients to be served
- the needs, wants, demands to be met
- the services or products needed to meet the needs.

The mission statement is often used to explore ideas of philosophy, commitment to the community, employee welfare, public good; such commentary is just fine talk – it is not part and parcel of the mission statement. Whilst we may want to explain why we think libraries are important or why information is a basic right, it does not help the organization's sense of purpose or direction to use broad generalizations. The mission statement should be precise, unadorned, and simple; we can refer back to it anytime to help us clarify decisions – it is the true business of the organization. The well-formulated mission statement offers us a sound basis for working out the objectives of the organization; we need also to remember that the customer base is not static, and that needs will change; the mission statement will require review and re-writing at regular intervals. In chapter 2 of this Handbook, *Scanning the environment*, we show how much change is going on in the external world; change must be recognized and assimilated into the mission if we are to keep ahead of the competition and go in the directions we want to follow. If the situation gets too far away from our control, it is almost impossible with limited resources to recover.

The objectives of the organization also reflect the business we are in, but are subordinate to the mission; they will be consistent with the mission and will support it, but there is a crucial difference – objectives will not be so focused. There will be many objectives for the organization, some will be short-term and some will be long-term; objectives for one department or service area may even be in conflict with those of another – and provided that both sets of objectives support the mission the apparent disparity is inconsequential. Management may determine at one time to stress one set of objectives, to the detriment of the other, and *vice versa* at another time.

The feature that will assist in the formulation of objectives is prioritization; if we draw up a hierarchy of objectives, it will be clearer what we should do first, and how to determine relative importance. Generally it is recognized that there are four levels in the hierarchy of objectives:

- corporate objectives (for the whole organization)
- divisional objectives (individual service sectors, locations)
- administrative objectives (financial, human resources)
- operational objectives (simpler targets, often short-term).

Two remaining points must be made before we leave the idea of the mission:

- measurement of achievement
- stakeholder analysis.

The mission statement will say what the organization is doing; in the same way that determining the mission requires careful, lucid thought, similarly determining how we decide if the mission is being achieved also needs careful and lucid thought. Often it is through the measurement of the achievement of objectives that we view success; maybe we should separately view the success of the mission – it may not be easy or relevant to adopt mechanical indicators. Chapter 6 (*Performance measurement and evaluation*) will be helpful here; recent work by Hernon and Altman (1996) and by McDonald and Micikas (1994) will also be relevant.

Throughout the process of writing a mission statement and formulating objectives, we are faced with the question: who is responsible for creating the mission and the supporting objectives? The answer in the context of strategic management has to be that everybody is responsible; the idea of the stakeholder is prevalent. All those people or organizations which influence our organization, or who are themselves influenced by what we do deserve a say in the process – customers, suppliers, fund-holders, employees, pressure groups, politicians. Openness in the creation of our mission demands that we explore our stakeholder community, assess their relative power, and involve them all in the process of thinking about what is the business we are in.

INPUTS TO THE STRATEGIC MANAGEMENT PROCESS

In chapter 2, we examined in detail the influence of the environment on our planning and management cycle; obviously we do not work in a vacuum, and the strategic process requires us to take account of what is happening outside our organizations. It is the world outside that provides us with our market – customers, clients; our raw materials – information in any of its formats; our workforce; our finance. Changes in any of these inputs will have an effect on our business. Secondly, there is the environment of our own organization; we shall discuss this aspect in the following section of this chapter.

Since a stable relationship between the components mentioned is unlikely, a part of our strategy has to be to react to change. In a slowly changing environment, response might seem to be a simple process: just keeping an eye on things and observing good administrative practices, watching costs and monitoring quality of services. In such a case, the environmental scanning would be low key – the existing strategy would suffice and need only to be maintained and gently updated.

However, we do not currently live in slowly-changing times – nor are we likely to in the foreseeable future; every aspect of the environment of libraries and the information industry has been changing rapidly and profoundly. There is not one aspect of our professional life that has not altered dramatically in the last decade, although it is questionable how much 'better' the services are that we can provide, and how far we have been able to respond to new demands.

Our client base is changing: in public libraries there are underlying social patterns of aging and unemployment; in academic libraries there are increasing student numbers and shifting patterns of attendance modes; in the corporate sector the information commodity is now almost wholly electronic and end-users predominate. Everyone sees economic and resource *205* problems which curb their abilities to respond; there is a growing crisis in human resources – failure of morale and insufficient recruits with the training and expertise now wanted.

Our reaction to this total raft of change cannot be passive; to a great extent, our current malaise results from a lack of response to environmental change over many years; our successes show how even in lean times it is possible to surmount the difficulties. Without citing obvious examples, we know professionally of services in all sectors which are close to collapse, and we know and read about conspicuous examples of thriving services.

The success stories are always in those services where managers have moved fast to alert fundholders of trends, and prepared strategic documents to illustrate the potential benefits and problems of emerging change. Watching what the others do and then moving is too slow; stakeholders are not convinced by a lack of decision, and good decisions are made on the basis of sound observation and accurate response to opportunities. We are in a competitive society, and funds do not flow to services that cannot be seen to have adapted their ways to a cost-conscious environment; part of this adaptation is to demonstrate environmental awareness.

CULTURE AND MANAGEMENT OF OUR ORGANIZATIONS

In the same way that the external world affects the strategic management of an organization, so too does the internal working of that organization. To know how successful we are within our own world, we need to analyse our organizations in respect of two factors – efficiency and effectiveness. Efficiency is the expression of how well, how economically, we convert our inputs – finance, people, premises, stock – into outputs – services and products. Effectiveness is the measure of the match of outputs to consumer demand – how well we apply our resources within the organization and how well we relate our outputs to the external world.

Features that we need to consider in this analysis will include financial performance over several years (trends, compared with other similar services), the relative performance of individual departments or functions (to identify bottlenecks, uneven quality), the structure of management (how fast and reliable is communication), and organizational attitudes and beliefs (because these can be indicative of intangible assets or liabilities).

A particular difficulty that faces libraries and information supply units is that although they are apparently simple functional units with small staff numbers, they are actually very complex organizationally; the reasons for this are twofold:

- the customer/client base and the external environment are amorphous
- they are usually parts of much larger organizations (local authority, academic, multi-national companies) that cloud the simplicity of control.

To find the answers to our questions on efficiency and effectiveness therefore, we need to be very careful that what we are examining are in fact parts of the structure, not imposed systems that we have to accommodate – that is, that they are not features of the environment which we need to acknowledge but which we cannot change.

As well as the organizational structure, the style of management or culture plays a part in the adoption of strategic thinking. Maybe a reluctance to move in certain directions – refusal to think of charging for library services at the point of use for example – may reflect organizational culture; opposition might be appropriate, but unless we accept the concept, cost it, argue its relative advantages and disadvantages, and come to a decision based on the evidence, we shall not be able to convince stakeholders that we are not simply reacting to a 'cultural' heresy.

The attitudes, value systems, perceptions and assumptions of the organization can be very powerful; if we are to introduce and use strategic management we shall need to get behind the established beliefs and argue on the basis of analysis and evidence. Otherwise we will be always on the defensive, always unable to show that we are genuinely facing up to all the alternatives in front of us.

The two most famous classifications of cultural roles in the organization are by Miles and Snow (1978) who found that organizational players fell into four categories:

- defenders (conservative, control enthusiasts)
- prospectors (innovative, decentralized)
- analysers (keen on planning)
- reactors (last-minute responses, minimal planning).

Handy (1992) saw cultures in four attitudinal categories:

- power (central control)
- role (bureaucracy; defined jobs and roles)
- task (emphasis on problem solving)
- person (human resource emphasis).

If we consider these analyses, we can see that the success of the strategic management approach would be very different in the eyes of the different participants identified by Miles and Snow, and that progress of ideas would be very differently handled in the four categories of culture suggested by Handy.

THE EMERGING OPTIONS

All the points we have mentioned so far in this chapter feed into the next stage of the strategic management process – the generation of strategic options. Complacency is reckoned to be a poor business attitude, so whatever the results of our analyses there will be some ideas that emerge that we must consider. The report from the Audit Commission (1997) particularly observed that decisions have to be based on clear priorities and this presupposes planning and choice. Nothing should be ignored as hopeless or impossible; everything that emerges should be listed as a possible option and treated in the same manner. There are probably no secrets in strategic management, just the re-working and re-examination of the same ideas that have proved successful *208* elsewhere; the biggest obstacles are our own inability to put everything on the agenda and our reluctance to appreciate that absolutely anything is a possible option. Maybe closing a service is one of the options that the strategic management process offers; if we refuse to put that on the list of possible actions, we are deluding ourselves and doing nobody any favours. If it is an option, we should recognize it.

Arranging options for consideration will need to be based on certain criteria; the most obvious could be importance – if an action is a fundamental point of policy then it would have to take priority over detailed points; or urgency – if financial collapse is imminent then fast action is required.

Consideration of the options will bring in various activities and involve renewed consultation; use of a SWOT analysis may be helpful, and we shall have to divide options into existing products/services/markets, new products/services/markets, diversification into other areas, and maybe lateral or creative spin-offs produced by the process of examination itself – totally new innovations that do not arise from the process but are thrown up by the challenge of re-thinking.

MAKING STRATEGIC CHOICES

Choosing between the emerging options is best tackled by itemizing criteria against which the options can be measured. A series of possible criteria can be suggested, which are based on existing knowledge of your organization and its current policies. For example:

- how well does the option fit into known corporate objectives? (If you have an objective to avoid capital investment, for instance, then no option which presupposes capital costs will be a choice.)
- does the option coincide with policies that remain part of the organization's culture? (For example, if revenues from external sources are necessary but the larger organization of which you are part vetoes such proposals, then that option is not a choice.)

209

- does the option address conspicuous strategic difficulties that you face? (If you cannot offer adequate opening hours, for instance, does the option preclude doing so because it diverts resources elsewhere. Such an option might be politically impossible.)
- does the option meet known environmental challenges? (Remember that external threats cannot be accurately foreseen, and some flexibility is essential.)
- if the chosen option fails to produce the advantage foreseen, what are the hazards of failure or partial success? (Are core services threatened if you are forced to withdraw from your proposed strategy.)
- is the option possible in terms of resources and finance?
- will the option be acceptable to all interested parties?
- are the advantages of success fairly stated, and not exaggerated?

Although options should not be emerging that are not sensible or viable economically, the changing state of the external world or of political control can invalidate certain ideas that seemed possible; the strategic management cycle embodies flexibility and encourages thinking the unthinkable – this is healthy at the examination stage, but needs to be tempered when actual choices are being made. Evaluation of the options may be assisted by drawing up charts that highlight plus points and minus points; arithmetic scores could be assigned, maybe weighted to demonstrate that certain factors are more significant than others.

At the end of the day, the value of the exercise is twofold:

- the collection of information about the organization, its analysis, discussion, and the selection of options is of itself amazingly revealing; this is adequate reason to explore strategic management even if little comes out of it
- the option chosen sends a message to all stakeholders about what the organization wants to do; this encourages further debate and raises the profile.

Choice is subjective – however much 'impartial' assessment is built in – and the opinions, attitudes and backgrounds of those making the choice will win out. The choice is not the end of the process, just a step on the way towards implementation and subsequent feedback to the next run of the whole process.

IMPLEMENTATION AND CONTROL

When there is agreement on steps that should be taken to further the strategic process, implementation must be tackled. The structure of the organization and its cultural patterns will affect the speed of change. Whatever the circumstances, training of personnel to reflect shifted emphases and changed attitudes will be essential. Chapter 4 (*Strategic planning*) also feeds into this process, and offers support to the opportunities that arise from change.

Centralized organizations will start with a programme that emanates from the centre – this will give ostensibly good control over the change, but may result in very uneven success depending on local managers and their varying enthusiasms. Looser organizations will delegate implementation, and clearly this demonstrates greater confidence but control remains uncertain. There will be resistance to change in many ways.

Textbook recommendations for implementation specify that one person should have overall responsibility for the implementation process; he or she should start by ensuring that there is clear understanding of the new strategy throughout the organization. There must be excellent communication systems, and a reporting structure is needed to monitor and control changes.

Bryson (1997) notes and explains the complexity of such a process; she itemizes features such as:

- leadership
- power, influence, authority, delegation
- decision-making
- networking
- group dynamics
- team-building

- motivation
- conflict management
- negotiation
- change management.

Programmes within the strategy will be the smaller steps that can be readily monitored; annual revisions of programmes will often result in feedback into the management process – organizational renewal never stops, and the cycles of planning, decision-making, implementation, monitoring will feed into a loop of unceasing activity. No process ever ends – if it does, the organization itself has become moribund. 'Completion' of the process is just the start of the next stage.

CONCLUSION

Libraries and information units are often seen to be at a disadvantage in comparison with commercial environments when it comes to assembling essential data to assist in strategic development; Hofmann (1995) points out that the lack of various details such as 'market price' makes it structurally difficult for a library to obtain high management productivity. Strategic management can help in reducing complexity, and recognizing risks and trends; but because of the structural lack of clarity decisive factors can remain unknown, and the inter-dependence between factors can be unclear. As library services are essentially a decentralized network, autonomous and independent yet all producing the same 'product', there is inevitable duplication and redundancy.

Monitoring and review procedures are an integral part of the strategic management process; Sutton (1994) quotes a sad comment on drawing up a mission statement – 'get it done and never have to look at it again' – and reminds us that strategic management and its associated documents 'because they are the products of complex decision-making processes, tend to possess a great deal of bureaucratic inertia... they tend to resist change'. We have to insist that the process continues and succeeds.

REFERENCES

Armstrong, M. (1990), *Management processes and functions*. London: Institute of Personnel Management.

Audit Commission (1997), *Due for renewal: a report on the library service*. London: Audit Commission Publications.

Bryson, J. (1997), *Managing information services: an integrated approach*. Aldershot: Gower.

Carr, S. J. (1992), Strategic management in libraries: an analysis of a management function and its application to library and information work. *Library management*, vol. 13, no. 5, pp. 4–17.

Handy, C. B. (1992), *Understanding organizations*. 4th.ed. Harmondsworth: Penguin Books.

Hayes, R. M. (1993), *Strategic management for academic libraries: a handbook*. Westport, CT: Greenwood Press.

Heeks, P. and Kinnell, M. (1992), *Managing change for library services*. London: British Library. (Library and Information Research Report, 89)

Hernon, P. and Altman, E. (1996), *Service quality in academic libraries*. Norwood, NJ: Ablex.

Hofmann, U. (1995), Developing a strategic planning framework for information technologies in libraries. *Library management*, vol. 16, no. 2, pp. 4–14.

Johnson, H. (1994), Strategic planning for modern libraries. *Library management*, vol. 15, no. 1, pp. 7–18.

Kinnell Evans, M. (1991), *All change?* London: Taylor Graham.

McDonald, J. A. and Micikas, L. B. (1994), *Academic libraries: the dimensions of their effectiveness*. Westport, CT: Greenwood.

Miles, R. E. and Snow, C. C. (1978), *Organization strategy, structure and process*. New York: McGraw-Hill.

Sutton, B. (1994), The modeling function of long-range planning. *Library administration and management*, vol. 8, no. 3, pp. 151–160.

Wilt, C. and Wilt, C. C. (1995), Library networking issues and strategic issue analysis. In Huston-Somerville, M. and Wilt, C. C. (eds), *Networks and resource sharing in the 21st century: re-engineering the information landscape*. New York: Haworth Press. pp. 33–48.

10 Information auditing

Feona Hamilton

As the importance of information as an asset has been realized, so
has the need for it to be properly and comprehensively audited.
The auditing of accounts is the basis upon which other forms of
auditing have been brought into being and information auditing
stems from this legal requirement, although there is no equivalent
legal requirement for it. Information assets have proved
particularly difficult to treat in this way, since costs are difficult to
define closely and much of their value is intangible. Add to this the
growing interest in the concept of 'knowledge' as an asset and the
problem is compounded even more.

It is surprising that the absolute necessity of good information in
order to function successfully has not been recognized long before
this. Money, staff, premises and equipment may all be available
but, without accurate and timely information and the knowledge to
analyse and use it, no business will survive and no profits are
possible. In fact, information is very much a – if not *the* – core
commodity. This is especially true in the late 1990s, when a multi-
million pound company can function without offices and very few
staff, existing only in virtual reality. This has been made possible
by the amazing growth of the Internet and the number of its users.
At the time of writing, most of the security problems associated
with trading on the Internet have been resolved and people are
becoming more comfortable with buying from Web sites.

Bookshops are apparently leading the way, but Internet banking is also becoming more acceptable.

Even before the Internet became such a feature of everyday business, computers and their use were an essential part of information management. Unless great care is taken and proper records kept, the information resources of any organization, whether it is a large multi-national corporation, or a small business, will not be fully known to that organization. This will lead to under-use on the one hand and needless duplication on the other. The term 'information resources' is a very general one, covering far more than may at first be realized. Ask most people what they think is meant by the word 'information' and they will usually be fairly specific. Their response will also depend on the context in which you ask the question – at home, in the office, during a discussion – and the circumstances of the person to whom you put the question.

Consider, for example, the professional soldier. To such a person, the term information is synonymous with 'intelligence', and will refer to troop movements and related data, whether in peacetime or during an involvement in fighting. To the intelligence officer on the other hand, involved in the mysterious and more or less legal activities of MI5 or MI6, the same word can mean something picked up concerning the similar activities of another country. For the rest of us, this aspect of information is usually something we read about rather than actually involve ourselves in.

KNOWLEDGE – THE 'FORGOTTEN' RESOURCE

There is another source of information which is only just being recognized as a specific resource. This is the knowledge and expertise built up during the course of carrying out the tasks connected with each individual's job. Knowledge management and knowledge systems are terms which are becoming more widespread to indicate that this more nebulous type of information must be included in information management. There is even a move to use titles such as Director of Knowledge Systems (shades of Big Brother) to describe the function of the most senior member *215* of the organization's support staff concerned with information resource management, most notably in management consultancies. This kind of information may take an infinite number of forms, among them:

- in-depth knowledge of a specific subject, gathered by a partner in the course of dealing with a client
- detailed knowledge of a company, gathered by the same means
- familiarity with a country and its culture gathered by making frequent trips to it
- details of previous projects undertaken by the organization
- a network of contacts built by attending conferences or training courses
- knowledge of the expertise held by those who have retired, or left the organization for some other reason, but who are still in touch
- specialist knowledge learnt during initial training and retained as a personal interest, but not necessarily used in the course of current work.

Knowledge held in this way is frequently not indexed anywhere, and the loss of access to it is only noticed when its source – the individual who knows it – has left the organization for some reason or another. If this happens, it can lead to a very noticeable gap in the organization's information resources, until the loss can be made good by someone else appearing with similar knowledge. But, even when another source does appear, the knowledge base itself will never be identical to that which was lost, if only because the original contacts and sources by which the knowledge base was built up have gone forever and will not be the sources used by the 'replacement'.

People as information resources

It is important to recognize that information resources include all
those working within the organization, and that a conscious effort

must be made to capture their specialist information in some retrievable form, whether printed or electronic. Needless to say, such an information bank will have to be indexed in the same depth as all the rest. If this is the first time that such an exercise has been undertaken, it will require a great deal of thought to set up a suitable system, and time and patience from both the holders of the – thus far – unindexed knowledge as well as from those trying to get at it.

A member of the information profession – who may be involved in any aspect of information management, including the technology which enables it to be stored, manipulated, and otherwise handled – perceives information and its management as their *raison d'être*. Information managers are beginning to realize that the term 'information resource' is not confined to the contents of the information service, wherever and however they may be obtained, nor does it refer only to the service provided by information staff. Information resources embrace the services provided, the materials used to gather the information included, and the equipment used to enable the research to be undertaken – plus the staff themselves, including not only information managers or IT managers, but any member of the workforce, including everyone from the Managing Partner to the porters.

THE INFORMATION RESOURCES INDEX

Very occasionally the impact of information in all its forms is recognized within the organization. More probably, those whose training and inclinations lead them to the information profession will find that they have the difficult task of persuading their colleagues of the priority which should be given to the formulation of a good information strategy. One of the first steps towards this is to ensure that a complete information audit has been undertaken.

The jargon used by and within the information profession has led to a proliferation of terms to describe the same thing – how information is obtained, accessed and used. There are references to information policies, business process re-engineering, knowledge engineering, knowledge systems, information *217* technology systems, networking, hardware, software and now groupware and wetware (human beings). The possibilities for confusion and misunderstanding are endless.

For the purposes of this chapter, information resources are as defined in *InfoMap* (Burk and Horton, 1988), since they seem the most succinct, and have yet to be supplanted, despite it being a decade since they first appeared in print, which is a very long time in the world of information:

> Information resources: 1. In general the information holding and information handling functions within or available to an organization. 2. Those information sources, services and systems under the control of, or available to, an organization, which constitute significant supply, support or aid in fulfilling its mission or in achieving its goals or objectives.

The reason for dwelling in such detail on the exact definition of an information resource is to underline the importance of listing every single resource, wherever it may be, and whoever has ownership, in an Information Resources Index. This should include all offices, both in the UK and, where they exist, in other countries. If the business is part of a larger group, its position within the group and any links – for example via an intranet, or a wide area network (WAN) – should be included. The information flow of specific areas – for example, internal flow within larger offices or within a geographical area – should also be given separately, if doing so gives a more accurate overall picture. Good use of flow charts giving graphic interpretations of the information flow within the organization will give the non-specialist a better idea.

The fact is that an information resource may be located anywhere within the organization. It may be:

- in any format, paper, print or electronic
- a small collection of specialist material in a partner's office
- a collection of journals available in the library
- an online service giving access to a wide range of databases containing, among other things, company information;

business information; constantly updating news services; financial information

- a collection of annual reports
- a current awareness service put together in-house and circulated by library staff
- the entire contents of the organization's intranet (see chapter 16).

It can, of course, include anything else, from a single sheet of paper on an individual's desk to an entire library or information centre, which contains anything of interest or relevance to anyone working in or on behalf of the organization concerned, and the equipment, whether IT-based or not, in which it is stored.

It will include all of the records relating to the day-to-day running of the organization itself, such as:

- personnel information
- financial information
- minutes of all meetings held in connection with the business of the organization
- the schedules of individuals
- the business and project plans drawn up for work to be carried out in-house, or on behalf of clients
- the reports put together and submitted at the end of a project
- best practice or know-how databases
- extra copies kept for reference in filing cabinets all over the place.

In order to be truly exhaustive, an index of information resources should also include detailed descriptions of:

- the individual computers in use throughout the organization, where they are situated and who uses them
- the network cabling that links them, and any servers used for the network
- other computer equipment such as CD-ROM jukeboxes, scanners, printers

- the software packages in use
- the telephone system, including every individual telephone, and the functions available to the users
- video-conferencing facilities
- photocopiers
- microfilm/fiche readers and printers
- operator or user manuals which come with the above
- equipment, such as filing cabinets, cupboards and bookshelves, used for storage.

Even the records of repairs and upgrades carried out on the computers and other equipment become an information resource in themselves, as they may well be referred to for information subsequently.

The completed Information Resources Index is the basis upon which the information strategy will be built. It is very important that it should show a complete list of all information resources within the organization. In order to ensure that the right questions are posed and answered, a database for the collection of the interview results should be designed and set up for use.

TOWARDS THE AUDIT REPORT

In compiling the information audit report for an organization, a number of stages must follow the creation of the Information Resources Index. In addition to designing a questionnaire, this includes a review of:

- computerized systems and their use
- information management staff
- costs of current services
- value of information resources.

In outlining these processes, the author has drawn upon experience in conducting the information audit for an accountancy firm. This involved visiting the 16 largest offices (out of a total of 47), speaking on the phone to 10 others, and conducting face-to-face interviews with over fifty people, over a period of three months. Other input was received by faxing copies of the questionnaire and asking the senior partner in each office to complete and return it. This latter method was applied only to the smaller offices. Overall, a very complete picture was built up. A pattern of resources and usage emerged quite quickly, with heavy duplication of some materials in every office – for example, those relating to personal taxation and to auditing. This was not surprising, since both of these are common services offered by accountancy firms, regardless of size or geographical siting. Duplication of this sort of material is perfectly acceptable, particularly where cutting back on the number of copies would affect the ability to carry out work required.

Designing the questionnaire

A questionnaire should be designed to collect the information; the headings below are intended to provide a fairly complete picture of the resources in the organization:

- *Resource name*: for example, letters of engagement file, short-form reports, technical library
- *Location*: individual offices, open access information centres, closed collections
- *Format*: cards, files, databases, printed, handwritten, floppy disk, hard disk, network server, CD-ROM, online
- *Security level*: private, open to certain groups, department confidential, open access
- *Subject coverage*: for example, personal taxation, corporate taxation, tax law, financial services law, pension planning, insolvency, audit
- *Timespan*: month/year at least from beginning to most recent item in collection, or 'current' if still building
- *Software used for access*: Word 6, Excel, Lotus Notes, CompuServe, Virtual Access
- *Hardware used for access*: Desktop PCs, network servers, CD-ROM jukebox, dumb terminals

- *Other access method*: manual files, card index
- *Used by*: public access, trainee accountants, senior partners only, personnel department, information centre, finance department, named individuals
- *Used for*: management information, current awareness, work-in-progress, research
- *Comments by users*.

This last item often provides the clue to the real usage and viability of the resource in question! Users should be encouraged to indicate the positive and negative aspects of each resource they use, and to propose alternatives and future developments for the enhancement of the service overall, as well as the specific resource. This type of input is extremely helpful, particularly when drawing up recommendations for implementation. It is clear that an individual, or group, which is making use daily of an online service, or an in-house database, will be familiar with the reasons for its use within the organization, and the problems encountered in using it. A relatively small amount of work on a product or service can often result in a huge improvement for the users.

Computerized systems and their use

This section covers the IT systems used throughout the organization, irrespective of their particular use. It should result in a comprehensive list of the hardware and software in all offices. If carried out thoroughly, the results of this part of the project will provide a complete picture of computer use in the organization, nationally, and if the organization has offices outside the UK, internationally. All incompatibilities will come to light here. If there are old, slow machines in use in one office, they will be affecting the efficiency of the partners and staff in that office. If there are mavericks using their own software, which does not allow data to be easily transferred in and out of the office, this should be noted.

Any networks installed, whether within a single office or
222 throughout the organization should also be listed, as should

methods of external access – modems used, type of access (X.25, ISDN, direct dial, Internet servers). It must be emphasized, during the gathering of this information, that no-one is being criticized, no fingers pointed, no mockery will be made of the systems currently in use. The whole point of the exercise is to find out exactly what people are using and why. This last point is particularly important: as with the request for comments during the compilation of the Information Resources Index as a whole, the astute interviewer will find pointers towards the final recommendations to be made by listening to the people actually using their own combinations of hardware and software. Positive and negative comments are both important and should be encouraged – even by conferring anonymity, if this is requested.

Information management staff

It would be foolish not to include a listing of all those involved in ensuring the easy flow of information throughout the organization. There is a case for considering everyone working within an organization to be an information resource in themselves, holding and using some pieces of information or 'knowledge' that contribute to the organization's operation. However, the active co-ordination and management roles are played by the information professionals. Highly trained and with an in-depth knowledge of the information needs and interests of everyone throughout the organization, from the most senior director to the most junior assistant, they are the prime information resource possessed by any organization. They are the unsung and ignored heroes of many successful projects completed, much new business undertaken, and the resource without which no organization can function properly. And yet they have been virtually overlooked, as IT professionals and generalist management consultants rush to re-invent the wheel. If information is indeed the core commodity, then the staff of the Information Centre are the key personnel within the organization, because they have the training and the methods of accessing, storing, analysing and disseminating all the information required by the rest of the organization.

223

In an increasing number of organizations, such expertise is being recognized and valued. In such organizations, the skills of the information staff are being passed on to the end-users. This is done by running training courses – either at the organization's own training centre, if one exists, or by information staff running courses 'at the desk' as it were.

Costs of current services

It would be wrong to assume that any organization, even one which exists to offer financial advice and information such as an accountancy firm, would be fully aware of the true cost of the information it uses. This is partly because of the ephemeral nature of much information, and the methods by which it is accessed, obtained, used and stored. There will, no doubt, be budget headings, particularly in the Information Centre's annual forecast, giving details such as:

- annual subscriptions for some online services
- estimated pay-as-you-go expenditure for online services using this method of payment
- annual subscriptions for CD-ROMs, journals, newspapers, loose-leaf services
- estimated percentage of telecoms costs allocated to service
- estimated percentage for heat and light costs
- estimated staff costs
- allowances for training and personal development
- equipment maintenance
- software updates, replacements, or additions
- estimated capital expenditure for renewing equipment, furniture and fittings
- estimated stationery costs.

All of these are costs incurred in the management of information, but they all relate to just one part of that management, and just one group of staff. How do you cost the time spent in actually acquiring information; in those people outside the Information Centre receiving and scanning, for example, a tailored current awareness service? How do you estimate the cost of two people exchanging information of great value to each other, while having a cup of coffee, or standing in the corridor? When does social chat become information exchange, in fact?

As a start, the Information Resources Index should, if it has been correctly compiled, give a complete list of all easily-costed information sources used within the organization. There should, equally, be a matching cost of some kind – a subscription, or estimated amount within the appropriate budget – which will provide some idea of the existing costs to the organization. However, it is unlikely that a first estimate of costs will be accurate to more than 70 per cent; with subsequent audits the figure will still not rise much above 80 per cent accuracy, as much information resource use will not have been recognized as such before the project began.

Value of information resources

Inevitably, the valuing of information resources is an extremely difficult task. While the costs of acquiring, storing and – particularly in the case of online pay-as-you-go services – accessing information may be more or less accurately assessed, the valuing of those same resources is a relatively new discipline. There are already some software products available to assist in this, but they are still very few. The problem lies with the perception of value, if it is narrowly defined as meaning only monetary value. A more accurate perception, in this context, is the meaning of 'information value' as defined by Burk and Horton (1988):

Information value: The value attributed to information produced or acquired by organizations, entities and persons, and delivered in the form of an information product or service. The values may be realized immediately or at some later time. For example, the values attached to information created by scientific research are often realized long after it is created. The risk of realizing future values must be weighed against present and continuing costs of creating, storing and accessing it.

Burk and Horton were among the earliest proponents recognizing the importance of assessing the costs and values of the information resources within an organization, and much of what they say is still of importance and relevance to any organization wishing to set up and implement a corporate information strategy, no matter which sector the organization may be in.

In order to help with the costing and valuation processes, the product *InfoMapper* was devised. This is a computer program which will prompt the user through the process, and calculate as accurate a result as possible, given the information put into the system. Obviously, inaccurate or incomplete data will result in inaccurate or incomplete results. *InfoMapper* has been on the market for some years, and has only recently had any competitors to contend with.

Another type of assessment for this purpose has been developed by Nick Willard, an active member of the Aslib Information Resources Management Network. This is a group of independent consultants and other interested information professionals who are looking anew at the work of Burk and Horton, and updating the methodology. 'The Willard Model' covers all the steps needed to create a corporate information strategy. Step 3 refers to *Cost and value: identifying information resources in money terms*. This utilizes a narrower definition than that given by Burk and Horton but, as part of the whole Willard Model, works well. It solves the problems of identifying and trying to value the more intangible aspects of information resource usage: whether this is acceptable or not rests with the organization for which the project is being undertaken. It should form part of any discussion during the project's lifetime, between the auditor and the organization's Task Force. Whichever model is used, a chart showing the estimated costs and values of each information resource should result, complete with explanatory notes.

PRESENTATION OF THE REPORT

This part of the project always proves to be extremely interesting and enlightening. The charts and the information contained in them will be the first time that any overall picture of information resources available within the organization will have been presented. Combined with the Information Resources Index, it should show exactly what and where the resources are, how much is being spent on them, and how great is their value. This is the point at which indications of the future policy should become clear.

Audit recommendations

Properly completed and presented, the Index and accompanying charts will show problem areas and enable the decision-making process to resolve these. Here is an example of the list which may result, with additional comments.

Gaps in existing provision

Most obvious when respondents frequently cite a source used and express the wish for it to be available in-house, or if an analysis of the questionnaire results indicates a missing resource. This does not refer to new resources only just available.

Duplication in existing provision

Some duplication may be deliberate but some may simply be the lack of awareness that a copy, or a subscription, is available elsewhere in the organization. Watch out for separate offices taking out online subscriptions without notification, as this can be extremely expensive.

Under-use of resources

Under-used resources may be unknown, as well as unnecessary. Check carefully for the actual reasons for under-use, before deciding to dispense with the item or service.

227

Incompatibility of IT systems

This can occur in different offices – perhaps within the same office – and is not as uncommon as may be thought, especially in very large organizations, or those which have grown through the merger of different companies or practices. The latter is particularly common in the legal and accountancy sectors. After ensuring that the audit has encompassed all the systems within the organization, the findings should be presented to the appropriate director or division head. There should be an internal rolling renewal programme – if there isn't, the findings should be sufficient to initiate one.

Use of outdated, slow and cumbersome systems

This relates to the incompatibility problem in one way, and to the lack of a renewal programme for hardware and software. The saying 'three months equals one Internet year' could almost apply to hardware. Up-dating systems is not just an excuse to spend money: new systems frequently save on costs and time because they work faster. There is, though, always the danger of installing new software before the 'bugs' have been ironed out.

'Jams' in information flow

Are these jams caused by systems problems (for example, insufficient memory on the server) or by an insufficient number of copies of journals, reference books, or even CDs? Hi-tech is exciting, but books are still vital and the place of printed information sources alongside the electronic formats must always be borne in mind.

Need for extra staff

If there is a real need for extra staff, the results of the information audit should provide strong arguments for the case. Growth in the information service may be a reason for extra staff, or it may be possible to get round the problem by increasing the access to information via the intranet. Talk to the IT department before making a presentation to the Board, to discuss the options available. Be prepared to be flexible and open to suggestions for changing the services already on offer, as well as expecting changes from the IT people. The system already installed may not be able to deliver the facilities required. However, like the information manager, the IT manager is well aware of the need to update services. This alone is sufficient reason for the existence of good relationships between the two departments most concerned with the organization's information needs.

Need for extra resources

Extra resources will be required for either more of the same, or totally new, services and systems; this is obviously one of the basic reasons for undertaking an information audit in the first place. Be guided by the results of the survey, then do the necessary research regarding the services and resources required, the costs, and their value to the organization, then put it all into a report on the future development of the information services!

Training needs

Deliberately left till last, the training needs of the organization, as well as the information staff, become clear after all the analysis is complete and the Information Resources Index compiled. Indicate where in-house training will suffice and where there will be a need for external training courses to be available.

CONCLUSION

Once all of these steps have been completed and the report presented, an information audit may be considered complete. Presenting the results of an information audit to the Board or senior management is often the first step to making them see what an important asset to the organization its information resources are. The opportunity to raise the profile of the information services *229* is one which should be seized upon eagerly, whether the audit is carried out by the information manager, or by an external consultant. While such an audit need not be carried out annually, it should certainly be included in any programme for the enhancement of the information resources within an organization.

REFERENCE

Burk, Cornelius F., Jr, and Horton, Forest W., Jr. (1988), *InfoMap: a complete guide to discovering corporate information resources.* Hemel Hempstead: Prentice-Hall.

FURTHER READING

Bryson, Jo (1990), *Effective library and information centre management.* Aldershot: Gower.

Gallegos, Frederick *et al.* (1987), *Audit and control of information systems.* London: South-Western University Press.

Hamilton, Feona J. (1996), *Corporate information strategy for accountancy firms.* Bath: Elan Business Publishing.

Johnson, J. David (1996), *Information seeking: an organizational dilemma.* Westport/London: Quorum Books.

Lawes, Ann, ed. (1993), *Management skills for the information manager.* Aldershot: Ashgate.

O'Brien, Bart (1995), *Information management decision: briefings and critical thinking.* London: Pitman.

Walters, Patricia (1996), *Corporate information strategy for management consultants.* Bath: Elan Business Publishing/ Management Consultancy.

Ward, John and Griffiths, Pat (1996), *Strategic planning for information systems.* 2nd ed. London: Wiley.

Wilson, David A. (1996), *Managing knowledge.* London: Butterworth-Heinemann.

11 Human resource management

John Pluse

It has become a truism to say that human resources are an organization's most valuable asset. This is equally the case where a single person is operating a facility or where hundreds are employed in a library and information service (LIS) spread over several sites. What is less widely acknowledged is that human resources are, as a general rule, less well managed than the other assets of LIS. They are also probably the most difficult actually to manage.

It is also a fact that, whatever the scale and scope of a particular LIS, it is almost always part of a larger organization – be it a commercial enterprise, a local authority or an academic institution – and therefore the policies and procedures relating to human resource management (HRM) will be those of the parent body. Although the ability of the average LIS worker to determine HR policy and practice is circumscribed, individual everyday interaction between managers and managed is not susceptible to central control.

It is therefore vitally important that everyone should be familiar with HRM, and this chapter seeks to set out a framework of understanding for the establishment of policies and procedures. The main headings under which this is done are:

- organizational culture
- recruitment and selection
- training and development.

ORGANIZATIONAL CULTURE

There are a number of general factors which form the backcloth to human interaction in an organization: understanding of these is an essential prerequisite to successful HRM. These factors may be grouped under the overall heading of organizational culture, which basically means, 'how does that organization work, and how do people work with each other within it?' Is it predominantly formal or informal? Is authority and creativity centralized or delegated? Does it embrace change readily or reluctantly? What is its vision, what are its values? Does it set standards for service? Has it achieved any national standards, such as the Charter Mark, ISO 9002, Investors in People or National Training Award? The infrastructure formed by the answers to these – and similar – questions has a profound effect on all human resource matters throughout the organization: it is the basis of everything.

A number of models have been devised to diagnose, in simple definition, the overall culture of an organization. The most widely known is by Charles Handy (1992) based on the work of Roger Harrison (1972). This model proposes four cultures:

- Power: in which a central power source dominates and all authority radiates from this centre. The archetype of this culture is an organization still run by its owner/founder, but there are also elements to be found where top managers do not have the skill or the confidence to delegate effectively. There are also likely to be traces in an organization blessed with a charismatic leader. In the last two situations there are likely to be problems as these elements of a Power culture collide with the organization's predominant culture, which may be Task but is most likely to be Role (see below).

- Role: this is what is usually styled a bureaucracy, and works by logic, order and rationality. It is dominated by clearly laid-down rules and procedures. Power and influence stem from an individual's role and place in the hierarchy, and communication follows – more or less rigidly – these hierarchical lines. The great majority of large organizations – especially but not at all exclusively in the public sector – have a Role culture. Such cultures find it difficult to respond quickly to change.

- Task: this culture revolves around the actual tasks to be done in the organization rather than individuals' roles and job titles. Communication relies more on networking and who needs to talk to whom to get the job done, rather than hierarchically between peers. Such a culture is better equipped to respond to change with necessary speed. A Task culture is characterized by project teams and *ad-hoc* work groups: a 'matrix organization' (Galbraith, 1973) has a Task culture.

- Person: in this culture the individual is the focal point, and self-orientation the norm. The only organizations which can operate in this culture are professional practices (for example barristers and architects) where the organization's only purpose is to facilitate each individual in doing their own thing. Significantly, the administrator of such an organization, necessarily operating from a Task or Role standpoint, usually has a pretty torrid time! Although a Person culture is comparatively rare, people hankering after elements of it – very self-centred, or wanting to do their own thing – are to be found in all organizations: such people are notoriously difficult to manage.

Handy (1992) reproduces Roger Harrison's diagnostic question-naire (p. 214) in sufficient detail for anyone to have a go, on a do-it-yourself basis, at assessing what people in the organization think its culture is, and what they would like it to be. Interestingly, the first answer is almost always Role, and the second is almost always Task.

This gives no more than an overall, quite simplistic, snapshot of what the culture may be. There are several other facets of the total cultural picture, not specifically dealt with above.

The learning organization

An important part of the culture of an organization is the extent to which it nurtures the learning and development of its members, harnesses that learning corporately and thereby makes itself more readily responsive to stimuli for change, improvement and development. At the same time, such an organization maintains a workforce constantly well-equipped to deliver the objectives of the organization. A learning organization is defined by Pedler, Burgoyne and Boydell (1996) as one 'that facilitates the learning of all its members and continuously transforms itself'.

The concept is further developed in Burgoyne, Pedler and Boydell (1994), by Garratt (1994) and – in what has become something of a cult book – by Senge (1994a). This is not just a matter of giving the best service, important as that is, but of survival. Reg Revans put forward the notion that for any organization to survive, its rate of learning must be equal to – or greater than – the rate of change in its external environment.

One useful pointer towards a learning organization is the achievement of the Investors in People Award (IIP). This is the UK national standard for HRM, particularly in relation to training and development. It requires an organization to show acceptable evidence that it:

- has made a top level commitment to develop all employees to achieve its objectives
- regularly reviews and plans the training and development needs of all its employees
- takes action to train and develop all employees on recruitment and throughout their employment
- evaluates its training and development investment to assess achievement and improve future effectiveness.

The author has written elsewhere (Pluse, 1994) about the benefits of IIP to LIS, and a detailed blueprint for applying the principles of IIP is given by Gilliland (1997).

Another important aspect of organizational culture is the degree to which individuals have their working lives enriched by self-determination. The shorthand term for this currently is 'empowerment'. It is not just a matter of delegation of specified tasks: even less is it what is termed 'boomerang delegation', characterized by 'take this piece of work and decide exactly how you will carry it out – but check back with me before you actually do anything'. An empowering organization is one in which all its members are aware of what the organization and its work are for – its 'mission' – and are clear about what is expected of them in their jobs, and how well they are doing in relation to these expectations; one in which comprehensive, interactive communication habits are entrenched. Empowerment at work is comprehensively dealt with by Foy (1997).

It would be a grave mistake to take empowerment simplistically as a total break with past ways of working, as the latest ephemeral panacea. Senge (1994b) points out:

> Right now the word 'empowerment' is a very powerful buzzword. It's also very dangerous. Just granting power, without some method of replacing the discipline and order that come out of a command-and-control bureaucracy, produces chaos. We have to learn how to disperse power so self-discipline can largely replace imposed discipline. That immerses us in the area of culture: replacing the bureaucracy with aspirations, values and visions.

An empowering organization and a learning organization are, if not identical, then certainly close cousins.

These cultural aspects are areas where organizations commonly pay lip service and utter fine slogans, but on closer examination are found to be bluffing. One indication that an organization is seriously working on these issues is where they have been awarded recognition after external inspection and evaluation. The three most common such awards are IIP (discussed above) the National Training Award and the Charter Mark. The international standard on quality in service design and delivery – ISO 9002: 1994 – is also seen by some as a valuable indicator, but this writer is less enthusiastic and certainly, in terms of HRM, it is of less significance than the three awards mentioned above.

RECRUITMENT AND SELECTION

If we accept that human resources are an organization's most valuable asset, then it follows that getting and retaining the most appropriate workforce possible is of fundamental importance. Before recruiting to any post, it is advisable to ensure that that job is necessary and viable. This applies equally to new and existing posts. This process is *job analysis*, and it consists of gathering information on the tasks and responsibilities of the job and the skills needed to do it effectively, and then analysing that information – particularly in relation to the specific needs and activities of the organization at that time. Although the term job analysis is used as a shorthand, the process, to be fully effective in today's workplace, must embrace the concepts of job, task and role. Pearn and Kandola (1993) define the process as 'any systematic procedure for obtaining detailed and objective information about a job, task or role that will be performed or is currently being performed'. Job analysis is useful in many areas of management, and embraces a wide range of techniques. The most commonly used in this context are probably observation, diaries/logs/self-description, job analysis interviews, job inventories and critical incident analysis. These techniques (all of which are detailed in Pearn and Kandola) are all relatively straightforward and manageable by the non-work study specialist. Other techniques require specialized expertise to be applied effectively and, in many cases, computer-assisted data analysis.

Once the content and structure of the job have been determined, or re-assessed, the next stage is to produce an appropriate *job description*. It is now fashionable in some circles to scoff at job descriptions as being too inflexible, a relic of defunct bureaucracy, and much besides. Any such instrument can be flexible or inflexible, not inherently, but according to how it is used by the parties concerned. Even in today's volatile working world, some relatively stable points of reference are needed: otherwise productive flexibilty becomes dysfunctional chaos. A job description should cover these areas:

236

- job title
- pay level
- location
- who postholder reports to
- who postholder is responsible for
- purpose of the job
- broad statement of duties and responsibilities.

Having established the viability and parameters of the job, the next question is: what sort of person do we need to do it? The *person specification* must set this out with sufficient detail and clarity for the selection team to be able to make their choice with confidence. There have been several frameworks published for the production of person specifications but the most enduring has been that of Rodger (1952): this is dated but can readily be adapted to present circumstances. It classifies the features of the ideal postholder under seven headings:

- attainments: including educational and professional qualifications, and experience. Basic literacy and numeracy are surely essential for LIS work – but how will an employer assess them? Are certificates earned in general education sufficient evidence, or will specific tests at the selection stage be carried out? This may well depend upon an employer's past satisfaction with recruits and upon the nature and clarity of their skill requirements.
- general intelligence: sometimes assessed by standard tests.
- special aptitudes: particular skills, attributes or competences called for in the job; again, sometimes assessed by testing.
- interests: both work-related and leisure, provided they are demonstrably relevant to the job.
- disposition: personal attributes relevant to working with others, and attitudes to work; personality testing is sometimes used here.
- physical make-up: particularly important for manual tasks while keeping in mind the special status of the disabled.   *237*

- circumstances: domestic/family commitments, availability to work unusual hours or patterns; particular care is necessary in this area today – items specified must be strictly relevant to the job and must be tested with scrupulous fairness as between candidates.

Under each of these headings, two categories of requirements must be listed – 'essential' and 'desirable'. It is important that 'essential' includes only requirements so crucial to effectiveness in the job that not possessing them disqualifies any candidate. There should be no fudging on this at later stages of the selection process, because to do so would be a gross breach of fair and objective selection: essential must *mean* essential.

This brings us to the point where we are ready to invite people to apply for the job. There are many ways – formal and informal – to build a list of job applicants but current opinion, particularly in the public sector, is that fairness and openness requires jobs to be publicly advertised. Where best to place such an advertisement will vary according to the nature of the job and will be fairly obvious to those involved: it might be a local or national newspaper, or it might be a professional journal. Wherever it is placed, a *job advertisement* must be clear, specific, concise – and attractive to its potential audience without being gimmicky, which often misfires. It is customary in job advertisements, particularly for more senior or specialist posts, to offer additional details to applicants. These should include the job description, the person specification and such further information on the organization in general as is thought appropriate. Overall the package must be informative and attractive: it is not just an aid to recruitment, it is an advertisement for the style and quality of the whole organization.

The question arises at this point: should applications be on a standard form or should applicants be allowed the creative licence of the *curriculum vitae*? The selection process is made easier, and probably fairer, if the essential information required from each candidate is presented in standard and comparable format. This

238   does not preclude there being opportunity for creative and

persuasive expression within an application form – in describing career history and giving reasons for wanting the job, for example.

Having thus attracted a number of candidates to apply for the job, the process of deciding which to appoint must begin. The applications must be matched against the person specification and any which fail to meet all the essential requirements must be eliminated at this stage. Further analysis should identify those applicants who best match the person specification as a whole: the aim must be to distil this number to somewhere between four and eight – this is the *shortlist*.

Imperfect though it is, the individual *interview* is the most common method of selection – and probably the least difficult to carry out. In the interests of fairness and consistency, the same people should carry out the whole recruitment and selection process for a particular job – from compilation or review of the job description and person specification right through to appointing the successful candidate. How many should be involved? – clearly, one is not enough; two is acceptable; three is ideal; four is manageable; five and above cannot normally be justified, and the motives and practical usefulness of all those claiming involvement should be rigorously questioned in such circumstances. The purpose of the interview is to clarify and supplement the information already given by each shortlisted candidate, and to help each to appear in their best light. Therefore, questions designed to trip up or confuse candidates serve no purpose other than to massage the ego of the interviewer. The culmination of the interview process is deciding which of the candidates to appoint – or, on occasion, none of them. There are other aids to this process, including taking up references – but these need to be approached with caution since they are not always clear or, indeed, totally honest – and various forms of test and exercise. Psychometric tests, very popular in some quarters, are an expensive way of gaining some insight into candidates' personality and attitudes: this author does not view them as particularly useful or cost-effective, but for those who wish to explore them Toplis (1997) is a helpful guide. Of more realistic value in selection decisions might be practical tests of skills and aptitude directly related to clerical *239* or manual jobs, say, or group discussions for candidates for more senior or specialist positions. Also, remember the value – in the interview itself – of situational questions of the 'what would you do if...' nature.

It is important that the selection processes seek to identify candidates' potential to develop in the job in question, and not just their off-the-peg readiness – which can prove static and of diminishing value.

Suitable reading for those wanting to go into recruitment and selection in more depth are Plumbley (1991), the more technical Smith and Robertson (1993) and the more recent Roberts (1997).

TRAINING AND DEVELOPMENT

Assuming an employer sets clear and focused skill requirements at recruitment and selects successfully against these, then subsequent training and development will revolve around what skills and knowledge need adding and/or updating from time to time. The learning organization, and the idea of the IIP Award as a yardstick of commitment to effective training and development for the whole workforce, are the backcloth against which the functioning of this activity in an organization should be examined.

Effective training activity in an organization is continuous and cyclic, taking in these stages:

- identification of training needs
- planning of appropriate responses
- carrying out training
- evaluation of the outcomes; transfer of learning to the workplace.

This classic training cycle can appear static and it is very important to remember that the loop of activity never ends: the final stage always leads back to the first stage of the next cycle. Constant development takes place as time passes.

This structured approach to training and development – which incidentally mirrors other learning-related cycles and also the IIP criteria – is in marked contrast with what actually happens in many organizations. This is characterized by large elements of chance – at best, serendipity – based on 'what comes up' in the way of training events within the parent organization and externally, and hurried consideration of 'who can we send on this?' This whimsical approach is usually a by-product of all senior managers being too 'busy' to give proper and systematic consideration to training and development overall, and results in the funds available for training being expended with little or no perceivable benefit either to the organization or its individual members.

Formal training programmes

The first stage in a properly considered and value-for-money training programme is a systematic and ongoing analysis of what training is actually needed to support the objectives, targets and activities of the organization. What knowledge and skills are needed by individuals to function effectively within those parameters, which of these do they possess and which do they still need to acquire or develop? This presupposes that the stages of the recruitment and selection process discussed above have brought clarity to all concerned about exactly what is expected of the postholder. Moreover, this foundation must be built on by regular communication between postholder and line manager in order that these expectations are kept clear and up-to-date, and in particular so that every member of the organization knows at all times how he or she is doing in terms of effective performance.

This regular, routine dialogue between managers and their staff is pivotal to the success of any training strategy – and therefore throughout the cycle described here. Its frequent absence is the biggest cause of failure in an organization's training activity – and indeed throughout HRM as a whole. Ideally this will all happen as part of a systematic process of individual performance review involving the whole workforce. This concept will be explored at the end of this chapter. There is a wide range of techniques available for determining training needs (Bartram and Gibson, 1997) but to be effective they must be based on dialogue between managers and   *241* those whose work they are responsible for. The aim would be to identify gaps in the skills they need to do their jobs effectively.

Situations which are usually indicators of training need include:

- new recruits
- job change (the training needs of those coming into supervisory/managerial work for the first time are frequently overlooked)
- below par performance
- new services, processes or equipment.

Training for individual development can be a difficult area in which to judge legitimate need: there is a fine line to be drawn between the demonstrable needs of the organization and its services and an approach which accepts all training as intrinsically good. The latter view shows an altruism which few organizations – particularly in the public sector – can afford. The example of the long and expensive higher qualification course, for which there can emerge a widespread demand, is one which will bring agonized debate to the most well-intentioned organization.

Readers of this chapter requiring further help and information on all stages of the training and development cycle will be well served by the *Training Essentials* series (Institute of Personnel and Development, 1996/7). The planning and delivery of training (the middle two stages of the cycle) will be best helped by a variety of approaches involving both internal and external sources. Even where the organization has the capability, which is very rare, it is inappropriate for all training and development needs to be met from internal resources: the result would be a very inward-looking workforce. Conversely, no organization can really afford to buy in everything from external sources, which would in any case overlook the challenge and refreshment to be found in taking responsibility for some training internally. It is always of benefit to have some appropriate members of the organization properly trained as occasional trainers.

The parent body to which a LIS belongs is an intermediate source for some training, usually less costly than totally external sources, but sometimes less focused than internal sources. It is important to get to know what is being offered externally, as far in advance as possible, so that use of such opportunities can be properly planned and matched to real need. It is easy to overlook the possibilities of 'cascade training', whereby one or two appropriate people are sent on an external course with the intention of them reproducing the training internally for so many colleagues as need it: this can be very cost effective, but does require the 'cascaders' to have had some training as trainers.

Internal training can also be a simple matter of placing the trainee with an experienced colleague to learn by doing: the 'sitting by Nellie' approach. This is scorned in some circles but there is no more effective way of imparting basic skills and procedures – provided, of course, that you have effective and competent 'Nellies' for the purpose, and that the process is properly monitored by the relevant line manager.

It is important that there be a strong feeling of ownership of training by those involved, and consequently a high level of commitment to successful outcomes. In appropriate circumstances this can be enhanced by building a high degree of self-direction into the learning (Pedler, 1990). The increasing spread of National Vocational Qualifications (NVQs) will emphasize this, because they essentially have a learner-focus (Herzog, 1996). Another form of self-directed learning – this time in groups – is action learning: small groups working semi-autonomously to solve work-based problems with no pre-determined outcome, and learning in the process (Weinstein, 1995).

Other training activities

Not all training and development is through formal training events, of course. Placements, shadowing and job enrichment can be very useful, as can guided reading. Active, positive involvement by managers and supervisors is important to the success of any training and development activity, and essential to this latter group.

A further stage of manager involvement is seen in coaching, and related activity. Coaching is a one-to-one dialogue on work-related *243* issues, aimed at improving performance and personal development. It may be part of a formal scheme, but is probably most effective when it is an ongoing, everyday part of interaction between line managers/supervisors and their team members. The technique is described in appropriate detail in Kinlaw (1997). A closely-related approach is mentoring, which has a similar one-to-one basis but is much less likely to involve the direct manager/supervisor. Typically, mentoring involves a senior manager acting as guide and 'god-parent' to a junior colleague from a different management line. More recently it has developed to encompass a much broader range of relationships, but all with one aim: the assistance and development of a junior colleague by confidential advice and support. Mentoring originated as informal and unstructured, but now can be formally set up as a structured – even compulsory – scheme covering the whole organization. The danger in this is that it can come to be seen by managers as a chore, to be paid lip service only. The classic text is Clutterbuck (1991), and Mumford (1993) deals with all aspects of inter-managerial development.

Evaluation of training

Much training and development activity is wasted because it is neither evaluated nor effectively used in the workplace. Managers taking proper responsibility for the training and development of their people will be the key to success throughout the training cycle. Most of us are familiar with the scepticism, indifference – even hostility – experienced from work colleagues by people returning from training events, making it unlikely that the workplace benefits at all from that particular investment in training, in terms of transfer of learning. Training evaluation is not of itself the remedy for this, but as part of a conscientiously followed training cycle it can be so: for instance, it is difficult to assess how successful a piece of training has been if, earlier in the cycle, clear and specific expectations were not agreed. Evaluation can be used to assess the value of training in relation to the objectives and targets of the organization; to assess the effectiveness of the mechanics of the systems and procedures relating to training in that organization; and to gather feedback to those organizing and delivering a particular training event. There are a range of changes in the trainees which evaluation can seek to measure:

- reactions of trainees, although this is too often confined to their immediate reactions – 'happiness sheets'. Longer-term reactions – say, four to six weeks after the event – will be more useful.
- improvements in job skills and level of relevant knowledge, measured particularly against expectations set when this training was agreed and planned.
- changes in attitude and behaviour, also measured against earlier agreed expectations.
- by cumulating evaluations, the impact of training on the achievement of the organization's objectives and targets.

Most aspects of evaluation are easily applied by informed managers, but some will require specialist skills. Bramley (1992) will be found useful, as will the relevant title in the *Training Essentials* series (Institute of Personnel and Development, 1996/7).

CONCLUSION

It can not be overemphasized that the cyclic process described here must be continuous, and it can only work as a total package: organizations will not succeed in creating an effective training and development environment by partial adoption of this model.

There is the final question of performance management, frequently called *appraisal*, which the author closely associates with training and development. Properly organized training and development systems and supportively-structured performance management procedures have the same objective, namely: good outcomes for the organization in relation to its objectives and targets by consistent, monitored and appropriate support and development to enable its members to optimize their contribution to these ends. Where appraisal is used as a control tool of hard- *245* nosed management in organizations with an authoritarian culture, there is no evidence of long-term success. Similarly where appraisal data is linked to a system of performance-related pay, there is little evidence that real fairness and objectivity can be achieved or that such schemes can run productively or peacefully over time.

In this context of personal development for better performance, the term *individual performance review* seems more appropriate than either appraisal or performance management. Whatever title is preferred, there are a number of pre-requisites for an effective, credible and acceptable system. These are:

- the appraiser should normally be the immediate line manager
- the system must be a partnership between appraiser and appraisee throughout, balancing the needs of each
- the system must be based on clear, agreed and achievable work targets
- performance review must be in terms of those targets
- the targets and reviews must be linked to consistent managerial support, and to opportunities for appropriate training and development related to agreed needs and work targets
- the system must be based on objective data throughout
- the system must be fully open and honest between appraiser and appraisee and totally confidential
- memories cannot be relied upon: proper records must be kept by both parties, but there is no real need for files to be kept by third parties (for example, personnel officers)
- agreed notes of review meetings should be seen (but not filed) by the manager's manager, to whom both parties must have equal access in cases of disagreement
- the agenda of review meetings must include all items both parties wish to discuss, and be as wide-ranging as necessary
- review meetings should be sufficiently frequent for issues to be dealt with within reasonable time of them arising (which probably means not less than two and not more than four per annum) and must be supplemented by regular, routine feedback in the workplace.

The spirit of the review process should be one of support to the appraisee in the interests of optimum performance, and this means a strong focus on reviewing and fulfilling training and development needs. For more detailed coverage readers may turn to Fletcher (1997) and to the classic but still useful Randell (1984).

REFERENCES

Bartram, S., and Gibson, B. (1997), *Training needs analysis.* 2nd ed. Aldershot: Gower.

Bramley, P. (1992), *Evaluating training effectiveness.* 2nd ed. London: McGraw Hill.

Burgoyne, J., Pedler, M. and Boydell, T. (1994), *Towards the learning company.* London: McGraw Hill.

Clutterbuck, D. (1991), *Everyone needs a mentor.* 2nd ed. London: Institute of Personnel and Development.

Fletcher, C. (1997), *Appraisal.* 2nd ed. London: Institute of Personnel and Development.

Foy, N. (1997), *Empowering people at work.* Aldershot: Ashgate.

Galbraith, J. R. (1973), *Designing complex organizations.* London: Addison-Wesley.

Garratt, B. (1994), *The learning organization.* Rev ed. Harlow: Harper Collins.

Gilliland, N. (1997), *Developing your business through Investors in People.* 2nd ed. Aldershot: Gower.

Handy, C. (1992), *Understanding organizations.* 4th ed. Harmondsworth: Penguin.

Harrison, R. (1972), How to describe your organization. *Harvard business review.* Sept/Oct.

Herzog, J. (1996), *Implementing S/NVQs in the ILS sector.* London: Library Association Publishing.

Institute of Personnel and Development (1996/7), Training Essentials Series. London: Institute of Personnel and Development:
Introduction to training. P. Hackett. 1997.
Identifying training needs. T. Boydell and M. Leary. 1996.
Designing training. A. Hardingham. 1996.

Developing learning materials. J. Gough. 1996.

Delivering training. S. Siddons. 1997.

Cultivating self-development. D. Megginson and V. Whitaker. 1996.

Evaluating training. P. Bramley. 1996.

Kinlaw, D. (1997), *Coaching.* Aldershot: Gower.

Mumford, A. (1993), *How managers can develop managers.* Aldershot: Gower.

Pearn, M. and Kandola, R. (1993), *Job analysis.* 2nd ed. London: Institute of Personnel and Development.

Pedler, M. *et al.* eds. (1990), *Self-development in organizations.* London: McGraw Hill.

Pedler, M., Burgoyne, J. and Boydell, T. (1996), *The learning company.* 2nd ed. London: McGraw Hill.

Plumbley, P. R. (1991), *Recruitment and selection.* Rev ed. London: Institute of Personnel and Development.

Pluse, J. M. (1994), Investors in People: a framework for all. *Information management report*, December, pp. 13–15.

Randell, G. A. *et al.* (1984), *Staff appraisal.* 3rd ed. London: Institue of Personnel Management.

Reid, M. A., Barrington, H. and Kenney, J. (1992), *Training interventions.* 3rd ed. London: Institute of Personnel and Development.

Roberts, G. (1997), *Recruitment and selection – a competency approach.* London: Institute of Personnel and Development.

Rodger, A. (1952), *The seven point plan.* London: National Institute for Industrial Psychology.

Senge, P. (1994a), *The fifth discipline.* London: Doubleday.

Senge, P. *et al.* (1994b), *The fifth discipline fieldbook.* London: Nicholas Brealey.

Smith, M., and Robertson, I. T. (1993), *The theory and practice of systematic staff selection.* 2nd ed. London: Macmillan.

Toplis, J., Dulewicz, V. and Fletcher, C. (1997), *Psychological testing.* 3rd ed. London: Institute of Personnel and Development.

Weinstein, K. (1995), *Action learning.* London: Harper Collins.

12 Preservation, access and integrity

Priscilla Schlicke

The preservation of information is an idea whose time has come. In the not too distant past preservation and conservation (PAC), both related activities, were of minor, if not insignificant, relevance in library and information services (LISs). If considered at all, they were deemed to be the province of those who had the care of rare books and manuscripts. But over the past fifteen years the view of PAC has expanded to become an integral part of the much wider area of collection management and a vital element in the provision of access to information. If the particular medium which records the information has been allowed to decay and disappear, then access to it is impossible. This increased perception of the essential requirement of preservation is perhaps related to the 'green revolution' generally. Global warming, pollution, the burning of fossil fuels, the world environment summits at Rio in 1992 and Kyoto in 1997 – and numerous other events – have all contributed to the growing awareness of the importance of preserving and conserving the physical environment; some of this concern has percolated into the thinking of library and information managers (LIMs) who are concerned with access to information and its provision to their users.

This chapter of the Handbook investigates preservation in particular and conservation to a lesser extent. The emphasis here is on the relation between preservation and access. If the 249 importance of preserving information is accepted, then it must be on the basis that, in order to maintain access to information for users, that information must somehow be preserved; very few information sources require to be preserved as artifacts. As one writer observed – with tongue in cheek – if preservation is the sole criteria, the cheapest and most obvious solution is to bury the material in Greenland. This might well serve to preserve the artifact forever, but it would not contribute much to easy and widespread access to information at the point of need. What is at issue in the current thinking about preservation is the preservation of content rather than object.

There are various definitions of preservation and conservation in the literature. Those provided in a 1992 glossary from the National Preservation Office at the British Library seem particularly comprehensive and appropriate:

Preservation: includes all the managerial and financial considerations including storage and accommodation provisions, staffing levels, policies, techniques and methods involved in preserving library archive materials and the information contained in them;

Conservation: denotes those specific treatments and techniques applied in protecting library and archive materials from deterioration which involves intervention with the object itself.

Preservation is a broader term than conservation and is a management process; conservation is a technical and/or craft process. This chapter will emphasize preservation because that activity is crucial for all LIMs; conservation is of concern where artifacts themselves, rather than just their contents, must be preserved. The chapter will explore the following issues:

- the background to the development of interest in PAC
- the reasons for the deterioration and decay of the various media which hold information

- the policy and planning required for the effective management of PAC
- the range of technical solutions applicable to the preservation of information, with particular emphasis on the rapidly developing area of digitization
- general, practical guidelines to help ensure the maximum useful life of materials.

A proper and effective preservation policy can help to ensure that the LIS gets maximum value for money from the information sources – be they books, journals, tapes, discs or whatever – which it acquires. And a policy which ensures access as and when required because the information has been preserved and is available can make a positive and significant contribution to the effectiveness of the organization.

THE BACKGROUND TO PRESERVATION AND CONSERVATION

There are, of course, more specific reasons than the general 'greening' of society for the heightened awareness of the need to preserve collections of information. An early one was the discovery of the 'brittle books syndrome'. Most books printed after about 1850 – and some even before that date – were produced on paper which was chemically unstable and these books were literally crumbling into dust on the shelves of thousands of libraries around the world. John Murray wrote to the *Gentleman's magazine* in 1823:

> Allow me to call the attention of your readers to the present state of that wretched compound called *Paper*. Every printer will corroborate my testimony; and I am only astonished that the interesting question has been so long neglected and forgotten. It is a duty, however, of the most imperative description; – our beautiful Religion, our Literature, our Science, all are threatened.

251

There are extensive discussions of the problem in the literature; a particularly good study was that undertaken by the Harvard University Library Task Group on Collection Preservation Priorities (1991).

The floods which devastated the city of Florence in 1966 caused enormous damage to the priceless documents in the Italian State Archives. Substantial donations of money poured in, but it quickly became apparent that there were not sufficient numbers of trained conservators to undertake the highly skilled work required for restoration. Most of the damage was repaired eventually, but the disaster revealed a serious gap in the knowledge of preservation management and techniques worldwide.

This gap was identified by the International Federation of Library Associations (IFLA), which set up its core Preservation and Conservation Programme in 1984 as a logical continuation of the earlier programmes of Universal Bibliographic Control and Universal Availability of Publications. The programme is based at the Library of Congress (LC) and encourages research into different methods of preservation and the formulation of policy and strategy at national and international levels. The LC itself has published several comprehensive handbooks on practical preservation techniques and funded extensive research into the mass deacidification of paper.

In the United Kingdom the Ratcliffe Report (1984) investigated preservation policies and conservation practices in British libraries. This report was funded by the British Library, which about that time also set up the National Preservation Office (NPO) to provide a focus for preservation planning and co-operation. Ratcliffe was influential in bringing about an awareness and discussion of preservation in the UK and succeeded in widening the concern beyond the rarefied world of special collections and antiquarian materials. It has also led to a number of subsequent studies, most recently *Preservation management: policies and practices in British libraries* (Feather, 1996).

Other European countries, in particular France, Germany and Spain, have begun to put considerable emphasis on PAC in recent years. UNESCO has also turned its attention to these issues with the publication of two key documents, *Guidelines on preservation and conservation policies in libraries and archives* (Chapman, 1990) and *Preservation and conservation of library documents: a UNESCO/IFLA/ICA enquiry into the current state of the world's patrimony* (Clements, 1987), as well as its 'Memory of the World' Programme.

All this activity provides evidence of the serious problem of decaying and disappearing materials on a global scale. The challenge for the individual LIM is to translate this concern – using the knowledge and techniques available – into a programme appropriate for the particular LIS and the information and materials which it wants and needs to preserve.

MEDIA DETERIORATION

Information is necessarily recorded on some kind of medium. McLuhan claimed that the medium was the message, but in preservation terms the medium is also the problem. All media deteriorate over time, at different rates and for different reasons. This section of the chapter provides a brief survey of the major media used for recording information and identifies the major reasons for the deterioration of each. Further details on the various threats are explained in chapter 13.

Paper

Despite the rapid developments of digitization, paper is still by far the most common medium for the recording of information. Early paper was made from rags, chiefly linen, and it was and is remarkably stable. During the nineteenth century, however, the demand for paper increased rapidly and the supply of rags could not keep pace. Wood pulp began to be used as the raw material for paper and it still is. Paper made using the mechanical wood pulp process, however, is chemically unstable and reacts to pollutants and ultraviolet light to become acidic, brittle and yellow. Brittle paper can crumble into dust while just sitting on a shelf and can crack and break when handled. When paper becomes damp it is *253* susceptible to mould and damage from micro-organisms. It is possible to deacidify paper, either in an individual volume or on a mass scale; but on the assumption that prevention is better than cure, LIMs should press for the use of permanent paper – an international standard was agreed in 1994 – in the publication of any information with a long 'life expectancy'.

Film

In contrast to paper, early film stock was much less 'permanent' and stable than most of that used today. Early nitrate stock was highly flammable and cracked and broke easily. Much of the early film in archives has been transferred to safety stock. The use of microforms in a preservation programme has led to the development of standards in the manufacture of film stock.

Magnetic tape

Magnetic tape decays over time. The tape itself is a plastic material and chemically stable, but the glue which holds the information (audio; visual; computer data) onto the tape deteriorates and the data quite simply 'falls off'. This phenomenon was discovered at NASA: magnetic tapes storing data collected through the space programme were kept in cupboards and when they came to be consulted some years later the tapes were unreadable, basically because they no longer held any data. The British Standards Institution (BSI) has set standards (BS 4783) for the cleaning and rewinding (6 months) and the copying (12 months) of magnetic tape to help ensure preservation of the data; these are likely to be similar to those required for digital audio tape when use of this becomes widespread.

Optical discs

The 'permanence' and stability of digital materials is not yet established. Early claims that CD-ROM discs might have a life expectancy of 500 to 1000 years quickly proved ridiculous; no one knows how long they might last. That they do deteriorate is evident: scratches, fingerprints and grime distort the information recorded on the disc; glues and inks used in labels can corrode the surface; careless handling causes damage. What is apparent with these media is that their machine dependence is highly volatile. Any specific hardware or software required to use them is changing and developing at an increasingly rapid rate. This has enormous implications for any preservation programme using digital technology; these will be considered in detail further in the chapter.

PRESERVATION POLICY AND PLANNING

Statement of purpose

The development of a preservation policy for a particular LIS will necessarily depend on its mission and purpose within the organization or community within which it operates. This process can be illustrated by statements extracted from the British Library document *For scholarship, research and innovation: strategic objectives for the year 2000* (1993). The Library's statement of purpose includes the following sentences:

Our function is to serve scholarship, research and enterprise. Our purpose is to promote the advance of knowledge through the communication of information and ideas.

One of the actions to enable this to be achieved states:

We build, catalogue and conserve the collections.

A more detailed statement about preservation expands on this statement of intent and defines the order of priorities:

* heritage material and unique or rare material including manuscripts, certain special collections, archives, rare printed material... or material classed as artifacts

255

- material comprising the national collection of British publications
- material that is heavily used now and has become fragile, or that may be expected to receive heavy use in the future and has already or is likely to become fragile
- material not available elsewhere
- material belonging to the research archives
- low-use material which is too fragile to be consulted or copied.

This statement clearly sets PAC within the larger context of collection management within the British Library. In their own organizations, LIMs decide what material to collect – or provide access to – which reflects the information needs and requirements of their users. LIMs then provide access to the collection by means such as catalogues and/or indexes, classification of the material and current awareness services. They will also provide facilities for users, including desks, equipment, lending procedures if these are appropriate and, increasingly, network access to the material required. And finally, it is necessary to provide storage for the collections; the environmental conditions of this storage have a significant impact on the overall issue of preservation, which will be considered in more detail later in this chapter.

Assessment of preservation needs

Once the statement of purpose for the LIS has been made it is necessary to consider other issues before a formal policy for PAC can be determined. A first step in this process often involves the identification of a stock retention policy – that is, a decision on how much of the stock is to be retained permanently. There are three basic options: retain none; retain all; retain some.

In situations where the answer is none – as might happen in a LIS involved in research in a rapidly developing field – then the question remains of how to maximize the useful life of the stock to ensure that it is accessible for as long as it might be required: binding and rebinding policies, for example. Also necessary is a clear policy and understanding of how long material should be kept, and when it can be disposed of or thrown out. This may seem negative but it does reflect conscious decision-making and planning.

If all material, on the other hand, is to be retained permanently a different set of issues arises. With the exception of the great national libraries, public record offices and other such organizations, very few LISs are likely to believe that they should attempt to keep everything. Where permanent retention is the case, however, it is necessary – as we saw in the British Library statement above – to set priorities for preserving and conserving the materials. The order of these priorities will depend on the needs of the organization and the condition of the materials which are to be retained.

The vast majority of LISs will have some materials in their collections which they intend and wish to retain permanently. In public libraries these might be local studies collections; in university libraries, special collections relating to a particular field of study or scholarship; in other types of LIS, possibly documents relating to the history and activities of the organization. Whatever the individual situation, these materials for permanent retention must first be identified and then priorities set for their treatment.

Managerial and technical resources

The next consideration in the formulation of a PAC policy is the availability of managerial and technical resources. The major issue is always finance. For a policy to be effective money must be allocated in the budget to achieve what is required. This can range from sums being set aside for binding journals and other materials and rebinding books, to grants being sought outside the organization for special microfilming and digitization projects. The Mellon Foundation has given substantial sums of money to a wide range of British libraries to microfilm special collections of material. Much of the literature on PAC highlights the challenges faced by LIMs in finding sufficient money to fund a preservation programme; convincing management of the value of such a programme is often a daunting task.

Staff resources are another issue. Few LISs will have – or need – trained conservators on their staff, but all staff will require some training in preserving materials. Where in-house binderies exist, decisions will have to be made about which material to bind there and which to send out; similar decisions need to be made if microfilming or, more recently, digitization projects are undertaken. A careful consideration of alternative costs will be necessary.

The impact on collections and service

An effective policy on PAC must consider the impact which it makes on the users of the LIS. Where information is provided in alternative formats – for example microforms or digitization – equipment for using them must not only be provided, but kept maintained in good working order. The provision of digitized materials, particularly, offers the LIS the opportunity to enhance access to the work by adding SGML and HTML links to the material so that it can be used in entirely new ways. Where original and valuable or rare materials are consulted directly by users, training should be given on how to handle them properly; any restrictions on use, such as no photocopying on flat-bed machines, should be explained so that they are understood. The timing for preservation work should be considered carefully; in a university library, for example, journals should be sent away for binding in the long vacation rather than in the weeks running up to examinations. Other types of LISs should try to identify appropriate times for such work so that inconvenience to users is minimized.

The development of an effective PAC policy, appropriate to the particular LIS, can only be made after careful and realistic consideration of all of these issues.

ELEMENTS OF A PRESERVATION POLICY

This section of the chapter considers the elements which make up an effective PAC policy; they are derived from the UNESCO *Guidelines* cited above. Some of these are routine tasks, which, nevertheless, if undertaken systematically can contribute much towards the preservation of information materials.

Preventive measures

Preventive measures are largely concerned with the control of the environment in which the materials are used and stored. For paper documents the temperature should be maintained at somewhere between 16 and 18 degrees Centigrade; this is somewhat cool for readers and staff, but where material is stored separately attempts should be made to achieve it. Relative humidity (the measurement of moisture in the air) should be kept between 50 per cent and 60 per cent, so that paper and bindings do not become too moist and run the risk of activating mould, or become too dry and brittle. Storage areas need to be well-ventilated and protected, by curtains or filters, from direct ultra-violet light.

Shelving should ideally be metal rather than wood (it doesn't burn and it won't harbour biological pests) with fitted, movable book ends to ensure that materials are supported upright. Cabinets are essential for large scale items, such as maps, plans or drawings which need to be kept flat. Appropriate storage for other materials – optical discs, computer disks, magnetic tape, microforms, slides, glass negatives – is also necessary.

Protective measures

These are more proactive than preventive measures and include binding, boxing and wrapping, as well as simple repairs to paper, to reduce wear and tear on materials. Binding is self-explanatory and most LISs will have a policy on which materials require binding and when this should be undertaken. Boxes can serve a variety of purposes. Open-top boxes – 'pamphlet boxes' – should be used for frequently consulted materials such as unbound journals, booklets and leaflets. A number of more sophisticated boxes – phase boxes; solander boxes – are available, made from acid-free card, which fit snugly around an item or a small collection of similar materials. Wrapping ranges from the simple use of a plastic jacket to *259* encapsulation, a reversible process where a single sheet is sandwiched between two pieces of transparent polyester which is then fused at the edges. Where protective measures are used it is essential that they are appropriate for the materials.

Housekeeping routines

Regular cleaning may appear mundane and uninspiring but it is an essential aspect of preservation and will serve to protect materials and extend their useful life. Books and other items should be regularly dusted, wiping away from the spine. This is particularly important in closed storage areas. Leather bindings need the application of a dressing at intervals to prevent them drying and cracking. Cleaning staff will need training on the proper way to treat and handle the materials and a procedure for reporting possible hazards.

Staff and user training

The LIS should develop programmes for both staff and users to promote preservation. These include instruction on how to handle books: for example, opening a new one carefully so as not to crack the spine; not leaving them open either face up or face down; and transporting them safely: it has been estimated that dropping a book on the floor causes about £5 worth of damage. It is important to shelve items correctly: not overcrowding so that books have to be tugged out by the top of spine, thus pulling it off; or left loose so they tumble over or fall off. Staff should also be trained to identify damaged materials and to make simple repairs where appropriate.

Conservation treatments

These are treatments undertaken to repair and restore damaged originals. Such treatments are likely to be expensive and time-consuming and thus usually applied only to items important as artifacts in themselves; not all LISs will be concerned with conservation. Conservation often includes removing the binding,

260

cleaning, washing and deacidifying the paper, repairing it where necessary and rebinding as appropriate. LIMs in most organizations would need to approach professional conservators for advice when such work needs to be undertaken.

Reprography

Reprographics covers the procedure for reproducing originals; in virtually all cases this means providing a photocopy. Current copyright legislation in the United Kingdom permits the making of a copy for preservation purposes as *long as the item cannot easily be replaced* – in other words, if it is not still available for sale.

Photocopying of material as part of a PAC programme can certainly increase accessibility; it may no longer be necessary for users to handle rare or fragile originals. But flat-bed copiers can cause enormous damage to the binding structure, especially with large, tightly-bound volumes, such as periodicals. When preservation is a concern, LIMs will have to develop a policy for photocopying – within the constraints of copyright law – appropriate for their service.

Substitution programmes

A substitution programme replaces documents – whether they are rare, valuable, fragile, bulky or whatever – with surrogate forms. Surrogacy programmes are of major importance in implementing preservation policies and have been one of the most important techniques in shifting emphasis from the preservation of books and documents towards the preservation of information for access by users. Microforms have traditionally been used for the production of surrogates, but these are rapidly being overtaken by digitization. These two processes are mentioned here and will be discussed in more detail later in this chapter.

Disposal programmes

The disposal of material which is no longer required is an integral   *261* part of collection management and hence of preservation. The usual procedure is to dispose of material that is no longer current or no longer required. In most cases this is an internal issue for the LIS; decisions will be made in relation to the overall purpose of the service and its users. Problems are potentially posed, however, when the material is rare or unique or is of potential interest to the wider community. There are implications here for companies, charities, private societies and others whose archives, records and other documents could provide valuable material for study, research and investigation in the future. In some cases, such as the Stationers' Company, the records have been microfilmed and made available commercially – an example of a preservation programme offering the opportunity of wider access.

The above discussion covers the most significant elements in an overall policy for PAC. Security and disaster management, larger issues which also impinge on a preservation policy, are considered in chapter 13.

MICROFORMS AND DIGITIZATION

As noted earlier, microforms and digitization are two technologies which make a valuable and important contribution not only to PAC, but also allow much wider access by users to the content. This section of the chapter will survey the technical processes involved in microfilming and digitizing and discuss the management issues which must be faced in undertaking projects.

Microforms

Microfilming was first introduced in the mid-nineteenth century and is an old and well-established technology. There have been a number of major microfilming projects in the United Kingdom and, indeed, worldwide. In the UK, NEWSPLAN is a nationwide co-operative project, funded from a variety of sources, to microfilm local and regional newspapers to ensure their continued availability. And, as noted above, the Mellon Foundation has made funds available for the microfilming of a range of special collections in various libraries and information centres throughout the country. Some public libraries have also microfilmed collections of local studies materials.

Certain procedures need to be followed if a microfilming project is to be a success. When considering microfilming, check first in various registers of microform masters – the National Preservation Office has produced one for the UK, and there is also a European register (Schwartz, 1996) – to see whether the material has already been filmed; if so, it is almost always cheaper to purchase a copy than to start from scratch. The major step is undoubtedly to secure the funding; this is likely to be a special allocation within the budget or, if lucky, an outside grant. In some cases, where the material has a potential sales value, it may be possible to get a commercial microfilm publisher to undertake the project.

In most cases, particularly for smaller LISs, the actual filming will be done by an outside organization. It should be one which has experience in filming to archival standards. Silver halide film must be used for the microform master, which should then be stored in acid free boxes or sleeves and kept in drawers; masters are then copied to diazo stock for use. Where volumes need to be unbound for filming, care should be taken to keep the sheets in the correct order for filming. When filming is complete, the quality should be checked carefully, ideally page by page; but for large projects a random check may suffice. It is sometimes necessary, and often essential, to prepare indexes and other 'finding aids' to the material to make access easier for users. These may be either microfilmed themselves or printed.

There are drawbacks to microforms, especially as regards access to the material. Users generally claim not to like them, but this may often be because of the quality of the reading equipment. Despite statements from manufacturers, reader/printers haven't really developed many sophisticated features. More seriously, all too often they are poorly maintained in the LIS; if they work – more or less – that is usually deemed to be enough, despite the fact that screens may be filthy and reels and winders not operate properly. Overall microform technology is not very exciting; the data cannot be manipulated or enhanced as it can with electronic formats. But *263* the process and its management have been going on for a long time and – at least in comparison to digitization – it is simple and straightforward.

Digitization

Digitization is the most recent technology to be adopted for the purposes of PAC and access to information. The process uses binary code to record and store information objects, including text, images, sound, movement, colour. The objects are converted to bit maps using a digital scanner or other such technology such as Kodak Photo CD. The process of creation often incorporates customized indexes and sometimes Query By Image Content (QBIC) for searching visual images on the basis of features such as colour or texture. HTML links are common as well, both to enhance the content of the material itself and potentially to connect it to 'outside' documents or objects which may be of interest and relevance. Editorial and explanatory matter and translations from the original language of the document may be added. The digitized image can be displayed on a computer screen, manipulated, stored on magnetic tape, optical disk or COM, and transmitted over a network, allowing for wider access. It can be copied endlessly with no loss of quality or integrity to the original digital work.

In many ways digitization is an ideal means of preserving information, while widening and easing access to it. The rapid development and expansion of digitization technology in recent years, as well as the relative drop in the costs of such technology, have led to a dramatic increase in the number of major digitization projects being undertaken. These range from the conversion of in-house, paper-based information systems to facilitate document and records management to one-off projects to digitize a unique work or the archival collection of an organization. Co-operative projects, also, for electronic archiving of disparate materials belonging to a number of organizations are beginning to emerge, particularly in the academic sector. The Research Libraries Group in the US has undertaken several; in the UK the Consortium of University Research Libraries (CURL) is beginning CEDARS (CURL

Exemplar for Digital ARchiveS), a digital preservation project supported by funding from JISC through the Electronic Libraries (eLib) Programme. CEDARS will address strategic, methodological and practical issues as they relate to digital preservation and will investigate strategies to ensure that the digital resources included in library collections may be preserved over the longer term.

There are numerous examples of smaller digitization projects undertaken in an effort both to preserve materials and to make them more accessible. The National Railway Museum in the UK has digitized the bulk of its photographic collection, much of it fragile images from the nineteenth century (Hopkin, 1996). A valuable collection for those studying, researching or just interested in the history and development of railway transport is now available. A larger scale project was undertaken by United Distillers (Campbell, 1996). This included the digitization of a sample of the company's archives including business records, marketing and advertising materials, photographs of the factories and retail premises, artifacts such as bottles and packaging materials, and other memorabilia and ephemera. A CD-ROM with HTML links, motion video and sound was produced. The result is a high quality 'living' archive, accessible in a variety of ways and used by the company in a range of marketing, promotion and publicity strategies. It also provides valuable documentary evidence for the study of social, economic and design history.

The management of digitization projects

The CEDARS project is right to focus on issues of management. Any organization undertaking digitization needs to plan very carefully and consider seriously the issues involved in preserving digital information. It is too easy in the initial enthusiasm for a new project to concentrate on the relatively straightforward tasks of capturing the data and determining the appropriate method of storage. More problematical are the longer-term issues of preserving the integrity and enhancing the accessibility of the material.

These questions have been addressed by a Report, *Preserving digital information* (Waters, 1996), instigated by the Commission on *265*

Preservation and Access and The Research Libraries Group in the US. The Report is a comprehensive survey into the complex challenges which surround all digitization projects.

THE INTEGRITY OF DIGITIZED INFORMATION

The central goal of any project should be to preserve the integrity of the information being digitized by defining and preserving those features of the object(s) that distinguish it as a whole and singular work – including content, fixity, reference, provenance and context.

Content

The notion of 'content' as text is familiar to all information users and LIMs. But it also necessarily includes material submerged in the text, such as page numbers, chapter headings and footers. The content of images and sound is more problematical because less inherently understood. Colour is an element, as is shape and form in the case of images, while tonality can be significant for sound. High resolution during scanning is essential for rich colour register; this means a larger file size and more expensive storage, as well as slower transmission across a network. Where the costs of a digitization project are a significant factor (as they are in virtually all projects), compromises may have to be made as to what is an essential level of 'content' for a particular information object as opposed to what would be ideal.

Fixity

'Fixity' is the relationship of the object and its content to other objects and to the outside world. LISs are accustomed to the concept of fixity in published and other works: a book may go through several editions; business records, invoices for example, relate to a particular transaction which is fixed and located in time. In other cases – the most obvious being financial databases – the digitized data is volatile and there are no points of fixity except in relation to the data itself. The integrity and value of such databases resides in their completeness and the fact of being up-to-date. But in order to identify significant shifts, a record of changes and a method for recording these needs to be built into the initial design of the database.

Reference

Reference is a third aspect which bears on the integrity of digitized information. Reference is a consistent method of identifying both what an information object is and where it is located. Such systems as authors, titles, ISBNs and catalogues have evolved over time to do precisely this for traditionally published materials. The challenge with digital information is to adopt such techniques which meet conventional citation requirements.

Among the most important developments are the Uniform Resource Locator (URL), the Uniform Resource Name (URN) and Uniform Resource Characteristics (URCs) but their use is far from standard as yet.

Provenance

The provenance of an information object also contributes to its integrity. Provenance identifies where an information object came from and how it got there. This is essential if users of the information are to have any confidence in it and corresponds to the familiar notions of relying on the reputation of a publisher and the peer review system as indications of quality, worth and authenticity. It is necessary in a project to document the sources of the data which have been digitized, and in some cases how they were measured and what instrumentation systems were used for their collection, as well as the use made of the information by the organization which created or collected it.

Context

The final attribute of information integrity is context, including technical and communication dimensions, links to other *267* information objects and wider social issues. Essential for any use of digitized material is the specification of hardware and software technologies for both creation and use. The storage method selected for the digitized material has obvious implications for how and where it can be used, as well as by whom. HTML provides a way both to link together the disparate parts of a single object and to link one object with another. Wider social and economic issues include the provision of the technical infrastructure in which networks and communication services operate, data protection, copyright and other legal requirements, and funding for major digitization projects.

Migration strategies for digitization projects

Digitization is an electronic technology and – as all LIMs know always to their cost – increasingly volatile. There may be some doubt and debate about whether a digitized object might be 'permanent'. There is no doubt about the short life-span of the equipment and software used to access the contents. It is essential that all digitization projects develop migration strategies so that the contents remain accessible and usable as the technology on which they depend becomes obsolete. A number of strategies are possible including a change of media – which may result in the loss of certain desirable features such as manipulation and computation capabilities – or a change to a more standard software system. Most effective of all, however, is to build in migration paths – and the funding for them – at the design stage of the project. This requires planning and preparing for the wholesale transfer of the digital information at regular intervals as hardware and software change and develop.

CONCLUSION

There has been much emphasis in this chapter on the use of digitization for the preservation and conservation of information materials and objects. This is not just because it is the most recent – and undoubtedly the most exciting – technology to come along, but because of the opportunities for almost unlimited access that it provides. Except for a few isolated artifacts which are of great intrinsic value, a PAC programme within a library and information service cannot be justified unless it is part of a wider policy of collection management with the emphasis on access to information. The preservation techniques discussed in this chapter – copying, microfilming, digitizing – all serve the dual function of preservation and access.

The key to a successful PAC project – whichever technology is adopted and used – is careful planning and management. The National Preservation Office in the UK, the Commission on Preservation and Access in the US and the European Commission on Preservation and Access can all offer support and advice to LIMs on preservation issues.

REFERENCES

British Library (1993), *For scholarship, research and innovation: strategic objectives for the year 2000*. London: The British Library.

Campbell, Jennie (1996), CD-ROMs: a tool for preservation and access. Paper given at the *National Preservation Office Annual Conference, Preservation and digitization: principles, practice and policies*, York, England, 3–5 September 1996.

Chapman, Patricia (1990), *Guidelines on preservation and conservation policies in libraries and archives*. Paris: UNESCO (PGI-90/WS/7).

Clements, D. W. G. (1987), *Preservation and conservation of library documents: a UNESCO/IFLA/ICA enquiry into the current state of the world's patrimony*. Paris: UNESCO (PGI-87/WS/15 rev).

Feather, John, Matthews, Graham and Eden, Paul (1996), *Preservation management: policies and practices in British libraries*. Aldershot: Gower.

Harvard University Library Task Group on Collection Preservation Priorities (1991), *Preserving Harvard's retrospective collections*. Cambridge, MA: Harvard University Library.

Hopkin, Dieter (1996), Shifting the focus: digital imaging and photographic collections management at the National Railway

Museum. Paper given at the *National Preservation Office Annual Conference, Preservation and digitization: principles, practice and policies*, York, England, 3–5 September 1996.

Murray, John (1823), Untitled letter. *Gentleman's magazine*, no. 93, (July), pp. 21–22.

National Preservation Office (1992), *Glossary (Preservation policies)*. London: The National Preservation Office.

Ratcliffe, F. W. and Patterson, D. (1984), *Preservation policies and conservation in British libraries: report of the Cambridge University Library Conservation Project*. London: The British Library. (Library and Information Research Report, 25)

Schwartz, Werner (1996), *European register of microform masters (EROMM) supporting international co-operation*. Amsterdam: European Commission on Preservation and Access.

Waters, Donald and Garrett, John (1996), *Preserving digital information: report of the task force on archiving of digital information*. Washington, DC: The Commission on Preservation and Access, 1996. (A World Wide Web version, mounted by The Research Libraries Group Inc., is available at <http://www.rlg.org>)

13 Disasters: prevention, rescue and recovery

Priscilla Schlicke

The word 'disaster' is a dramatic term; it conjures up catastrophic, unexpected events – often acts of God – which wreak havoc and cause enormous damage. Within a library and information service (LIS), the most likely disasters are fire or flood, but those caused by wind, earthquakes and other natural phenomena can also happen. Acts of sabotage or terrorism may occur which can destroy, or seriously disrupt, the LIS. But disasters, or more accurately accidents, also happen on a smaller scale: burst pipes; leaking roofs; vandalism; other events which cause damage to parts of the collections in library and information services. And with more and more information being held in an electronic format, computer disasters, whether caused by system failure or unauthorized access and hacking into files, are likely to become more common. Disasters, by their very nature, are impossible in all instances to prevent, but they can be prepared for; such preparation may not in itself minimize damage and loss, but it can make reaction more efficient and recovery easier.

In the context of library and information services disaster management – or disaster planning as the process is sometimes known – covers:

- identifying possible risks in order to avert or minimize the chance of disasters happening

- making preparations to deal with disasters that do occur
- reacting to those disasters
- and recovering from them.

This chapter of the Handbook outlines disaster management and surveys the issues which need to be considered by LISs when developing a disaster plan.

THE DEVELOPMENT OF DISASTER MANAGEMENT

Several factors over the past ten to fifteen years have served to bring about an awareness of the importance of disaster management within the thinking of library and information managers (LIMs). The biggest impact has undoubtedly been made by the catastrophes themselves, and the reports of them published in the professional literature. In 1986, fire – started by an arsonist – devastated the Los Angeles Central Public Library, causing millions of dollars worth of damage, including the destruction of 400,000 volumes (Butler, 1986); the library was again hit by another fire shortly after the first one. Two years later, a fire in the Academy of Sciences Library in Leningrad (now St Petersburg) similarly destroyed 400,000 volumes, while thousands of others were damaged by fire, water and smoke (Matthews, 1988). In August 1994 the Norwich Central Library was totally destroyed by fire. Along the San Andreas fault in California, earthquakes in 1989 caused serious damage to the libraries at Stanford University and the University of California, Santa Cruz. At Stanford, something like 750,000 volumes fell off the shelves; it sounds an absurd problem, but teams of volunteers had to be organized to re-shelve them before the library could again provide a service. The IRA bomb which exploded in the City of London in 1992 severely disrupted commercial activity, and the effect on the Commercial Union Library highlighted the need for disaster plans to take into account electronically stored information (Saunders, 1993).

Nearly as important as the disasters themselves in raising awareness of the problem, however, has been the work on disaster planning done by various bodies within the library and information world. This work has been publicized and distributed throughout the information community resulting in a heightened awareness of the need to plan for how to deal with a disaster – or, for that matter, a small emergency. In 1985 the National Library of Scotland published a *Planning manual for disaster control in Scottish Libraries and Record Offices* (Anderson, 1985), which is generally regarded as a model of its kind and has been used by many libraries in the UK as the basis of their own disaster plans. Two years later the British Library produced an outline disaster control plan (Jenkin, 1987). UNESCO published guidelines on disaster planning in 1988; these specifically included security (Buchanan, 1988). The National Preservation Office's (NPO) annual competition for 1988 was disaster control planning (National Preservation Office, 1989) and the NPO also produced a video cassette on the subject (National Preservation Office, 1988).

These two broad strands have combined to convince many LIMs of the importance of forming a plan for use in the event that they have to deal with a disaster. Disasters, and even small emergencies, require quick responses in order to minimize the damage, to facilitate the salvage of materials and to ensure the resumption of the service as quickly as possible. In certain specialized information and records departments, an effective disaster plan may be essential; it has been estimated that 40 per cent of companies who suffer a major disaster to their IT systems subsequently go out of business (Awade, 1997). This is not an issue for the majority of libraries, of course, but the goal of minimizing disruption is essential. This requires careful formulation of policy and planning.

DISASTER PLANNING

Planning and developing a strategy for coping in the event of a disaster involves more than just preparing an action manual with emergency telephone numbers. The process requires:

* a statement of policy
* disaster prevention

- preparation for disaster
- action, reaction and rescue
- recovery.

The task of preparing a disaster plan is not particularly lengthy or time consuming, but it does require some expenditure of staff time for preparation and subsequent review and updating, as well as money for the purchase of a stock of essential supplies for reaction and recovery.

Statement of policy

The first step in the development of a strategy for disaster management is usually the establishment of a committee or working party to undertake the work required. In most organizations this group is unlikely to have much personal experience of dealing with disasters, but the knowledge gap can be overcome by consulting both the literature and outside experts. The 1988 NPO competition, mentioned above, was won by Glasgow University Library; this document on emergency planning can serve as a useful model (Ashman, 1989).

The new committee will initially need to develop a statement of policy, which sets out the LIS's – and probably the parent organization's – commitment to preparing for disaster. The policy should provide some background information on why the disaster plan is being developed; for example, mention of previous emergencies or crashed IT systems or whatever can strengthen requests for funding. The statement needs to identify the main purposes of the LIS and the range of particular materials in the collection, with specific mention of important and unique items; there needs to be an awareness that not all materials damaged by a disaster need to or should be salvaged. It should also specify the appointment of members of staff as disaster co-ordinators and salvage team leaders. It does not, however, need to include detail on the actual work of disaster management or of the planning which will go on; the policy statement should focus the thinking and actions of the working party and provide a basis of support for them.

274

DISASTER PREVENTION

Not all disasters can be prevented, but it is possible both to reduce the chance of them happening and to minimize the damage which might be done. The main hazards are fire, flood and slack security, in relation both to buildings and to electronic information systems. Probably the best way to minimize hazards is to conduct a detailed inspection and survey of the facilities and to seek professional advice from the fire brigade, the police and experts in computer security. The survey will identify and locate potential hazards in the building; the potential risks of these can then be assessed and decisions taken about how to eliminate or at least minimize them.

Fire

An analysis of fire hazards and effective protection against them should be undertaken in conjunction with local fire prevention officers. The following list includes some of the issues which need to be considered:

- the position and location of fire extinguishers and the most effective type to use – far more library and information materials are damaged irretrievably by water than by fire; fire extinguishers need to be checked regularly and staff need to be trained to use them
- the safe storage of flammable materials, preferably in metal cabinets
- safety checks for all electrical wiring and electrical appliances, including any evidence of damage from rodents
- clear and enforced regulations about areas, if any, in the building where smoking is permitted
- a regularly tested fire alarm system
- smoke alarms
- clearly posted fire escapes, exits and procedures, with regular fire drills
- overall general tidiness and the regular removal of hazardous clutter and rubbish.

There is some debate as to whether the installation of a sprinkler system is a good idea; it can certainly help to prevent a small fire from spreading, but may cause serious water damage if it goes off accidentally.

Fire prevention officers can also advise on the best place to store particularly valuable and unique materials. A purpose-built, fire- and bomb-proof strong room is ideal, but expensive. Where such facilities are not available – or not warranted – it is best to consult with fire officers, who will, rightly, not risk lives trying to rescue documents stored inaccessibly in the roof space.

Water

Water does far more damage to library and information materials than fire. It washes ink from paper, turns some kinds of coated paper into solid white bricks, breaks down bindings, and can destroy the data held on tapes and disks. Even a small amount of water for a short time will cause sufficient humidity for mould to begin growing on paper and microfilm. Protection against floods of all sorts is essential. Where possible, materials should be stored well away from water mains and tanks and drainage pipes. And they should never be stored on the floor; if possible, the bottom shelf of a book case or press should be left empty. Buildings need regular maintenance to protect against leaks through roofs and windows; flat roofs are a particular challenge. All possible sources of water leaks – washrooms, drainpipes, gutters, water tanks, air conditioners – need checking regularly. In cold climates, minimum heat should be provided through the winter months to guard against broken pipes. Hydrographs and hygrometers should be installed where valuable material is kept so that any water penetration can be detected. Careful and regular maintenance of the fabric of the building can do much to prevent accidental water damage.

Natural flooding is more problematical. The easiest way to prevent it is undoubtedly not to build the LIS beside a river which regularly floods its banks. Or, where there is no choice in the question of location, avoid storing information materials in the basement or on the ground floor.

276

Much of the reaction to an actual disaster involves dealing with water-damaged materials. This is a complex area and will be considered in detail later in this chapter.

Security matters

The question of security in helping to prevent disasters or malicious damage involves buildings, LIS property and computer security. Security is an issue which needs to be considered at the design stage of a new building and advisors in the police force can provide help on this. The interior design and layout of the LIS can also make a contribution to security. Shelving should be arranged in such a way that staff can observe the public; expensive equipment should be security marked and, if practicable, bolted down; procedures for the issue and return of materials need to be stringent. Where possible, users should not be allowed to take bags into areas where special materials are consulted. The NPO has produced a series of short pamphlets on security matters, including design, security surveys and dealing with criminal and anti-social behaviour (National Preservation Office, 1996, 1992, 1994).

Security for electronic information is something which probably needs to be considered in consultation with systems engineers. Electronic copies of vital documents can be made (copyright legislation permitting) and stored off-site; backing-up files should be done on a regular basis. Vigilance is needed against hackers and viruses.

The *Records management handbook* (Penn, 1994) suggests the following security precautions:

- staff responsibility for locking windows and doors at closing time
- automatic security alarms
- locks on all doors and windows
- strict control of all building keys, with locks changed when keys are lost
- strict supervision of non-staff who enter the building, especially of cleaners and maintenance workers

- bars or toughened glass on ground floor windows (but ensuring bars or grills can be opened in case of a fire)
- nightly locking of all rooms which contain mainframe or personal computers
- limited access to systems, either by use of passwords or, with personal computers, power locks
- data encryption
- auxiliary generators and surge protectors for computers
- control of static electricity near computers.

The above precautions will not necessarily prevent a disaster, which by its very nature is unpredictable, but they can help to prevent accidents and to keep those accidents which do happen from escalating into something far more serious.

Insurance

Insurance coverage needs to considered in the context of disaster management and planning. Organizations vary in the way in which they insure themselves and their property; one wonders how many LISs have no coverage whatsoever for their collections or equipment – not a very sensible practice. Where insurance coverage for information materials is provided, policies should be checked carefully; ideally, they should specify that, in the event of a disaster, the costs of replacement, salvage (including staff, facilities and materials), conservation and restoration, and recovery are met. A comprehensive catalogue of the collection is certain to be necessary to substantiate claims about material lost. Where the catalogue is in an electronic format, storing a copy off-site is simple; in other circumstances, the fire brigade might be instructed to save the catalogue first. Complete insurance coverage is likely to be expensive, but it may be possible to negotiate savings if the LIS can demonstrate that substantial disaster preventive measures have been taken.

In addition to insurance, business recovery services are beginning to be offered (Awade, 1997). These are not directed specifically at LISs, but may have some application where continuous operation is perceived as essential for the existence of the organization.

PREPARATION FOR DISASTER

The disaster plan

Disasters, by their nature, require fast and efficient responses. Effective preparation requires a written plan which identifies the procedures to be followed and lists the names and telephone numbers of emergency personnel, sources of equipment, stores and supplies, and also provides a basic guide to salvage procedures. The plan needs to be brief, but comprehensive, and each member of the disaster salvage team should have a copy.

Part of the work of preparing for a disaster involves contacting various organizations willing to provide the equipment and services which will be required during the salvage operation. The following services should be arranged:

- blast freezing
- coldstore
- transport (most likely refrigerated trucks)
- freeze drying facilities
- spaces for air drying
- document conservation services
- data rescue services
- plumbers
- electricians
- pest controllers.

The following equipment is likely to be required and suppliers should be arranged:

- dehumidifiers
- portable fans
- portable generators
- electric pumps

- heavy duty extension leads
- emergency lighting.

A small stock of emergency supplies – for example, rubber or polythene gloves; cling film or other plastic wrapping material; crepe bandages; protective sheeting; tie-on labels; newsprint; blotting paper – should be purchased and kept where it is readily accessible, so that the salvage process can begin as soon as it is safe to do so.

Further stocks of these and other materials are certain to be needed as the salvage operation proceeds. Sources of supply for the following should be identified:

- protective clothing (coats; trousers; footware; helmets; gloves)
- cleaning materials (mops; buckets; squeegees; sponges; kitchen roll)
- marking pens for labelling damaged materials
- plastic crates and sturdy cardboard boxes for packing damaged items
- adhesive tape and dispenser
- polythene sheeting
- tape recorder and tapes (for making verbal notes – easier and faster than writing everything out)
- refuse sacks.

Local circumstances will doubtless suggest other items which will be necessary in a particular situation.

As noted earlier, it is essential that the disaster plan be brief and easy to consult; attention should be paid to the design and layout of the document so that the information is clear and easily located. In the aftermath of a disaster there will be neither time nor inclination to consult a bulky, cumbersome volume. The plan must also be reviewed on a regular basis – usually annually – so that contact names for staff and suppliers can be updated.

Training

It is also necessary to organize training seminars for disaster co-ordinators, salvage team members and other interested staff members and potential volunteers. These seminars need to cover the initial actions required when the emergency begins, the overall co-ordination of the salvage operation and particular salvage procedures. Hands-on practice in handling damaged materials should be included in the training.

Disaster reaction flow chart

The disaster reaction flow chart was first developed by Anderson and McIntyre at the National Library of Scotland (Anderson, 1985); it is reproduced here – Figure 13.1 – with permission granted from the Trustees of the National Library of Scotland. It provides a schematic diagram of the course of action to be followed in the event of a disaster. In a highly commended entry for the 1988 NPO competition, Anderson-Smith (1989) at Aberdeen University Library usefully linked the specific stages in the flow chart to particular suppliers of services, equipment and supplies in the library's disaster plan; for example, under the heading 'Blastfreeze' and 'Coldstore' the contact details for several local companies prepared to provide these services are given. This focuses attention on precisely what needs to be done at any stage and also ensures that nothing vital has been left out of the plan.

ACTION/REACTION/RESCUE

When preparing for a disaster, priorities need to be set for the order in which damaged materials should be salvaged. The following questions need to be considered:

- can the material be replaced? easily? at what cost?
- is the material itself of intrinsic value? is it an artifact?
- is the information available elsewhere?
- would the cost of replacement be more or less than the cost of restoration?

281

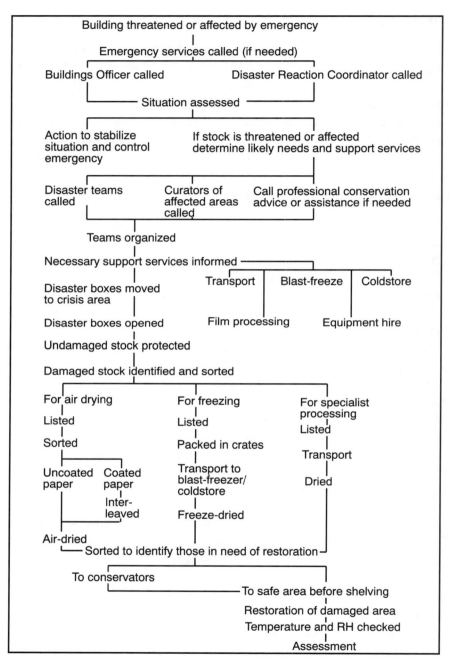

282 **Figure 13.1 Disaster reaction flow chart**

Salvage and recovery procedures need to begin as soon as the disaster area is safe to enter. The environment should be stabilized using fans, humidifiers and pumps to prevent further damage to the materials while the salvage work is being undertaken. A stable, cool temperature and circulating air will do much to prevent the growth of mould.

The salvage operation

In most disasters fire and water will be the major causes of damage – and water damage is likely to be more serious than fire. Different information media need different treatments.

Paper

Paper documents charred by flames or smudged by soot and smoke do not need immediate attention. They can be wrapped in plastic or even just set aside to await further treatment by trimming around the edges or wiping clean to become usable again; they will come to no further harm by being left in an environmentally stable storage area.

Water-damaged materials are likely to be the major focus of any salvage operation. Wet paper is very heavy and can be damaged further by careless handling; if left for more than 48 hours, mould and other fungi begin to grow and spread quickly.

Where only a small number of items have been damaged, the best solution is air drying. To air dry materials, interleave absorbent sheets (paper towelling, blotting paper or unprinted newsprint) about every 50 pages – or more where the humidity is high and the book very wet. Sheets should be changed every two or three hours to hasten drying and discourage the growth of mould. In addition the leaves can be carefully fanned out and the books stood in a wind chamber or tunnel. Pamphlets and small volumes can be suspended over a thin nylon washing line to dry naturally.

Where there is a larger quantity of very wet materials, it will be necessary to freeze them and then dry them later. Freezing itself does not in any way restore the damaged materials, but it does   *283* stabilize them and stop any further deterioration. It also buys time, so that decisions about replacement, restoration and other issues can be made when the situation is calmer and the financial details and implications are clearer.

Sodden, water-logged books need to be wrapped – open or closed, as they are found; they should be handled and moved as little as possible – in plastic cling film or placed in plastic bags, labelled, crated and taken as soon as possible (within 48 hours, or less) for blast freezing. The two options for drying frozen materials are freeze drying or vacuum drying. Vacuum drying is faster and therefore likely to be cheaper, but both are effective for drying large quantities of material and cause no further damage in the process.

Coated papers need to be frozen immediately if they become wet. It allowed to dry, they bond together to form what is virtually a clay brick. And because of the way in which they are usually printed, any attempt to separate the papers by hand is likely to remove the colours and inks.

Microfilm, negatives, photographs

The salvage of film stock will require professional help in most instances. Freezing is not advisable because it may damage the images on the film. When film has become wet, it should be kept wet. Wet, muddy negative film and prints can be sealed in plastic bags and put under clean, running water. Microforms which have become soaked should be put in clean plastic buckets with fresh water; they should then be reprocessed, preferably within 72 hours. Ideally they should be kept in their original containers to assist in identification.

Magnetic media

Magnetic media which have been exposed to or damaged by fire and excessive heat can only rarely be salvaged. Attempts can be made, however, where the tapes have been stored in canisters and properly wound. Clean all fire debris, ash and smoke residue from the canister, remove the tape carefully and do two wind/rewind passes while inspecting the tapes for warping, adhesion or shedding. If there does not appear to be too much damage, give the tapes two cleaning passes and rewind them onto new reels. After about 48 hours perform a read and re-copy pass.

Wet magnetic tape, on the other hand, can usually be rescued provided it is moved quickly out of areas where water is standing. Canisters should be checked for water, drained and dried; tape reel hubs should be shaken and rotated to empty the water. Hand dry all external surfaces which are wet, then air dry the wound tape by separating the reel flanges with spacers to allow airflow through. Wet tapes can also be run reel-to-reel on a tape cleaner or winder to facilitate drying. As soon as possible, it is a good idea to copy the tapes because of the potential for glue degradation due to water absorption.

Salvage after a disaster is dirty, tiring work, usually stressful and always dispiriting. It is essential to provide the salvage team workers with hot drinks and refreshments and allow for frequent breaks. If there are enough salvage workers, it is probably best to organize the work in rotas or shifts so that they get plenty of rest.

RECOVERY

Recovery from a disaster includes the following:

- a review of the options for substitution and conservation
- rehabilitation of damaged premises
- assessment of the disaster.

The options for substitution and conservation will have to be considered in conjunction with the financial and other resources available, including insurance claims. Time will be needed to determine exactly which items need to be replaced, as well as what formats (for example, photocopying, microfilming, digitizing) are appropriate for particular substitutes. Professional help and advice will probably be needed for items which require to be conserved and restored. Items which have been salvaged and dried *285* should ideally be kept in an interim area where their physical condition, especially in relation to mould, can be monitored.

The damaged area will need to be rehabilitated and restored. It must be dried thoroughly and kept well-ventilated. It is also likely that it will require treatment from professional pest controllers to minimize the risk of fungus and mould. The physical environment needs to be closely monitored for some weeks to ensure that it is stable before returning the stock.

As soon as possible after the disaster, the co-ordinators should call a meeting of the reaction team members and other concerned individuals to discuss the successes and failures of the control procedures. In the light of this discussion recommendations for improvements should be incorporated into the formal disaster plan. Emergency stores and supplies should be replenished. And all those who helped in the salvage operation and recovery should be thanked.

CONCLUSION

Disasters cannot be prevented. Careful planning and preparation, however, can go some way towards mitigating their effects on the library and information service. Every LIS should spend some time planning how it would react to and recover from a disaster.

REFERENCES

Anderson, Hazel and McIntyre, John E. (1985), *Planning manual for disaster control in Scottish Libraries and Record Offices*. Edinburgh: National Library of Scotland.

Anderson-Smith, Myrtle (1989), Aberdeen University. In *Keeping our words: the 1988 National Preservation Office Competition*. London: National Preservation Office.

Ashman, John (1989), Glasgow University. Emergency planning. In *Keeping our words: the 1988 National Preservation Office Competition*. London: National Preservation Office.

Awade, Priscilla (1997), Planning for disaster. *Information age*, July/Aug, pp. 30–34.

Buchanan, Sally A. (1988), *Disaster planning. preparedness and recovery for libraries and archives: a RAMP study with guidelines.* Paris: UNESCO. (PGI-88/WS/6)

Butler, R. (1986), The Los Angeles Central Library fire. *Conservation administration news*, no. 27, pp. 1–2, 23–24.

Jenkin, Ian Tregarthen (1987), *Disaster control planning and preparedness: an outline disaster control plan.* London: British Library.

Matthews, Graham (1988), Fire and water: damage at the USSR Academy of Sciences Library, Leningrad. *Library Association record*, vol. 90, no. 5, pp. 279–81.

National Preservation Office (1988), *If disaster strikes!* London: National Preservation Office.

National Preservation Office (1989), *Keeping our words: the 1988 National Preservation Office Competition. The winning and two 'highly commended' entries.* London: National Preservation Office.

National Preservation Office (1992), *Carrying out a library security survey and drafting a security policy.* London: National Preservation Office.

National Preservation Office (1994), *How to deal with criminal and anti-social behaviour.* London: National Preservation Office.

National Preservation Office (1996), *Designing out crime.* London: National Preservation Office.

Penn, Ira A., Pennix, Gail B. and Coulson, Jim (1994), *Records management handbook.* 2nd ed. Aldershot: Gower.

Saunders, Margaret (1993), How a library picked up the pieces after the IRA blast. *Library Association record*, vol. 96, no. 9, pp. 100–101.

Part V
ACCESS AND DELIVERY

Access and delivery

INTRODUCTION

The electronic environment is now such an integral part of our professional, domestic and cultural lives that it is hard to believe our working days were filled (and fulfilled!) without considerations of Internets, intranets, extranets and bandwidth, not to mention the particular negotiations with publishers which the electronic world has forced upon us. So this final section brings together some of these important issues.

This gathering together should not be interpreted as our attempt at saying the electronic world is separate from other aspects of information management. Indeed, the digital domain creeps over much of the Handbook in a manner similar to the Web robots described in chapter 14: the ever-hovering issues of copyright in an electronic environment have already been considered in chapter 8, and chapter 1 provided a look into the technological future. This final section is simply a recognition of the importance of these issues and a bringing together of some contemporary themes.

Closing the information net takes as its starting point the use of Internet search engines but quickly moves to a review of developments from the library and information community aimed at providing managed access to the multiplicity of information resources. Issues such as metadata, the UK eLib 'Clump' projects *291* and the MODELS Information Architecture are all considered in this broad-based view of Z39.50.

In *Electronic publishing* that uneasy alliance between the information profession and publishers is brought to the fore, detailing the implications from both sides of the digital divide. It also makes clear that the technology of electronic publishing is changing and developing at a faster rate than the skills for using it.

Much is known (or assumed) about the Internet but intranets still have a mystique associated with them even though in some ways they can be viewed as simply an extension of the more familiar LAN, or Local Area Network. *The intranet as an information management tool* should dispel any myths as it explains how the technology has been implemented in a range of situations.

Finally, with *New paradigms in access and delivery* there is a look to the future while still keeping one foot on the firm ground of the digital present. Some of the, by now familiar, issues of access to information resources and the dilemmas of electronic publishing are raised again in moving to a realization that there must be changed perceptions of the role of information managers in the future. Perhaps all we can be sure about is that nothing is certain.

14 Closing the information net: gateways, brokers and Z39.50

Peter Stubley

In the Internet age no information service is an island. One of the prime driving forces for individuals and groups of all sizes – societies, companies, organizations, pressure groups, universities, governments – is communication, even when much of the time this does take place on their own terms. If there is anything that can be discussed, displayed, disseminated, enjoyed, shared – sold! – then information about it can almost be guaranteed to be found somewhere on the Internet, even if this information is just a record pointing to other sources.

Leaving aside – for the moment – the variable quality of information, one of the main issues is the ever increasing size of the Internet and the difficulties of locating relevant content in an increasingly fluid environment: a site that was useful today may very well have disappeared by tomorrow leaving no trace or forwarding address. Internet statistics, once so shocking, mesmerizing and downright impressive, have now become almost commonplace; but it is still useful to throw in a few figures to support one's case. For example, Poulter (1997) noted that by mid-1996 nearly 12 million computers were connected, while just one year later – July 1997 – Lottor measured 19.5 million connected computers in 214 countries and territories. This represented a transition from exponential to linear growth, while the proliferation of World Wide Web (WWW) servers indicated continuing *293* exponential expansion, increasing by an annual rate of 256 per cent to a total of 755,000 hosts.

A range of strategies has emerged for coping with the problems of accessing resources on the rapidly expanding Internet that include keyword search engines and subject directory services. Inevitably, many of these have emerged from enthusiasts and commercial concerns (or have started life as products developed by enthusiasts which then act as seed beds for commercial concerns). A more recent development has seen active involvement from librarians and information professionals who are bringing their expertise to bear directly on large scale resource discovery issues. This chapter focuses on these information professional-led initiatives and, after a brief consideration of Internet search engines looks in more detail at subject gateways, metadata, and developments surrounding the Z39.50 protocol.

SEARCHING THE NET

Keyword search engines

To cope with the information overload presented by the expansion of the Internet, a range of WWW search engines have appeared to give the user a range of (related) possibilities for accessing information with relative ease. Poulter (1997) refers to these as 'keyword search engines' and discusses their operation in some detail. Simply put, these engines rely on 'robots' that traverse the WWW following links between pages and copying relevant information – in some cases titles and links, in others the whole page or sets of pages – to create a database which is then indexed to form searchable keywords. In a particularly quantitative approach to the topic, Gudivada *et al.* (1997) describe the methods used by a number of search engines, including AltaVista, Excite, HotBot, InfoSeek Guide, Lycos, OpenText, WebCrawler and the WWW Worm.

There are probably few Web users who don't search using one of these engines on a regular basis, in spite of the decided lack of precision in the search results. And while advanced search modes exist, it seems likely that the vast majority of users simply try out a few keywords to see what is 'thrown up' from a quick and dirty approach. It could be argued that the embedded complexity of search engines is a further argument for librarians and information professionals to be involved in future skills training (see, for example, chapter 5 on *Customer care*) but even advanced search techniques fail to circumvent the problems of massive variability of content caused by the many personal and commercial pages on the Web. In these circumstances, a search on almost any topic will invariably produce results with a low level of precision. The problems arise from the attempt at comprehensiveness. As Weibel (1995) points out, 'indexes are most useful in small collections within a given domain. As the scope of their [search engines] coverage expands, indexes succumb to problems of large retrieval sets and problems of cross disciplinary semantic drift'.

Subject directories and gateways

An alternative to keyword search engines are subject directories, listings of Uniform Resource Locators (URLs), sometimes annotated, grouped together usually under broad subject headings. These have the advantage that they are browsable though, as the Internet has grown, this browsability has necessarily been combined in many cases with search engines. In addition to the WWW, many subject directories also cover other Internet facilities such as Usenet news, ftp and Gopher sites, and e-mail addresses. The earliest subject directory was the World Wide Web Virtual Library, based at CERN, though the most successful and well-known is probably Yahoo! <http://www.yahoo.com>. Yahoo! gathers its data through user submissions and through the use of robots that retrieve new links from well-known pages.

It might be argued that the links section of most Web sites act as subject directories but, though many of these have been compiled systematically, they can suffer from a flabbiness that can be traced back to 'link-trading' and a desire to be comprehensive at the expense of quality. While obviously not essential to Web site creation, the skills of the librarian and information professional can *295* provide real value in building-up subject gateways that are focused, independent and user-oriented.

SUBJECT GATEWAYS AND eLIB

Stimuli in the higher education (HE) community in the UK have been the cause of particular developments in this area in the last few years. The main incentive came from the Follett Report (Joint Funding Councils' Libraries Review Group, 1993) which, through a particular emphasis on the need to actively involve HE libraries in what is now termed C&IT (Communications and Information Technology), led to the creation of the eLib (Electronic Libraries) Programme. At the time of writing eLib is in its third phase – of which more later in this chapter – and has funded approximately 60 projects listed at its Web site <http://www.ukoln.ac.uk/services/elib/projects/> and which fall into the following broad-based areas:

- Access to Networked Resources
- Digitization
- Electronic Document Delivery
- Electronic Journals
- Electronic Short Loan Projects
- Images
- On-demand Publishing
- Pre-prints
- Quality Assurance
- Training and Awareness.

The programme area Access to Networked Resources – ANR for short – was established to create innovative subject gateways to reliable and key resources in a range of subject areas and the funded projects have included:

- ADAM: Art, Design, Achitecture and Media Information Gateway <http://www.adam.ac.uk/>
- Biz/ed: Business Education on the Internet <http://www.bized.ac.uk/>

- CAIN: Conflict Archive on the Internet <http://cain.ulst.ac.uk/>
- CATRIONA II: approaches to university management of electronic resources <http://catriona2.lib.strath.ac.uk/catriona/>
- EEVL: Edinburgh Engineering Virtual Library <http://www.eevl.ac.uk/>
- IHR-Info (Institute of Historical Research) <http://ihr.sas.ac.uk/>
- OMNI: Organizing Medical Networked Information <http://omni.ac.uk/>
- ROADS: Resource Organization and Discovery in Subject-based services <http://www.ukoln.ac.uk/roads/>
- RUDI: Resource for Urban Design Information <http://rudi.herts.ac.uk/>
- SOSIG: Social Science Information Gateway <http://sosig.ac.uk/>.

All the eLib gateways emphasize the high quality of the resources to which they provide access; the resources have normally been evaluated and selected by experts working in the discipline – generally a mix of librarians and academics – and most include an abstract describing content and coverage. In this way the gateways should provide real working resources for researchers, teachers and students both in higher education and in the wider community. Many of the gateways emphasize their international perspectives: SOSIG includes resources from any country, written in any European language, with a particular emphasis on European resources; OMNI aims to be comprehensive for UK resources but also link to the best resources worldwide. The EEVL page states that it:

collaborates with similar services in other countries, and has connections with UK-based engineering professional institutions... As well as providing access to resources, EEVL encourages the creation and provision of new engineering resources, and gives assistance to non-networked engineering organizations for this purpose.

An example of the coverage of ANR gateways is provided by SOSIG:

- electronic journals
- digitized books
- reports and papers
- scholarly mailing lists and archives
- educational software
- databases
- electronic newsletters
- datasets
- home pages of key social science organizations
- bibliographies.

ROADS

In the ANR programme area, ROADS stands out as not being a gateway as such, but rather generic, highly configurable 'toolkit' software from which subject-based Internet directory services can be readily constructed. Utilizing a database approach, ROADS enables detailed information about resources – for example, URL, title, description, keywords – to be entered via a 'cataloguers' interface' and stored for end-user browsing or searching via a customizable user interface; alternatively, existing records can automatically be converted into the ROADS format. Automatic indexing is carried out based on these inputs and, a particularly frustrating and time-consuming element of manually-maintained subject gateways – moving and disappearing resources – is also handled automatically via a link checker. Some technical knowledge is required for installation and setting up a ROADS-based subject gateway but various levels of support such as a problem centre, mailing lists, and meetings and workshops are available. Background information can be found at <http://www.ukoln.ac.uk/metadata/roads/what/>.

As already indicated, gateways are especially useful for bringing topics on a particular subject – or related subjects – to a single place for scanning or searching. But much current research is inter-disciplinary and does not fall easily within subject boundaries, however broadly defined these are. This provides difficulties for both gateway organizers – does this resource fall within my remit? – and end-users, who may be faced with the time-consuming task of searching a number of gateways. Within ANR, ADAM, Biz/ed, OMNI and SOSIG are all ROADS-based gateways, and this arrangement provides particular advantages for inter-disciplinary researchers by enabling the interoperability of gateways and transparent, simultaneous searching across them from a single query. This is achieved in ROADS by using centroids, locally-held compressed, inverted indexes of each gateway which constitute the first search point and from which the search can then be (automatically) broadened out to consider just those gateways relevant to the query. The results across all relevant gateways are consolidated and presented to the user as if from a single resource.

METADATA

At the centre of the effective retrieval of Internet data – by whatever means, keyword search or directory search – lies resource description. Of course, as the Internet stands currently, all search engines utilize data in a standard yet uncontrolled way, creating index terms from titles or even from whole pages. But as the debilitating effects of search engines on network speeds are recognized, as more focused results are expected from searches, and as searches based on specific attributes such as author are required, so enhanced methods of resource description are under demand. Elements of the commercial community, who have been known to be guilty of trying to 'weight' results of search engines in their favour are also recognizing that a different approach is needed: one (unspecified) site categorically states that 'meta tags are the most important part of Web page promotion; the absolute #1 "must have" of Web site advertising'. These tags can, with reasonable ease, be incorporated into all standard Web documents (see, for example, Miller (1996)).

In its simplest definition, 'metadata' is data about data, and for librarians and information professionals the obvious comparison is with a bibliographic record: a MARC record is metadata. The *299* problem with the MARC format, in a network context, is its complexity and the particular knowledge required to implement it. It may be possible for this format to be understood and utilized by the experts building specialist services but if an attempt is to be made at something approaching universal resource description over the Internet, a much simpler format, easily understood and applied by Web page authors, is required. Weibel (1995) points to the advantages of this approach, so that 'if the description followed an established standard, only the creation of the record would require human intervention; automated tools could discover these descriptions and collect them'.

Of course, there is a tendency to lump more and more attributes together to improve resource description and discovery and one of the difficulties is that, as greater demands of functionality are made on metadata, so it becomes more of a specialized entity, moving it back into the realm of experts for implementation – towards just the type of complaints raised about MARC. Dempsey (1996) outlines a metadata spectrum along which data become successively fuller, more structured, specialized, and expensive to create. Some kind of middle ground is therefore necessary, permitting substantially more functionality than a simpler robot indexing of pages, but still being simple enough to be author-generated. One approach that has created much interest is the Dublin Core Metadata Element Set – usually abbreviated to 'Dublin Core' – thirteen elements (since expanded to fifteen) agreed at the 1995 Online Computer Library Center (OCLC) and National Center for Supercomputing Applications (NCSA) Metadata Workshop (Weibel, 1995). Miller (1996) explains how Dublin Core can be added to Web pages – though if his descriptions are typical, it is difficult to see authors implementing it in this form! – and Thiele provides a review of the literature up to September 1997.

Heery (1996) presents a review of metadata formats that includes IAFA/Whois++ templates, MARC, TEI (Text Encoding Initiative), Dublin Core, and URCs (Uniform Resource Characteristics). IAFA (Internet Anonymous Ftp Archive) templates were originally created for use by ftp archive administrators in describing resources on local servers and, coupled with the Whois++

directory service software, search and retrieval of databases is possible as well as searching across multiple databases. This approach to metadata is being used in ROADS.

Z39.50

The availability of gateways to provide co-ordinated access to library OPACS (Online Public Access Catalogues) is not a new phenomenon. In the UK, NISS (National Information Services and Systems <http://www.niss.ac.uk>) provides an excellent service, offering direct links to the Web OPACS of most universities and, pre-dating the Web, telnet sessions could be initiated from the addresses held by NISS. This piecemeal approach to resource discovery is not assisted by the seeming multitude of automated library systems, each with its own characteristics and methods of searching and then displaying retrieved items from the catalogue. Of course, due largely to the proprietary nature of library systems, no parallel access is possible, so that if a search requires the consultation of a number of catalogues in a geographic area or with a known subject bias, this is extremely time-consuming and unlikely to be pursued by any but the most persistent end-user.

Possibilities for a more streamlined access to multiple library catalogues have become available from the early 1990s using Z39.50, 'a retrieval protocol which allows client applications to query databases on remote servers, to retrieve results, and to carry out some other typical retrieval-related functions' (Dempsey, Russell and Kirriemuir, 1996). Turner (1995/97) presents a particularly lucid and straightforward description of this protocol:

Z39.50 corresponds to the client/server model of computing. In this model, two computers interact in a peer-to-peer relationship with each computer having specific tasks for the function being performed. In Z39.50 the client is known as the 'Origin' and is that part of the local system which performs all the communication functions relating to initiating a search, sending a query and requesting the return of records. The Z39.50 server part is known as the 'Target'. It interfaces with   *301* the database in the remote system and responds to messages received from the Origin system, such as providing records that correspond to the search query.

A searcher enters a query into the local system using that system's set of menus and command language. The Z39.50 Origin module located in the local system translates the query into a standardized format defined by Z39.50 and sends it to a database system that has a Z39.50 Target. The Target presents the commands and search queries to the database and returns the results in a standardized format to the Origin which initiated the search.

The advantages available through the implementation of Z39.50 include:

- a consistent interface can be offered to users because the translation of search terms into the form required by the database takes place at the Origin; the difficulties of having to grapple with many search interfaces and methodologies are therefore removed.
- parallel searching of databases. This is not a feature of the protocol *per se* but a number of suppliers of Z39.50 systems are building in this facility (see the descriptions of UNIverse and RIDING below), permitting a single query to be formulated and then simultaneously transmitted to multiple databases/library catalogues.
- ability to include descriptive information about the databases to be searched. This feature became available through the EXPLAIN service in Version 3 (1995) of the protocol and enables a client to discover a wide range of information about a server. In a real world situation with multiple Z39.50 targets, it will not be practicable for the end-user to search all known servers and some knowledge of the specialisms associated with particular catalogues and databases will be requried to focus the search. Metadata from EXPLAIN could be used in this way, creating 'collection

level descriptions' that are utilized by the end-user manually or, preferably, enable the software client to automatically point to servers of key interest.

- retrieval of bibliographic records. In response to a search, Z39.50 returns complete, structured records and, licensing issues notwithstanding, a number of libraries view one of the chief advantages of the technology not in terms of search rationalization but through the availability of cheap (free!) MARC records.

In spite of the many advantages, Z39.50 is still a technology in development and not all is plain sailing. Lunau and Turner (1997) itemize some of the problems associated with building the Z39.50-based vCuc, the virtual Canadian union catalogue: one of the main drawbacks to true usefulness (and probably end-user acceptance of the technology) is that 'there is no agreed method for the provision of location, holdings and circulation information in response to a Z39.50 query' and, while at the time of writing the ZIG (Z39.50 Implementors Group) has developed a proposal for taking this forward, it will be some time before implementation occurs.

Much more information on Z39.50 can be found at the UKOLN Web pages <http://www.ukoln.ac.uk/dlis/z3950/> including a glossary and background papers from Hakala (1996) and Lynch (1997).

UNIverse

Dempsey, Russell and Kirriemuir (1996) describe the 'state of the art' of European Z39.50 projects as it stood at the end of 1995. UNIverse is a successor to a number of projects mentioned in that paper and is a project funded for 30 months from October 1996 by the European Commission under the Telematics for Libraries 4th Framework Programme. It grew from the assumption that a requirement of the distributed library model will be the provision of a 'single point of contact for information'. This single point of contact would include an interface that hides the physical distribution of information, its inevitable duplication, the *303* heterogeneity of storage and access methods and even language. In other words, it should present global information resources as a single virtual database. UNIverse aims to create a pan-European large-scale network of Z39.50 connected catalogues and, in doing so, deliver a number of advanced library services for both the end-user and the librarian:

- search and retrieve – very large scale, transparent multi-database searching
- multi-media document delivery – integrated to the search and retrieve process
- inter-library loans – integrated to the search and retrieve process
- collaborative cataloguing/record supply.

The consortium includes organizations across six member states and the demonstrator service is intended to be tested by 50 libraries across Europe. These libraries will broadly function through five Special Interest Groups or SIGs: three national (Greek; Irish; UK) and two subject-based (Environmental; Technical). The UK SIG is being co-ordinated by the British Library Document Supply Centre, assisted by the University of Sheffield Library. More information on UNIverse can be found at <http://www.fdgroup. co.uk/research/universe/>.

Clumps: eLib phase 3

Just as the creation of subject gateways had received a stimulus from the first phase of the eLib Programme in 1995, so did the utilization of Z39.50 in UKHE twelve months later, this time through a combination of MODELS and eLib phase 3. MODELS (Moving to Distributed Environments for Library Services) is an initiative of UKOLN (UK Office for Library Networking) supported by the Electronic Libraries Programme and the British Library and 'is motivated by the recognized need to develop an applications framework to manage the rapidly multiplying range of distributed heterogeneous information resources and services being offered to libraries and their users'. An introduction to the work of MODELS is provided as the Appendix to this chapter.

It was in July 1996 at the 3rd MODELS Workshop – *National resource discovery: organizing access to printed scholarly material* <http://www.ukoln.ac.uk/dlis/models/models3.html> – that the term 'clump' was coined to describe an aggregation of catalogues. The clump may be 'physical' – in traditional terminology a union catalogue, though preferably a broad-based one such as COPAC, the CURL (Consortium of Univiersity Research Libraries) OPAC – or it may be 'virtual', being created at the time of searching. It was recognized that a virtual clump could be many things but that it would normally exist as a result of libraries having related subject collections, being in the same geographical area, or serving similar types of user. The possibility of virtual clumps being 'hard wired' or alternatively created 'on the fly' in response to individual searches was also considered, as was the further complexity of clumps being connected to clumps. Around this time, the phrase 'Large scale resource discovery' also became used in an attempt to describe the notion of fully exploiting the enormous scholarly bibliographic resources available to the HE community in the UK.

It was recognized that a national initiative was required to move the implementation of Z39.50 forward in the UK and this came early in 1997 with the call for proposals for eLib phase 3 (Joint Information Systems Committee, 1997). The section devoted to large scale resource discovery pointed out that:

> one of [the] aims in this programme area is to kick-start a critical mass of use of Z39.50, through funding a small number of pilot virtual clumps ... [the] assumption is that setting up the pilot clumps will produce model technical and other agreements that will allow subsequent clumps to be justified regionally or by subject on their own merits, with funding from partners as appropriate.

In this way the pilot clumps should in the medium term move towards the formation of a national virtual union catalogue. Four clump projects were approved for commencing in January 1998:   *305*

- CAIRNS: Co-operative Academic Information Retrieval Network for Scotland
- M25 Link: Access to London Libraries
- Music Consortium (a geographically split subject clump)
- RIDING: Z39.50 Gateway to Yorkshire Libraries.

At the time of writing (February 1998) all four clumps were firming up their Project Plans, establishing Web presences and recruiting staff and as a result very little was available in printed or electronic form; however, plans were in place to ensure that 'flyers' for all projects would be available from the eLib Web site <http://www.ukoln.ac.uk/services/elib/>. The following information is provided by the author as Project Director for RIDING.

RIDING: Z39.50 Gateway to Yorkshire Libraries

RIDING is a project supported by the UK Yorkshire and Humberside Universities Association (YHUA), a group formed in 1993 by the Vice-Chancellors of the region's universities to provide a forum to enhance and promote the HE contribution to regional development. The Association comprises:

- University of Bradford
- University of Huddersfield
- University of Hull
- University of Leeds
- Leeds Metropolitan University
- Lincolnshire and Humberside University
- University of Sheffield
- Sheffield Hallam University
- University of York.

Prior to the project, the university libraries of the YHUA institutions already had formal co-operative arrangements providing reciprocal access and borrowing rights for academic staff and research students with many examples of less formal arrangements, particularly among libraries in the same city. The collections represented by the participating institutions are of outstanding value regionally, nationally and internationally and enhancing access was expected to have far reaching benefits.

The virtual union catalogue – or clump – that is the focus of the technical stream within RIDING will comprise the OPACs of the nine YHUA university libraries. In addition, two other libraries are RIDING members and bring particular databases, expertise, scope and breadth: Leeds Library and Information Services (the public library in Leeds) and the British Library Document Supply Centre (BLDSC). In developing the proposal, RIDING members funded a feasibility study into the technical and service issues associated with clumping and this confirmed their capabilities to support the required technologies and standards. Six different automated library systems are currently in use at member libraries.

The key to the technical implementation of RIDING is the Z39.50 broker or gateway which will act as the electronic mediator between users of the system and the library catalogues. This software will reside on a single server. The broker will provide parallel heterogeneous database searching, hold profile knowledge and record syntax and schema knowledge; and allow authentication of users. The feasibility of individually configurable user interfaces or 'landscapes' will also be investigated. Access to the RIDING broker will be via a Web browser, the minimum configuration being 'frames' capability. The broker software will be developed by the remaining RIDING member: Fretwell-Downing Informatics who led the UNIverse project, which included as partners BLDSC and the University of Sheffield. RIDING member libraries will also form the core of the UK Special Interest Group for UNIverse, giving a special European dimension.

While the building of the broker is essential to the success of RIDING, the project is not simply a technical exercise. At an early stage improved ways of co-operative working, different service scenarios and alternative business models will be investigated, particularly in relation to the introduction of automated document request services made available through the RIDING software. The project will also actively develop collection level profiles, taking account of the national activities in this area.

The deliverables of RIDING are:

- large scale demonstration of Z39.50
- enhancement of existing collaboration
- demonstration of cross-sectoral collaboration
- development of collection level profiles
- development of configurable user interfaces
- development of costing models for collaborative options.

BRINGING IT ALL TOGETHER

A number of emergent Z39.50 services – UNIverse and RIDING among them – utilize the concept of a broker for mediating and adding value to transactions between client and server. Z39.50 does not require this – it can create an 'association' between a single origin and a single target – but the broker concept offers a number of advantages for large scale resource discovery and the services arising out of it: location; request; and delivery. One of the obvious advantages offered by a broker is the ability to do parallel simultaneous searching from a single query but there is great scope for adding other user-oriented services. In this context, the broker may be seen as a pro-active software application, in contrast to Internet gateways which are generally a passive collection of links though, as indicated earlier in this chapter, the incorporation of centroids into the ROADS software presents a brokered type of approach to cross-gateway searching.

MODELS Information Architecture

Out of a combination of the broker concept and the user need and requirement to search multiple information resources has grown MIA, the MODELS Information Architecture. This recognizes that, in a world of ever-expanding information resources, real efficiencies can be built into the search process if a single intelligent interface could be provided for the end-user. This interface would form the front end to a software broker that generated parallel searches to
all relevant resources that could include:

- the local library catalogue, through a Z39.50 service
- other catalogues within the local clump
- other clumps available as Z39.50 servers
- networked CD-ROMs provided with Z39.50 access
- electronic documents
- Web indexes and other information repositories with Z39.50 indexes. For example, Z39.50 access to ROADS Internet gateways is under development.

As results are returned, the broker would integrate them, manage different server response rates, and display the results to the end-user.

This scenario should work where end-users have experience of those information resources from the multitude available that are of particular relevance to them. Another layer within the MIA broker aims to provide 'forward knowledge' of collections so that naive users or those undertaking research in new subject areas could locate, or be informed about through software, resources of interest. Collection descriptions will be created through combinations of metadata, though at the time of writing there is little practical experience of this; it is one area that will be explored by a number of eLib phase 3 projects and UKOLN is co-ordinating a study on behalf of eLib <http://www.ukoln.ac.uk/dlis/models/studies/>. At the same time, forward knowledge of collections could be combined with user profiles to create a real match between person and resource; this could be achieved by an individual interaction at the user interface or through software. The term 'information landscape' has been given to this concept of providing, via a broker-configurable interface, access to information resources that match the needs of individual users or groups.

Discussions on MIA took place at the 5th MODELS Workshop (Dempsey *et al.*, 1998) and further details were explored at MODELS 6 in February 1998 <http://www.ukoln.ac.uk/dlis/models/models6/>. Though there are some elements of MIA in RIDING, the architecture lies at the centre of AGORA, an eLib phase 3 Hybrid Library project whose partners are the University of East Anglia Library, UKOLN, CERLIM, and Fretwell-Downing Informatics.   *309*

CONCLUSION

This chapter has reviewed recent developments aimed at providing managed access to the multiplicity of information resources now available to libraries and end-users. In particular, it has focused on those developments that are being spearheaded by the library and information community. The eLib 'Clump' projects will provide UK exemplars of Z39.50 implementation before the millennium and the MODELS Information Architecture, MIA, provides a vital stepping-stone into the world of managed large scale electronic resources.

REFERENCES

Dempsey, Lorcan, *et al.* (1998), Managing access to a distributed library resource. Presented at the *MODELS workshop: A distributed national electronic resource?,* held 5/6 February 1998, Bath. *Program*, vol 32, no 3, July 1998. Provisional version at <http://www.ukoln.ac.uk/dlis/models/models5/report.rtf>.

Dempsey, Lorcan (1996), Roads to Desire: some UK and other European metadata and resource discovery projects. *D-Lib magazine*, July/August <http://www.dlib.org/dlib/July96/07dempsey.html>.

Dempsey, Lorcan, Russell, Rosemary, and Kirriemuir, John (1996), Towards distributed library systems: Z39.50 in a European context. *Program*, vol. 30, no. 1, (January), pp. 1–22. <http://www.aslib.co.uk/program/1996/jan/02.html>.

Gudivada, Venkat N. *et al.* (1997), Information retrieval on the World Wide Web. *IEEE Internet computing*, September–October, pp. 58–68. <http://computer.org/internet/>.

Hakala, Juha (1996), Z39.50-1995: Information Retrieval Protocol: an introduction to the standard and its usage. <http://renki.helsinki.fi/z3950/z3950pr.html>.

Heery, Rachel (1996), Review of metadata formats. *Program*, vol. 30, no. 4, (October), pp. 345–373.

Joint Funding Councils' Libraries Review Group (1993), *Report* [Chairman: Sir Brian Follett]. Bristol: HEFCE.

Joint Information Systems Committee (1997), *Electronic information development programme: eLib phase 3*. (JISC Circular 3/97).

Lottor, Mark (1997). Taken from an e-mail noting the results of this author who works for Network Wizards, Menlo Park, CA, US <http://www.nw.com/>.

Lunau, Carol and Turner, Fay (1997), vCuc pilot project: status report and preliminary identification issues. *Feliciter*, vol. 43, no. 6, (June) <http://www.nlc-bnc.ca/resource/vcuc/earticle.htm>.

Lynch, Clifford (1997), The Z39.50 Information Retrieval Standard Part I: a strategic view of its past, present and future. *D-Lib Magazine*, April <http://mirrored.ukoln.ac.uk/lis-journals/dlib/april97/04lynch.html>.

Miller, Paul (1996), Metadata for the masses. *Ariadne*, no. 5 <http://www.ariadne.ac.uk/issue5/metadata-masses>.

Poulter, Alan (1997), The design of World Wide Web search engines: a critical review. *Program*, vol. 31, no. 2, (April), pp. 131–145.

Thiele, Harold (1998), The Dublin Core and Warwick Framework: a review of the literature, March 1995–September 1997. *D-Lib magazine*, January <http://www.dlib.org/dlib/january98/01theile.html>.

Turner, Fay (1995/1997), An overview of the Z39.50 Information Retrieval Standard <http://www.nlc-bnc.ca/ifla/VI/5/op/udtop3.htm>.

Weibel, Stuart (1995), Metadata: the foundation of resource description. *D-Lib magazine*, July <http://www.dlib.org/dlib/July95/07weibel.html>.

SUMMARY OF WEB SITES

ADAM	<http://www.adam.ac.uk/>
Biz/ed	<http://www.bized.ac.uk/>
CAIN	<http://cain.ulst.ac.uk/>
CATRIONA II	<http://catriona2.lib.strath.ac.uk/catriona/>
D-Lib magazine	<http://www.dlib.org/dlib/>
EEVL	<http://www.eevl.ac.uk/>
eLib	<http://www.ukoln.ac.uk/services/elib/>
IHR-Info	<http://ihr.sas.ac.uk/>

MODELS	<http://www.ukoln.ac.uk/dlis/models/>
NISS	<http://www.niss.ac.uk>
OMNI	<http://omni.ac.uk/>
RIDING	<http://www.shef.ac.uk/~riding/>
ROADS	<http://www.ukoln.ac.uk/roads/>
RUDI	<http://rudi.herts.ac.uk/>
SOSIG	<http://sosig.ac.uk/>
UNIverse	<http://www.fdgroup.co.uk/research/universe/>
vCuc	<http://www.nlc-bnc.ca/resource/vcuc/>.
Yahoo!	<http://www.yahoo.com>
Z39.50 pages	<http://www.ukoln.ac.uk/dlis/z3950/>

APPENDIX

An introduction to MODELS (MOving to Distributed Environments for Library Services)

This is reproduced here with the kind permission of UKOLN; further information and details of all MODELS Workshops is at <http://www.ukoln.ac.uk/dlis/models/>.

MODELS is a UKOLN initiative supported by the Electronic Libraries Programme and by the British Library Research and Innovation Centre. It is motivated by the recognized need to develop an applications framework to manage the rapidly multiplying range of distributed heterogeneous information resources and services being offered to libraries and their users. Without an appropriate framework, use of networked information will not be as effective as it should be. MODELS is providing a forum within which the UK library and information communities can explore shared concerns, address design and implementation issues, initiate concerted actions, and work towards a shared view of preferred systems and architectural solutions.

To allow progress to be made, the project has been partitioned into several project lines. A workshop is being held for each line. These inevitably involve overlapping concerns and none will

312   deliver a universal view, but we hope that by progressively working

towards a model that incorporates the insights of each, we are helping to contribute to future developments. At the same time, each is of self-standing interest.

It will be seen that the lines have been chosen because they present issues to services and systems developers at the moment and because they provide useful ways of highlighting general issues of moving to distributed library systems. It is not suggested that there are not other application areas demanding attention. The following workshops have been held in Phase I:

- *Article discovery and request.* The first line looked at the discovery, location and request of journal articles. It is especially interesting because of the highly fragmented and variable levels of metadata content (abstracting and indexing services, catalogues, ...) and the hierarchical nature of the information resource (title, volume, contribution). Accordingly, many of the necessary issues were raised in this line. This line was useful in that it oriented future discussions and set the scene for the consideration of multiple services. It also introduced the technical architecture which is described above. It directly led to proposals for further studies and meetings, funded by JISC. The findings of the workshop have also influenced the course of several projects. Recommendations from the workshop are available on the UKOLN Web server. This workshop was chaired by Richard Heseltine, Director of Academic Services, University of Hull.

- *Metadata for network information objects.* The second line looked at current approaches to metadata for network information objects. This built on previous work with the Dublin Core, a simple set of metadata elements, and introduced the Warwick Framework, a container architecture for aggregating metadata. The outcome of this work, jointly carried out with OCLC, was reported in *D-Lib Magazine*. It formed the second of the global Dublin Core workshops, which are a primary focus for international metadata discussion. At the time of writing four of these workshops have been held. *313*

- *National resource discovery: organizing access to printed scholarly material.* This line examined the problems of providing access to existing catalogue data based on the heterogeneous, fragmented resource that currently exists in the UK. The focus was on discovery, not on request or delivery of materials. A significant outcome was the recommendation for a National Agency for Resource Discovery. The British Library and JISC agreed to fund a scoping study for such an agency and, after a competitive tender, the study was carried out by a consortium of Fretwell Downing Informatics and CERLIM (University of Central Lancashire), with support from Geoffrey Hare (Essex County Librarian) and Index Data (a Danish software company). The report is available on the UKOLN Web server. The workshop also introduced the influential notion of 'clumps'. A clump is an aggregation of catalogues. A clump may be 'physical' where it has a continuous physically aggregated existence. Example of physical clumps are COPAC (the CURL OPAC), the BL OPAC (made up of BL catalogues), the SLS and BLCMP union catalogues, Viscount or Unity. A clump may also be 'virtual', where the records from the participating catalogues are not physically brought together, but are assembled in a distributed search. This workshop was also chaired by Richard Heseltine.

- *Integrating access to resources across multiple domains.* User interests do not naturally fall into neat compartments which are coterminous with existing curatorial or professional sectors. There are user interests which may be satisfied by documentary resources, time-based media resources, geospatial resources, and so on. They may be interested in museum objects, in archival materials, in books, and so on. It quickly became apparent that libraries, museums, archives, galleries, electronic text archives, and others responsible for selecting and organizing parts of the intellectual record have shared concerns and this workshop looked at some of these issues. This workshop firmly introduced a 'cross-domain agenda'. The workshop report is available on the UKOLN Web server. This workshop was chaired by Chris Rusbridge, Director of the Electronic Libraries Programme.

- *Managing access to a distributed library resource.* Recent developments have encouraged renewed attention to resource sharing at various levels. The current library systems environment does not support unified access to a library resource distributed across several libraries with heterogeneous systems. This project line examined some of the applications infrastructure which would support effective resource sharing, with a special focus on public library developments. This workshop was chaired by Richard Heseltine.

MODELS Phase II started at the beginning of 1998. At the time of writing one workshop had been held:

- *A Distributed National Electronic Resource?* This workshop discussed management and access approaches to the growing mass of currently unconnected resources provided by libraries, data centres, archives, subject gateways, electronic journals, clumps and others. It introduced the MODELS Information Architecture (MIA), a framework for talking about distributed library and information resources with a shared vocabulary and set of concepts. It suggests some components of such systems and arranges them within a logical architecture. Another significant theme was 'information landscapes'. Landscapes will hide some of the underlying differences between resources, collate returned results, and support a higher quality of service than unmediated access to the end-resources themselves would provide.

MODELS is supported by direct funding for seven workshops and consultancy from the Joint Information Systems Committee of the Higher Education Funding Councils and for one workshop by the *315*

British Library Research and Innovation Centre. Technical consultancy is provided by Robin Murray of Fretwell Downing Informatics. The project manager is Rosemary Russell.

15 Electronic publishing

Priscilla Schlicke

'The Gothic sun sank behind the great press at Mainz' – Victor Hugo.

When printing with movable type was invented – probably by Gutenberg, probably in Mainz around the middle of the fifteenth century – it paved the way for the modern, industrial age. The invention of printing led to the development of what we call the publishing industry and to the mass production of the wide range of books, journals, newspapers, tracts, pamphlets, reports and other publications which contain the literary and informative works which record and document mankind's collective history and experience. The existence of this material in turn led to the development of library and information services (LISs) to provide for the collection and recording of the material and to make provision for access to it by users.

The history of printing and publishing has itself been well documented by a number of scholars, in particular Steinberg (1961). For about 500 years printing and its companion activity, publishing, evolved and expanded at a reasonably steady, even pace. There were, of course, major innovations – for example, the rotary, steam-driven press of the nineteenth century – which caused upheaval, not least in trying to find the capital necessary for investment in the new machinery. Librarians, often working with publishers, were required to develop tools – bibliographies, *317* indexes, abstracting services, among others – for coping with the 'information explosion'. But the output of the process – print on paper, folded, probably bound in some form of codex – would have been immediately recognizable to those journeymen working at Gutenberg's premises. Printers, publishers, authors, librarians and readers were all operating in an environment which remained familiar, if not always comfortable.

The advent of what we call electronic publishing (EP) has put paid to that cosy environment. Electronic publishing has been defined, in a recent study from the European Commission, fairly simply as: 'any non-print media material that is published in digitized form to an identifiable public' (Andersen Consulting, 1996). The reality is, of course, more complex. The media in an electronic publication can be text, numeric, graphic, still or motion pictures, video, sound, or, as is frequently the case, a combination of any or all of these. Generally, too, there is a software interface to provide for interactivity with the material. There are numerous other issues as well:

- the question of 'platform', that is, the material for holding the publication (as paper is the platform for holding print)
- the vehicle for the transmission and delivery of the publication
- the tools necessary for effective access and manipulation
- new policies of costing and charging for electronic publications
- the vexing problem of copyright protection in an electronic environment, where copying is easy and fast
- new strategies and methods for marketing
- new requirements for training information users, both intermediary and end.

The EP industry is embryonic and the capabilities of the technology which enable it are changing rapidly; thus, there are no absolute certainties and much speculation about the form which the industry will take in the next few years. What is certain is that EP will have a revolutionary impact on the kinds and forms of information which we get from publishers and on the ways in which it is accessed.

This chapter seeks to explore the wide range of activities which make up EP and has three objectives:

- to investigate the beginnings and development of EP
- to identify and explain the various processes, including the creation of content and the transmission/delivery, which comprise EP
- to examine the implications of EP for librarians and information managers, for users of information and for publishers and producers.

The emphasis of the discussion will focus on the implications of the developments of EP for information management and concentrate on information sources rather than entertainment or mass communication, but something of a wider perspective is necessary to provide an appropriate context.

THE GATEKEEPER

Before we begin to investigate EP, however, it is necessary to consider the role of the publisher in making information available. Put simply, the activities and processes of publishing are straightforward. Authors submit manuscripts to the publishing company, either on speculation or commissioned. Some are selected for publication, by in-house editors or by external reviewers; others are rejected. The text is prepared and extra material may be added – illustrations, diagrams, indexes, whatever. The document is printed, bound, distributed and sold.

This bald description is a gross over-simplification, of course. The process is infinitely more complex: marketing strategies are evolved and undertaken; rights to material are bought and sold; costs are carefully calculated. Underpinning the entire process, almost unconsciously, is the notion or idea of the publisher as the 'gatekeeper' of knowledge. He – or she – stands at the gate which represents the barrier between the chaotic world of untested *319* ideas, unstructured opinions, unproven knowledge and phoney research and the ordered, structured environment of literary value and accurate information. It is the publisher's responsibility, working with external subject experts and formally constituted editorial boards, to decide what is 'worthy' to be published.

Those who tend the gate are in an extremely powerful position. But in most cases this power is exercised carefully, and it provides a kind of quality assurance for those who use the information which has been verified and passed by the gatekeepers. As information managers we know that we can trust information from certain publishers: HMSO for government information, for example; and Elsevier Science, Blackwell Scientific Publications, the American Chemical Society and others for scientific and technical information. Gatekeeping does, however, slow up the process of publishing; seeking the opinion of outside experts takes time, as does the subsequent printing and distribution. And it is expensive. The use of computer technology can speed up the process of production for traditionally published materials, but it cannot entirely eliminate the role of the gatekeeper. It remains to be seen what sort of quality mechanisms will be put in place when the Internet and the World Wide Web allow anyone and everyone to become a 'publisher'.

THE BEGINNINGS OF ELECTRONIC PUBLISHING

Over the past thirty-five years there have been several significant developments in EP covering both 'cargoes' and 'carriers'. In this discussion the term 'cargo' refers to the content of the publication – what it says and what it does – while 'carrier' refers to the platform which holds it and the means by which it is delivered to the user.

Online databases

The access and use of information stored in an electronic format is certainly not new to librarians and information managers (LIMs). For many years now, certain publishers have been producing their content in an electronic format, in addition to paper and sometimes microfilm or microfiche publication. The earliest widespread use of these in an LIS context was the production of electronic database versions of traditionally published abstracting and indexing services. Major publishers in science and technology – for example the American Chemical Society with *Chemical Abstracts* and the Institution of Electrical Engineers with *INSPEC* – were among the first to provide data on magnetic tapes for mounting onto computers and to include tools, based largely on Boolean logic, to search these databases. An essential element of this searching is the concept of interactivity: the user interrogates the database and, depending on the response, asks a further 'question' or makes some other type of request. All this continues until the information need has been met. The tapes could be purchased or hired by libraries and loaded on their own computers, but it was much more common to access the data tapes, by way of a telecommunications link, held on computers at remote locations. The first online industry thus grew up, with host companies like Dialog offering access to an increasingly large number of databases – full text as well as bibliographic; with subject matter going far beyond science and technology – as more and more publishers throughout the 1970s and 1980s began to produce their information in an electronic format.

These first online databases suddenly made information searching much faster than it had been in the days of a long, slow trawl through volumes of printed abstracts. But they also raised certain challenges. Strategies for searching needed to be precise and to match the structured vocabulary of the database if appropriate, useful information was to be retrieved: finding information was not a problem, locating precise, relevant information was. Browsing slowly through the database was seldom an option because of the high level of connect costs and telecommunications charges. There were changes in the pricing mechanisms of the new service, too. Information sources were no longer purchased and owned by the LIS as they had been in the past, but instead 'hired' for a short time; the cost of information related to how much it was used, not how much it cost to buy. This *321* question of costs and charges continues to be important in current developments in electronic publishing and will be considered further in this chapter. New training and skills were required for LIS professionals, particularly in light of the increased responsibility of their role as intermediary between the information and the end-user; in the early days end-users did little searching themselves because of the specialized skills required and the relatively high (and attributable) costs involved.

CD-ROM

The next major development in electronic publishing was CD-ROM (Compact Disk-Read Only Memory), which began to be widespread in the mid-1980s. Publishers of abstracting and indexing services, who had been the first to make their information available on online databases, quickly began to offer it on CD-ROM as well. New types of information became available on CD-ROM. Early online databases tended to restrict themselves to bibliographic and numeric data; full text tended to be restricted to newspapers and a few journals and reference works like encyclopedias. Literary works, such as those of Shakespeare and Conan Doyle, and an ambitious database of pre-twentieth century English poetry from Chadwyck-Healey, began to appear later on CD-ROM. It quickly became apparent that the computer screen was not an ideal way to read extensive text, but the search facilities did allow the works to be investigated and studied in new and imaginative ways.

CD-ROM also made it possible to include pictures, graphics, motion video and sound in an electronic publication easily for the first time. The early attempts to produce multimedia were all too often crude and unsatisfactory, as well as sometimes very slow to load onto the screen, but they did provide an indication of just how sophisticated EP might become. Scientific, technical and medical (STM) publishers now produce highly complex CD-ROM versions of their standard reference titles, as well as original works which would not be possible in a printed version.

CD-ROMs are usually purchased, either as a one-off or on subscription, by the LIS. End-users are thus able to search for themselves with no constraints of time; browsing and detailed reading are available in a way not possible with online databases. They are also capable of being run on a local area network or an intranet (subject to the payment of an appropriate licence fee), so can be accessed by a number of users at one time. Responsible LIMs will ensure that users who need it receive training so that the advantages of the CD-ROM information can be maximized.

When CD-ROMs were first introduced there was much speculation as to whether these were an intermediate technology in the development of EP which would be quickly superseded by something else. There is little evidence of this so far; space on a single disk is limited to 550Mb, which is sufficient for most single multimedia works and for the smaller databases. When updates are necessary, as with abstracting and indexing services, these are issued as new disks, incorporating the older material where space permits. Using CD-ROM to provide a service in a subject area where the quantity of information is vast (for example, one which relies on *Index Medicus*) is more problematical; the sheer management of the number of disks is slow and cumbersome. In these instances it is often better and easier to rely on online databases. Web-based Internet sources are in most cases not yet as fast or as reliable as CD-ROM for the same information, though they can be considerably cheaper if that information is only sought by one or two users. CD-ROM, while not ideal in all situations and while possibly transitory, has yet brought the advantages of electronic publishing – speed of searching, interactivity, applications of multimedia, manipulability of information – firmly into the LIS and to the end-user.

The Internet and the World Wide Web

The Internet and the World Wide Web are the most recent developments in EP – and the most problematical. The difficulty is that much activity on the Net and on Web sites is not publishing as we understand it. There is quick communication via e-mail and electronic notice boards; there are advertisements and announcements and information available from a burgeoning *323* number of commercial and individual Web sites; there is, increasingly as financial transactions grow more secure, electronic commerce. Anyone, with access to the technology, can make almost any material available on the Net; can 'publish' it, if you like. Traditional, established publishing organizations are beginning to use the Internet to publish and distribute their titles, often in a form slightly different from that conventionally used: for example, as a single article rather than an issue of a journal. But what is missing from much of the material on the Net is any assurance of its quality or value. There is, so far, little evidence of gatekeepers – or whatever they might come to be called – operating in the environment of the Internet. And, it must be said, that the idea of a gatekeeper – of restricting access and not allowing material to appear because it is not good enough or hasn't been evaluated – is anathema to the ethos of the Internet, with its promise of access to any and all.

Anyone can make information available on the Net. 'Making information available' is a necessary but not sufficient condition for publishing. It also requires ordering, structuring, enhancement, literacy, accuracy, assurances of truth and validity. Publishers have traditionally contributed all of this to the material which they produce. The Internet is a very fast carrier for electronic publications, but it requires quality assurance mechanisms before it can become more than a delivery vehicle.

Despite this drawback, the Internet and its World Wide Web sites have become a valuable source of many different kinds of information and are essential in LISs. European Community, government and some commercial reports abound; bulletin boards provide quick and easy communication for selected groups of researchers and scholars; rare and unique documents have been digitized and enhanced and loaded onto the Net by the libraries which own them, thus allowing access by hundreds of users who would not otherwise have the opportunity to study them; computer software is available for downloading; LIS catalogues can be searched. There is no shortage of information on the Internet, but by no means is all of it 'published' in the sense of being quality controlled.

CONTENT AND DELIVERY OF ELECTRONIC PUBLISHING

Content/cargo

In traditional, paper-based publishing the concept of content is quite straightforward. Content consists of the text or data, along with any illustrations, diagrams, graphs, tables, charts or whatever which accompany it. In most cases the content is approached linearly, although indexes do allow a thematic access to the material. The carrier is paper and the distribution is physical: an object – book, journal, research report – is delivered to the user.

With EP the situation is immediately more complex and raises implications for both producers and users of information. A recent report to the European Commission Directorate General XIII Telecommunications, Information and Exploitation of Research undertaken by Techno-Z Forschung & Entwicklung GmbH (1997) argues that content is the key driver and the most important asset in EP and interactive media; the concept must expand to mean a targeted bundle of information, communication and transaction services. Content is thus a combination of smart texts, intelligent graphics/simulations, motion in images and texts, sounds, all linked and working together. Hypertext Markup Language (HTML) is the standard format for providing links between various elements of the content, which allow for browsing and interactivity. HTML can also provide links to related documents and thus more information. The term 'cargo', I think, effectively describes this new and complex mix of elements which encompass the concept of content.

The essence of cargo within EP is that it is 'media-rich' (multimedia) and capable of being manipulated in ways impossible with print. This has implications for the users of an electronic publication. With a print publication a single skill only – literacy – is necessary to be able to use it. Some subject knowledge may be necessary to extract any sense or meaning, but for use the passive activity of reading is sufficient. Skills training, both for information managers and end-users, will be essential in order to be able to use the electronic publications efficiently and to extract the maximum value of the information from them.

Transmission/delivery – carrier

There are a number of ways in which electronic publications are currently delivered or carried to the user: online databases via telecommunication lines; in-house CD-ROMs; the Internet and other networks, including local area networks and intranets. The next few years will probably see rapid developments in other modes of delivery; there is an extensive discussion of these, in particular digital broadcasting, in a report on the impact of technology on interactive digital media (Informed Sources, 1997). Some research and experiments have been done on using the spare capacity of cable broadcasting to deliver information sources but this has made little impact. The introduction and expansion of digital television and digital video broadcasting will enable electronic publications to be delivered more easily to a much wider audience. This audience, however, is likely to be domestic consumers and the content/cargo will be oriented to entertainment and leisure to reflect their interests. It is unlikely that digital broadcasting will have much impact on the delivery of information to LISs.

CD-ROM and the Internet are likely to remain the most important carriers of information to LISs for the foreseeable future. CD-ROM is a mature and tested technology and LIMs have developed successful strategies for its management and implementation. The Internet is more problematical. The rate of growth in the use of the Internet for all manner of purposes has been nothing short of astronomical and predictions show no hint of this increase levelling off. The Internet can become very congested and popular sites inaccessible at certain times and it can also be very slow when trying to transfer complex illustrative and graphical material.

Technical improvements, such as the use of optical fibre cable and broader bandwidths, should in time help to relieve congestion on the Internet and speed up the transfer of information. Academic consortia in North America are working to implement Internet 2 to ease the situation, and Internet+ is developing an Internet Protocol system to enable multicasting, where the same information is sent to many users at the same time, thus making the data delivery faster. Some work is also being done on establishing hybrid systems which will use different carriers (for example, broadcasting and telecommunications) for different strands of the interactive information transaction. It is essential to keep in mind, however, that any technical development in the carriage and delivery of information has an increasingly short life. Changes, not all of them improvements, come upon the LIM at an increasingly rapid rate. And these changes require careful analysis and evaluation to identify whether they are relevant and applicable to the LIS.

THE IMPLICATIONS OF ELECTRONIC PUBLISHING

Implications for librarians and information managers

As noted above, EP in itself is not new to the LIS; what is new is the plethora of publications available in this format, the variety of ways in which they can be used and the methods for delivering and accessing them. With the increased awareness of information as an important resource have come more users. The rise in the student population and the development of student-centred learning has put heavy demands on the academic library (or learning resource centre). Intranets within organizations have made a wider range of information available to more employees and extended the use that is made of it. The only resource not growing in the present scenario is the budget.

All this has implications for those responsible for providing the information service. There is the challenge of not only identifying the most appropriate source(s) of information for given situations – that source which has the best cargo mix – but also determining the best way to provide access to it.

Other factors need to be considered:

- How many users need access at a single time? Multiple access, with licence fees negotiated for networked CD-ROMs and where Internet-based sources are loaded onto an intranet, will be more expensive than single or one-off use. The media-rich electronic publications are laden with copyright-protected material, the use of which must be paid for.

327

- What are the challenges of managing an information service within a distributed environment? These range from how to support users based outside the physical LIS premises (online and onscreen help is one way – but this has to be written) to how to allocate and control costs.

- How to select the most efficient and cost effective source for any given information need? Electronic publications with similar, if not identical, content are available from a number of different sources; they vary in the amount of information given, the frequency of updating and so on. Tools for evaluation and selection are needed so that the most appropriate source for the organization or the situation can be selected. Lists of appropriate Web sites probably need to be compiled and kept up-to-date.

- How to cope with the rapid changes in technology? It is essential that LIMs – few of whom are information systems engineers – have training not only in the use of new technical innovations, including various software search engines, but also on how to apply these developments to their own situation. Lateral thinking and particular application is often a bigger challenge than is appreciated.

Information, unlike finance, is not a scarce resource. Control of the sheer quantity is essential to prevent not just information overload, but suffocation. The challenge which EP raises for the LIM is how to achieve the maximum benefit from information for the organization and for the users of that information. This means being able to identify precisely what is needed and to provide it when required – restructuring and refining when necessary, within the constraints of copyright legislation.

Implications for the users of information

The arrival of electronic publications has not suddenly made every end-user an information scientist. The ability to surf the Net, whizzing from one site to the next, is no guarantee that whatever might be found is going to be relevant. Experienced Net users, already part of an established cohort of the like-minded with shared interests, will be familiar with the province of information and are likely to know where pertinent material can be found. Those new to the game, including students, will need training, not only to use the technology but to identify and evaluate the material discovered. The provision of training programmes and tutorials is likely to fall on the LIS. Depending on the organization and the numbers of people to be trained, these can be simple one-off sessions or more extensive, formal programmes.

Implications for publishers

From the discussion of the content/cargo of an electronic publication above, it is clear that there are numerous and significant implications for publishers in this area. The media-rich cargo of such a publication demands skills and competencies which are outside traditional publishing expertise.

Publishers will need to learn how to incorporate motion video and sound within their products in a way which adds real value rather than as simply a gimmick. This does not mean hiring video photographers and sound engineers, but rather outsourcing or subcontracting this work. The programming of software interfaces for using the electronic publication interactively is also necessary. The use of freelance workers, particularly for editing, within the publishing industry is already extensive, and printing is often carried out at a location some distance from the publishing company, so the management techniques for handling a distributed operation are already in place. The management process of adding diverse media and software to a publication is more complex, but not inherently different.

An area likely to cause publishers tremendous difficulty is that of intellectual property rights and their management. These rights are among the most valuable assets of a publishing organization and the task in an electronic environment is both to exploit and to protect them effectively. Payment will most likely have to be made *329* to other organizations for use of copyrighted material as part of the cargo (for example, a sound track or a video sequence such as a recording of a medical consultation or a scientific experiment); on the other hand, publishers will seek payment for the use of their own copyright material in an electronic document produced by another company. This use of protected material from diverse organizations is likely to increase as more and more 'customized' documents are produced.

In education, for example, teachers and lecturers are more frequently producing their own packages of learning material by downloading chapters and articles from a range of books and journals. This use must be paid for and can generate a tidy sum for the publisher holding the copyright. But this multiple use of material is an administrative nightmare and publishing organizations are going to have to devote much time and energy and many resources to developing procedures for copyright protection and collection of payments. And given the ease of electro-copying and distribution over the Net, the risks of illegal use of material are greater than ever. These and other associated copyright issues are explored more fully in chapter 8.

One recent initiative by publishers through an Information Identifier Committee has been to create a Digital Object Identifier (DOI) system. It assigns a unique and permanent identifying number to a digital object; the number is managed by a directory and links to specific content, thus setting the foundation for automated mechanisms. These serve to ensure the integrity and authenticity of materials distributed within electronic publications and facilitate the management of electronic copyright by linking the user to the object's current copyright owner (Prytherch, 1997).

A third implication for publishers of electronic publications is the question of how to charge for them. Publishers traditionally sold products, unique items capable of being used by one person at a time. If items in a LIS were in great demand extra copies were usually bought. Journal subscriptions are usually much higher for organizations than for individuals, to compensate – to an extent – for photocopying. Copyright licensing and clearing services collect revenues from copying and pass these to publishers.

But with the development of EP it is possible for the first time to measure the actual use that is made of a publication. Commercial publishers need to investigate alternative methods of charging for publications and collecting revenues – methods which relate more closely to the actual use made of them rather than simply their sale. One possibility is a charge per view, for example when a Web site is visited; if material is downloaded a further charge could be made. Another development for publishers might be to charge for a single article in a journal, rather than an issue or an annual subscription – or a single chapter in a book or section of a report, for that matter. New pricing models, including payment for use, were surveyed by Boelio and Knight (1997). Whatever costing pattern emerges, security for the financial transactions within electronic commerce will be essential. These changes in pricing structures will also have an impact on the provision of the information service; LIMs will have to analyse carefully the most cost-effective way of getting the information their users require.

CONCLUSION

The world of electronic publishing – and digital interactive media – is evolving at a whirlwind pace. Much that is likely to develop over the next five years will be directed towards the home consumer, with emphasis on entertainment, leisure pursuits, and electronic shopping. The extent to which it penetrates this market effectively will depend on the rate at which digital broadcasting is introduced and digital television sets with interactive capacity are purchased and used in the home.

But for information managers electronic publications are already an integral part of the information service – and certain to become much more significant. As with so many things, the technology of EP is changing and developing at a faster rate than the skills for using it, to say nothing of the strategies and techniques – the knowledge base – for its effective management.

REFERENCES

Andersen Consulting (1996), *Strategic developments for the European publishing industry towards the year 2000: Europe's multimedia challenge (Executive summary)*. Brussels: European Commission DG XIII/E.

Boelio, David H. and Knight, Nancy H. (1997), Creating new pricing models for electronic publishing. *Digital publishing strategies*, vol. 1, no.5, pp. 6–8.

Informed Sources (1997), *Interactive digital media: the impact of technology to 2003*. Brussels: European Commission DG XIII/E.

Prytherch, Ray (1997), EU and STM choose Frankfurt to launch major initiatives. *Information management report*, December, pp. 12–14.

Steinberg, S. H. (1961), *500 years of printing history*. Harmondsworth: Penguin.

Techno-Z FH Forschung & Entwicklung GmbH (1997), *The content challenge: electronic publishing and the new content industries*. Brussels: European Commission DG XIII/E.

16 The intranet as an information management tool

Feona Hamilton

An intranet has become the one thing every organization must have and, during the past year or so, there has been a flurry of short courses, conference sessions and exhibitions to go to, as well as a positive flood of journal articles, books, and chapters in books (like this one). Much that is currently available is written from the point of view of either an IT fanatic or a consultant, with the result that a good deal of it tends to be full of jargon. This chapter, since it forms part of a handbook of library and information management, is deliberately written from an information professional's viewpoint. Any jargon that it contains is there simply to be explained. There are also some suggestions for further reading, and (since the whole topic sprang from it) some URLs (addresses) from the Internet for guidance. A single chapter can only give the broadest picture of intranet use and it should be borne in mind that this is only a starting point for a very complex subject.

What is an intranet? Think LAN (Local Area Network), think shared databases, think Web browsers, and one is practically there. An intranet is one of three concepts which, taken together, form what might be called the 'net' family. They are terms which are being used with increasing frequency and are:

- intranet – the network within a single company, regardless of how many offices there may be

- extranet – the links between businesses
- Internet – the links between everyone and every organization that has a modem and an Internet Service Provider (ISP).

The whole point of an intranet is to enable the people who work within an organization to gain easier and faster access to the information that they need, by using Internet technology. More specifically, it means having Web technology available on the desktop PC. This gives not only the facility of using a Web browser to search in-house databases, but also the ability to publish 'on the fly' (that is, as you put together the screens you want to display), using HTML. The resulting screens and databases may be held centrally or – more likely – are scattered throughout the organiz-ation, sometimes in offices all over the world. So, the full capacity of an intranet will include publishing, networking, communication and information management throughout the organization.

Access is as possible outside the office, using a laptop with a modem, as it is from the user's own desktop inside the office. This last is becoming an outdated concept anyway, as more and more people are able to work in different locations, and more and more organizations realize the space and cost saving that is possible, simply by distributing laptops among the staff and encouraging them to work, at least some of the time, from home.

Successfully implementing and using an intranet from the information management angle does depend on three initial provisos:

- that there is a good IT department staffed by people with the necessary skills
- that everyone will have to be familiar with Internet technology in the first place, or that training will be available to get them to that point
- that the corporate culture is such that the sharing of information in this way is accepted and not perceived as 'giving away good stuff to the competition'.

THE INFORMATION CENTRE AND THE IT DEPARTMENT

Most organizations still keep these two departments separate, but much of the animosity which once existed between them is disappearing. This is as it should be, since both professions are involved in ensuring the information flows in, out, and through the organization as smoothly as possible and in the most cost-effective and efficient manner. If this is not yet the case where you are working, then try and ensure that relations improve as fast as possible. As soon as the idea of an intranet is mooted, both departments should have at least one representative on the working-party that should be set up to handle the design and implementation process; if the intranet is already in place, both sides should have input to its successful management. As an information manager, your skills will be needed to decide what data should be available, what levels of security should apply to access, and how updates and new services are to be integrated. The IT people will be the ones to say what software and hardware configurations are best for the purpose and to actually carry out the installation and setting-up processes. So you really do need each other. If you don't make this effort, the Information Centre will find itself side-lined and the importance of the skills embodied in information management will be ignored.

TRAINING NEEDS

In many large organizations, especially in the financial services and management consultancy sectors, training in intranet use is already offered in-house, along with all the other training in using the software which is now an integral part of working within these sectors. Although there may be tutorials offered as part of the intranet service, actual attendance at a course for beginners is a better method of getting started. Information professionals can also find courses specifically tailored to their needs, advertised in the professional press. Most people will benefit from attendance at such a course, however experienced they may be in search techniques, as there are always new techniques to learn about. If *335* there is organizational in-house training, do make an effort to attend – you may be the one running the course another time. This is another opportunity to build a good relationship with the IT staff so that more influence can be exerted on how the intranet is managed and what goes on it.

Mention has already been made of tutorials available via the intranet and the fully developed intranet may make available training programmes in other skills for people to access and use when they have time. This has the advantage of lessening the need to timetable training courses, and expecting people to adjust their workloads in order to make time to attend a course at a specific time and place. Many organizations will follow the same philosophy for introducing new software and simply make the tutorial attached to new software available on the intranet, leaving it to the individual to find the time to use it. It must be emphasized that, while this works well for some subjects, it does not replace the need for training in groups, particularly for those subjects where role-play is part of the course.

THE PROS AND CONS OF SHARING INFORMATION

This idea of giving everyone access to all the organization's information is a fine theory, but it depends on two things at least. First, that everyone feels comfortable about sharing all their information with everyone else, and second, that they remember to save everything that they obtain from other sources, or write themselves, in the correct directories and files.

Despite the best efforts of IT departments in setting up a system that defaults to a specific information source at a click of the mouse on the 'Save' or 'Save as' line in the menu, there is still nothing to stop someone changing the directory and file to another place. Being expected to share information has an odd effect, even on members of the information profession, when it comes to it. It can feel like an invasion of privacy, or even, for some control freaks, like a loss of power in the workplace. A change of attitude is needed in order to appreciate that sharing information by holding it in a central resource actually gives more control over the ability

336

to organize the work than it removes, since it means that anyone can also access the material they need directly, instead of going to ask someone else to get it.

In addition to this useful facility, the intranet will do some other things: it will hold standard forms and templates centrally, so that they can be accessed and printed off as needed. These may include expenses forms ready for filling in, or contracts to send to new clients, or fax sheets ready printed with the company name and details. One of the most common templates is a simple piece of headed notepaper, containing all the details which would formerly have been printed by a printer, at considerable cost.

Among the most useful databases (if kept up-to-date) will be the diary, or organizer, so that everyone can check to see who's available when, and who's on holiday or out of the office for some other reason. Another will be the corporate, or organization's, contacts and mailing list.

The e-mail function, which is so often the main reason for installing a network in the first place, also comes into its own on an intranet. Those familiar with using an ISP such as CompuServe or CIX will be comfortable with the concept of discussion groups or conferences – that is, the facility for people to join in discussions on subjects in which they have a particular interest, by sending e-mails to the group address. Intranets can also have discussion groups on them, sometimes accessible only to a particular group of people (for example, partners and managers in the same department), or generally accessible for anyone within the organization. These latter are often used to ask for help to find information on a particular topic, to find out if anyone has particular expertise, or, perhaps, if anyone has a contact within a different organization. Once accepted as one of the facilities available, this becomes one of the most valuable information resources available to the organization.

As well as all this in-house information being available at the click of a mouse button, the intranet will also have the facility to launch the user onto the Internet and right out of the office information source into the World Wide Web and the millions more pieces of information available via its ever-increasing Web sites. Everyone (it *337* seems) wants to have a home page on the Web. It is becoming easier and easier to design one and load it. The problem is to find a way through the dross until you reach your very own seam of pure gold. Like desktop publishing in its infancy, the facility to design Web pages in the wrong hands is leading to some truly appalling examples of the home page. The frustration of trying to find exactly the right address, despite the facilities offered by search engines such as Yahoo!, Infoseek, Lycos, Excite, AltaVista *et al.* is leading to another service which recently became available via the Internet and the organization's intranet straight to the desktop.

PUSH TECHNOLOGY

Push technology enables the user to select topics of interest – geographical areas, news services – 'tell' the Web browser that these are of interest, and anything relating to that will be automatically downloaded and stored on the user's desktop PC, just waiting to be read when there's time.

Anyone with more than a few years' experience in information management may find this a strangely familiar scenario – sharing information and making it available from a central source may raise faint echoes in your mind and a growing sense of *déjà vu*. Surely, you think, this is what you have spent your life doing: collecting information into a central repository and then making it available to all who need it. Isn't this exactly what information management is all about? And finding out individual areas of interest, then keeping people informed when material relating to these comes in – isn't this user profiling and current awareness services? Yes, of course it is – so there are no mysteries relating to intranets on that score, because you have been running a current awareness service anyway, just without the fancy technology and with a press cuttings service. User profiling has long been a bedrock of information provision, since it is the best means of knowing what people need and what their special interests are.

Push technology leads to another problem – information overload. Having access to everything, and having the ability to set up a personal profile and use push technology to send it all to the desktop, without any intermediate sifting, leads down yet more familiar paths. We are once again in the situation of having to spend too much time reading and not enough time doing the job. The solution can only lie with the individual, who must practise a form of self-censorship by choosing only those news services which contain the most relevant material and possibly dropping personal interest and chat groups, or consulting them only from home.

THE INFORMATION CENTRE AND THE INTRANET

So far we have considered the general role of the intranet within the organization, and the information which may be available on it from different departments. The Information Centre will also have many uses for the intranet, as a promotional tool and for offering specific services. Some files almost suggest themselves, but the following is a fuller list than might at first come to mind:

- *The catalogue*: partly as a check for the user to see whether an item is available, but also as a promotional tool, to show what's on offer.
- *Information centre news bulletin*: to list new additions to stock, introduce new members of staff, give details of changes in opening hours and any other news about the services offered.
- *Current awareness service*: despite the presence of push technology, some organizations will still prefer a current awareness service from the Information Centre. This may be divided into different sections, to coincide with the departments within the organization, or by topic, or may consist of a straightforward listing of articles in A–Z order. The last option works only when a small number of topics are covered.
- *Information Centre brochure*: an electronic form of the brochure giving a list of services, items available, staff and their specialisms, opening hours, phone numbers and room numbers, and, perhaps, a plan of the centre, or centres, if there are several. Any charges made for services from the *339*

Information Centre should also be shown, as should any rules (such as length of loan, number of items on loan at one time).

- *Networked services*: provided you have the correct licences, CD-ROMs and online information services may be networked throughout the organization and accessed via the intranet. As well as giving easy end-user access and getting rid of the problem of queues in the Information Centre, this will also free the information staff from the tedium of answering simple queries, such as the address of a company's head office, or the latest currency exchange rates, many times a day.

- *Web guides*: most organizations are aware of the dangers of allowing end-users freedom to surf the Net. The resulting telephone charges and time wasting on game playing, or visiting sites of no relevance to the work of the individual concerned can be enormous. While the actual monitoring of Internet use will be the job of the IT Department, the Information Centre can help by compiling a list of relevant sites and putting them up. Making the list a series of hotlinks will also make it less tempting to just surf around – it's all too easy to be distracted by the results of a slightly wrong search!

The other concern of the information manager is that giving access to the end-user – that is, every desktop PC in the organization, whether a laptop or a desktop – is going to mean that there will no longer be a need for an information profession at all. This is the half-empty glass attitude: the half-full glass attitude sees this as the opportunity for information professionals to come into their own. Leave the boring routine bits (like selecting press-cuttings, circulating journals and so on) to the computers. Let's get on with the research and analysis bit! In any case, no computer can really cope with anything more than the most basic routines. Remember always that a computer will only do what it's instructed to do, or 'learnt' by doing it before. Anything new or deviating from the commands within the software will not be done, because the software won't be able to sort it out for itself. Now that software

340

has become so sophisticated – which makes it easier for the non-expert to use – it has been half-forgotten that it is still software. Computers still don't actually think like humans, even if it sometimes appears that they do.

MANAGING THE INTRANET INFORMATION CONTENT

Throughout the chapter, the need for updating the content of individual facilities, such as the diary and sales catalogues, has been referred to. The information professional is probably more aware of the need for updating than most other staff within any organization. The other side of the updating function is the archiving function. Overall, these two form the document management aspect of the whole intranet.

Document management is a skill taught as part of a course in information studies, but it is not necessarily a normal part of training and development for other professions. A look at many of the Web sites on the Internet will soon show examples of out-of-date information and documents which should have been removed, but have not been. Updating and archiving are both equally important functions and should, preferably, be managed by someone with the necessary training, such as a member of the Information Centre staff. A system by which all new material is sent to the intranet manager at regular intervals should be part of any proposal for an intranet and certainly should be in place as soon as the necessary systems have been installed.

Updating

The frequency of update will depend on the material involved. Library catalogues should be updated at least once a month and sometimes as often as two or three times a week, if the amount of new material justifies this. News files should be updated daily – some organizations, such as banks or broking firms, will have constant news feeds from outside the building. Sales catalogues are often updated once a quarter, but some sectors, such as the IT sector itself, may issue updated catalogues every month. This is *341* because the nature of the product changes constantly as new models are issued. The example of hardware and software catalogues has an inherent warning in it – don't put items in the catalogue if they're not yet available, in the interests of good customer relations!

Archiving

The apparently limitless space available on the Internet has led to the assumption that the same holds true of an intranet. This is not so: storage available on the latter is dependent on the size of the combined hard disk space. Although this may seem enormous, there are equally enormous amounts of information which will be produced and kept on the system. Some decision will have to be made as to which material should form part of an active archive and therefore available in-house via the intranet, and which should be part of the dormant archive and physically stored off-site. Material in paper format has been stored off-site in warehouses for decades. The same has also become the norm more recently for material in electronic form (data files). It is, in fact, a simple extension of the early appreciation of the need for back-up copies of databases to be stored off-site for safekeeping and in case of a disaster such as a fire or flood, which could result in the loss of the on-site data and/or equipment (see chapter 13 for further details).

There will often be an existing policy for archiving documents, particularly as there are often legal requirements to do so, and the simplest thing to do is to extend the same rules to the storing of material in electronic format; the same warehouse may be equally suitable for the storage of archives in electronic format. The storage medium is often still tapes, although there has been a move towards storage on CDs. The one problem regarding the use of CDs for this purpose is that no-one knows as yet how long the life of a CD may be, as it is still a new medium. The question is: will it last as long as paper – several hundred years – or only as long as early film – which begins to decay after about 20 years, particularly when stored in the wrong environment?

THE NEED FOR GOOD SECURITY

The picture of intranets that is painted by the IT industry is a rosy one, and, in some respects it is a very valuable addition to an organization's information- (or knowledge-) sharing capability. Unfortunately, there is also a downside, and the disadvantages must be carefully considered. The most obvious problem is security: if anyone from within the organization can hop from the intranet on to the Internet, then, it follows logically that it would be possible for anyone on the Internet to hop on to the intranets of any organizations that possess them. Preventing this happening means using a 'firewall', or a piece of software that handles access management. Computer security is a problem that will be with us as long as there are people who think it's fun to try and break into someone else's information. This is perceived by most hackers, as they are called, as harmless. Unfortunately, there are others who see it as a useful method of conducting industrial espionage or, possibly, endangering state security.

The firewall works as a barrier between the intranet and the outside world. Anyone wishing to use intranet-based information has to switch on and log on – that is, they will not be able to gain access to any of the intranet applications without first keying in a user ID and a password. If they try too many times, the whole system will simply close down, as the software is set up to give only a certain number of tries before failing. Most firewalls also require users to change their passwords after a certain length of time – sometimes as often as once a week, but more usually every three months or so. While this helps to guarantee security, it can be a nuisance if you have problems remembering your password, or thinking of a non-obvious one.

CASE STUDIES

Just to prove that an intranet is useful in different types of organization, here are three case studies. One is a multi-national accountancy firm, one is a supermarket, and one is in an academic environment.

343

The accountancy firm

Most of the large accountancy firms are also management consultancies, and it is probably this that has encouraged them to be at the forefront of IT developments. Certainly this firm moved rapidly from groupware to an intranet, and has a very large Web site with thousands of pages on it. About one hundred of these pages are generally available to anyone surfing the Net, and these give a good flavour of the content of the rest. Well designed, the external (Internet) pages contain information about the firm, career paths within it, sample job applications and interviews and an example of the best practice database. This is the most tantalizing as it gives a small sample of the thousands of pages available to internal users. There are plans for it to become a commercial product, available to those paying a subscription. However, there are some difficulties, and it is not simply a matter of taking off the security software. Naturally, the firm wishes this product to be commercially viable – in crude terms, it must make a profit. This means that there must be an administration module added, or the existing one must be modified, so that external users can key in a user ID and password. There must be some way of monitoring (a) those accessing the system, (b) how long they stay on, and (c) how many items they download. That's the simple, administrative side of things, but it's not all.

The best practice database has its own classification system. This has been devised by the firm's own information specialists. It is logical, but not based on any recognized existing classification system. Instead, it relies on job descriptions within the different divisions of a typical organization. There are section headings related to sales and marketing, personnel, finance, and so on, with progressively smaller sub-sections. The personnel section contains the obvious headings such as managing staff, contracts, and training systems, plus less obvious headings on, for example, reward schemes. The knowledge management section embraces both information management and IT as separate, but related, areas.

Much of the material added to the system over the five or six years that it has been running contains confidential material –

confidential either to the firm, or to its clients. A sanitizing process must be gone through. Sanitizing involves at least removing the name of the client: some companies who have been clients will require a complete sanitization job, which means changing the industry sector, too. This takes careful editing, so that nothing at all slips through which might indicate the company. The editing process must also make sure that the new company and sector description is consistent all the way through. This is a highly specialized task; further, the resulting best practice case study must be thoroughly checked by at least two other people to ensure that the changes have been correctly made.

There are currently some twenty thousand pages on the best practice database, covering more than five hundred companies and public sector organizations worldwide. It is a very valuable tool for internal users, and has obvious commercial potential. The rest of the intranet databases do not have much commercial potential, but certainly contribute to more efficient communication within the firm. These include a worldwide discussion database which works in exactly the same way as a forum service on a commercial ISP such as Compuserve. Anyone may post a discussion, request for information, or statement on this service. Additionally, each separate section of the firm – for example, Tax, Energy, Hospitality – has its own forum, not available to anyone else, unless it can be proved that they need access. Different groups, such as partners, managers, seniors, also have forums. Finally, there is a contacts list, and, of course, an e-mail facility, both operating on a worldwide basis.

The supermarket

The needs for the supermarket's intranet were very different to that of the accountancy firm. The major need originally was for details of stock supply and demand for hundreds of stores throughout the UK, ranging from a small site in a town centre to large, out-of-town superstores. Bar coding for goods initiated the installation of the first network, but this has now grown to a full intranet function. Other departments have added to the databases *345* now available to differing groups of staff. Most departmental files – for example, the personnel and accounts databases – are available only to staff within the department, their line managers, the appropriate senior managers and the Board of Directors. The latter are the only group having access automatically granted to all databases.

In 1996, the decision was made to launch an experiment in Internet shopping, the success of which was monitored the following year. Only five out-of-town superstores were involved, but a roll-out plan to increase the number of stores offering the facility was to be implemented thereafter. Obviously, the service is only available to people who already have access to the Net, and the necessary software is made available for downloading, rather than by sending disks through the post. The list of FAQs (frequently asked questions) indicates some confusion, particularly with the ordering function, which users apparently think performs as a normal e-mail service, rather than a link simply to the supermarket's own Web site.

Although this shopping via the Net function is not an intranet, it is worth including in this chapter as an example of a commercial organization seeing a natural progression from its own in-house administrative needs to an external sales and marketing function.

The academic intranet

The introduction of intranet functionality within an academic environment has been easier than elsewhere, because of the familiarity with networks that JANET (Joint Academic Network), and subsequently SuperJANET, has already instilled within the community of users. The addition of Web browsers and the use of a more attractive interface between the user and the system has made an intranet very acceptable. The main function is to link individual college libraries to the main university library. It makes registration for students, and administration of the loans service, very much easier for library staff. The planned addition of all the library catalogues will make a huge database available at every terminal. This part of the plan has not yet been completed, due to

346

the problem of getting all the special collections throughout the university catalogues in electronic format. Many smaller collections still rely on card catalogues placed within the room housing the collection itself. Fund-raising, including Lottery money, has been necessary, in order to provide the cash to hire temporary staff for the transfer of card catalogues into the centralized system and – in some cases – to catalogue material for the first time.

As well as the usual bibliographic details contained in a catalogue, the Web publishing functions now available have made it possible to include illustrated entries. Beautiful examples of medieval illumination can be shown as high-resolution graphics, as can examples of rare bindings. Built up sufficiently, this will allow scholars to examine pages and bindings of items which would otherwise be restricted or unavailable for viewing. Other items, which are currently available but which inevitably suffer from the effects of handling, will now be placed on restricted access in order to preserve them, and researchers will be encouraged to view them on screen.

Once completed, the full catalogue will provide a valuable research tool, as well as a checklist for the contents of the individual libraries and the whereabouts of an individual item. The extent of the collections are such that the catalogue will rival that of the British Library as a record of the history of publishing in the UK.

CONCLUSION

The use of an intranet is becoming more widespread, and is not limited simply to global firms within the financial services or management consultancy sectors. The skills of the information professional are such that the responsibility for maintaining the content side of the intranet should certainly include a representative from the information services of the organization.

Intranets are another tool for the flow of information throughout the organization. The promotional opportunities which an intranet offers to the information manager should not be under-estimated. The accessibility of information via the desktop to the end-user is a positive addition to the services available from the Information Centre and exploitation of the system is to be encouraged. In order to do this, proper training is a necessity, both for end-users and for information staff (who are themselves end-users in one sense).

It is essential for the information manager to be involved in the planning and installation of the organization's intranet from the very beginning. If an intranet already exists, ensure that the Information Centre has the facility to make full use of it, both as a means of publicizing the services available and of providing those services.

FURTHER READING

The most relevant computer magazines have articles about intranet developments in them from time to time:

Computing
Internet business
Internet magazine
PC Pro.

The information press also has articles on the same topic, for example:

Information management report
Information world review
Interactive media international
Managing information.

Books and reports proliferate all the time, but it is difficult and dangerous to list too many, because of the pace of change in this area. Better to rely on journals, which are issued monthly, and can inform you of the latest changes. At the time of writing the following are available and give reliable advice:

Bernard, Ryan (1997), *The corporate intranet: create and manage an internal Web for your organization.* London: Wiley. This is rapidly becoming the standard text for this subject and has been updated to keep pace with changes since it was originally published.

Henricks, R. J. (1997), *Intranets: what's the bottom line?* Mountain View: Sun Microsystems Inc.

Hopkins, Bryan (1997), *How to design and post information on a corporate intranet.* Aldershot: Gower.

White, Martin (1997), *Business information in the intranet age.* London: TFPL.

USEFUL WEB SITES

The site that was most useful in researching this chapter was <http://www.intrack.com/intranet/> where there are pages and pages of information. The subjects include: why intranets? introduction to intranets; FAQs (frequently asked questions); what's new; and a contact point. This is an American site, but the information it contains is useful wherever you are accessing it, especially the FAQ section and the 'why intranets?' page, which gives some good arguments in favour of the intranet, should you wish to pitch the idea at work.

Naturally, Microsoft is in there, but their site is excellent, so it's definitely worth looking at. Go to <http://www.microsoft.com/office/intranet> where you will find a large site containing, among other things, a promotion for their own intranet kit. Apart from this, there are case studies, and links to many more intranet sites.

Many organizations use Lotus Notes on their networks. Lotus has developed Domino as a Web server, and new, or experienced, Webmasters might like to look at the site for ideas. It's at <http://domino.lotus.com/>. You'll have to register to get at some of the pages, but there's plenty to look at before you do that, with loads of useful links to other Lotus pages.

Finally, Infoseek Software has a good home page at <http://software.infoseek.com/> where there is information about their 'products and services for adding search capability to your network' and where you can download a free trial version.

17 New paradigms in access and delivery

Colin Steele

The rise of the information society by the early twenty-first century and the infrastructures on which it is based will dramatically alter access to 'infotainment' by the individual whether he or she be at work or at home. All sectors of society will be affected by the 'telecosmic' changes which will occur.

The era of Internet 2 and its equivalents outside the USA promise bandwidth between 100 and 1000 times current speeds and support for such features as high quality audio and video, instant bitmap images and telephony. Developments such as virtual medicine and universities will be more easily accessible.

Gates (1997), in his keynote speech to the Special Libraries Association meeting in Seattle in May 1997, indicated that the two key initiatives in moving the Internet forward would be scaleability and manageability. Cost and ease of access will be the essential determinants of change. Some products will be available at a price, others will be 'free to air' and this will be as true for information content provision as well as entertainment.

Tapscott (1997), who coined the term 'paradigm shift' to describe the impact of the information society, has indicated that as the current generation has grown up 'bolted in bits', they will not only be familiar with the Net environment of non-sequential access, but they will also demand highly customized products.

Future generations will reflect their use of computer games, multimedia and the Net in their habits of accessing information. As Manguel (1997) has said, the cyber generation returns from the book-centered Hebrew traditions of Augustine to the bookless Greek tradition.

Castells (1996) urges us to address the cultural and institutional effects of such rapid changes in the access to and exchange of information. The segmentation of knowledge encapsulated in the Net may be reflected, Castells argues, in an extreme flexibility of work patterns and the individualization of labour. Will societal structures be fragmented in consequence? Castells writes:

> the struggle between diverse capitalists and the miscellaneous working classes is subsumed into the more fundamental opposition between the bare logic of capital flows and the cultural values of human experience.

Turkle (1995), has argued in similar vein.

If globalization of information access is inevitable then individualization of access will follow along with the Net collaboration of like minds and subject interests. Groups of users in the future will be linked more by their global subject interest than loyalty to their institutions. Most scholars, for example medieval historians or chemists, will prefer the interaction of their collective global group rather than the local technocratic demands and accountabilities practised by most Vice-Chancellors of Western society universities.

Personal information access systems are essential in the two-way flow. One process will deliver the relevant information required for leisure and professional work and the other will block out the flood of information available. As Brin wrote as far back as 1991 in his novel *Earth*:

> And to think, some idiots predicted that we'd someday found our economy on information. That we'd base money on it! On information? The problem isn't scarcity. There's too damned much of it. The problem usually wasn't getting access to information. It was to stave off drowning in it. People bought

personalized filter programs to skim a few droplets from that sea and keep the rest out.

A wider societal role for information may be required for the information needs of the general population and lifelong learning. The California Digital Library Initiative, Ohiolink and other state initiatives provide various models from the USA which may be easier to replicate within the federal structures of other countries. The two tendencies – availability of knowledge on a widespread scale and the fragmentation of knowledge to select groups – will need to be counterbalanced. The roles will be to acquire, disseminate and to be able, most importantly, to interpret knowledge.

Most users agree that in the future most students will have access to computing Internet facilities in the form of institutional work 'sweat stations', personal laptops or wired homes. Japanese researchers have recently indicated that laptop computers will have the capacity of 1997 supercomputers in the twenty-first century. Whether users require such computer power is debatable but for multimedia Net use they do need effective access and delivery modes. In this context, paper will be an output mechanism rather than an original format. The Net will be the initial source of information rather than the physical library. The convenience of the Web is the key, compared with the physical inconvenience of most of the information currently stored in libraries.

Material in university settings will be increasingly global in terms of access to courses offered by 'megastars' of the Net, and the potential 'dumbing down' of education in the mass provision of core material. The UK Dearing Committee Report in 1997 <http://www.leeds.ac.uk/educol/ncihe/> indicated the need for effective information and communications infrastructures in universities and predicted that by the middle of the first decade of the twenty-first century each individual student will or should possess laptop computers. Plug-in facilities will be as necessary in university libraries as photocopying machines have been in the past.

Peter Drucker has recently stated (Gregg, 1997) that 'higher education is in deep crisis… the cost of higher education has risen as fast as the cost of health care'. The 'dumbing down' of education can lead to the American model of basic undergraduate source material and a system where various levels of instruction and education are on offer, unlike the basic 'forced' homogenization of Australian education.

INFORMATION PROVISION

Ubiquitous satellite provision of information via consortia, such as Microsoft, Intel and Boeing have formed, will provide relatively cheap distribution mechanisms while local area wireless networks will allow niche redistribution. In that environment and with 'slim line' computer facilities the cost of some infrastructure provision will drop, although it may be counterbalanced by the rising cost of information if current scholarly communication patterns remain in place in the context of offerings from commercial publishers such as Reed-Elsevier and Springer Verlag.

In an era of increased co-ordination, the constituent elements will include electronic library facilities, multimedia interactive classrooms, virtual reality laboratories, and design and innovation centres which sit within or by the side of traditional print libraries. Twenty-four hour electronic reference 'intelligence' services could be available from our libraries but how many currently offer them on an interactive basis? They could be funded on a fee-for-service basis. In other areas of electronic access services, where funds are tight, there have been established definitions between 'core' and 'value added services'.

The convergence of functions is essential as the teaching/ learning process changes. Librarians will need to decide whether they want to be more involved in the instructional process in the virtual arena. As Ferguson (who has the intriguing title of Assistant Dean for Redesign of Subject Libraries) and Burge (1997) have indicated, now is a time for librarians to dramatically reassess the way libraries provide services, the way they interact with clients – 'the network compels librarians to seek new alliances, to radically change their perspective on user needs, and even to transform the ways in which they organize themselves to serve these needs'.   *353*

What is knowledge access in an information environment? Lyman (1996), one of the best thinkers on this topic, and perhaps not coincidentally a non-librarian, has outlined the massive changes encapsulated in the term 'digital library'. Another overview by the same author can be found in a collection of essays arising from Harvard University Library's 'Gateway' symposium (Dowler, 1997) which address some of the issues which are embodied in electronic library access.

Lynch (1997), Director of the Coalition for Networked Information, reflects on the need to move to personalized systems of access to knowledge, and the emergence of a set of new genres of communication as we move away from the 'tyranny of text'. As voice and video streaming via terminals and handheld devices becomes an economic technological norm in the early days of the twenty-first century, then multimedia information access will supplement or even replace the textual environment.

Is information access to be push or pull or a mixture of both? At the 1997 *Computers in libraries conference*, Paul Pinella of Individual Inc. (Maloney, 1997) described his company's software product that uses in-house intranets to filter information on the Web in both push and pull modes. Documents are ranked, tailored to each person's organizational requirements with a maximum ten minutes reading brief. Relevant items are pushed, within that time frame, to the individual's e-mail with links in place to pull down further information. Such operations are relevant to most current information management forums. This format allows relevance ranking, timeliness and a stable but evolutionary information requirement.

'Distributed knowledge work environments' is probably a better collective term for this learning environment than digital libraries, and the emphasis has to be a user-centered environment rather than a collective one.

HIGHER EDUCATION FUTURE

In a higher education market, research collections will have to be linked at a global co-operative level as the basic information for undergraduates will be limited, albeit flexible in a Web context. As banks have been reducing staff because of automation and online transactions, so information access will follow suit in traditional service downsizing. There will, however, be an associated growth of specialists in organizing knowledge and the development of niche markets. The basic problem to date is the segmentation of educational institutions and the competitive nature of education provision both nationally and globally, *vis-à-vis* the probable dominance of corporations such as Microsoft in this process.

Sir David Puttnam at the Singapore Virtual University Conference in August 1996 compared the development of the video industry with that of global virtual education and called for visions for the twenty-first century. Puttnam cited his desire in the early 1970s to gain venture capital to buy up the Rank film library and was asked by the British banks for what purpose. His response – rights for video dissemination – was treated with disdain, but film rights are now major bargaining chips. If, as he now states, the British film industry is an oxymoron then what will be left in the virtual university and global information arena? Will a university and student education be in the same state in the early twenty-first century?

Some of the best thinking on electronic publishing and access to information has come from outside the traditional profession; Odlyzko (1997) argues the pace of change is growing more rapidly as the decade reaches its end. He quotes J. R. R. Licklider who once stated that people tend to overestimate what can be done in one year and to underestimate what can be done in five to ten years. Such dimensions, however, make it extremely difficult to prepare forward plans more than three years out in the IT environment.

At many research institutions print information is largely held in a diversity of locations, accessible only when libraries are open unless items are borrowed. Twenty-four hour access is relatively rare unless material is electronic and Net accessible. One can easily discern the trend line of the future. As Lesk (1997) indicated in his Atlanta 1997 Mellon Scholarly Communication and Technology Conference speech, 'the goal is to use university Web publishing, information searching mechanisms, and rewards for a new kind of creativity to build a new kind of university community'. *355*

SERVICE PARADIGMS

McLean (1997), the Librarian of Macquarie University, has stated in a keynote address to a UK/Australian Seminar on Co-operation in London in July 1997 that new service paradigms will include:

- the capacity to influence both the form and make-up of information consumed
- the personalization of information/communication services
- location should not be a distinctive barrier to access
- transparent access is expected to a range of information resources
- the ability to access a number of remote information sources at the same time
- the ability to mix different media in real time
- the provision of a choice in suppliers
- the ability to interact with other colleagues in a collaborative networked environment.

There also need to be appropriate technology platforms to deliver information. There is no point in requiring the latest software releases of, say, Netscape and Adobe to deliver Web text if clients do not have sufficient capacity on their desktops to access material. Local concerns such as Internet access have to be taken into account. In Australia major providers are being encouraged to establish mirror sites, as AARNet 2 (a local university and research microcosm of Internet 2) has reduced local costs, in comparison with accessing sites directly overseas.

ROLE OF LIBRARIANS AND INFORMATION MANAGERS

Access to information is far removed from the print environment of the mid-1980s, but how many libraries have moved their mindsets to accommodate the changing information environment? It has been a contention of this writer for some time that the breakdown of the library profession into self-contained enclaves such as cataloguers, reference and acquisition librarians is no longer valid as different modes of information access demand radically different structures to provide them. To give one example, serials acquisition work will change dramatically in terms of the shift in information delivery patterns of the Web (Duranceau, 1997). The print environment is linear while the digital world is cyclical.

Are librarians indeed the only people to be involved in the provision of information in the twenty-first century? How many cataloguers are metadata or Webpac experts? Webpac links to full text from OPACs (Online Public Access Catalogues) are as much a responsibility of collection managers as they are of cataloguers. Development of electronic link specialists, including the evaluation of automatic link checkers, are as vital as classification expertise in the traditional modes of UDC, Dewey or Library of Congress. How many colleagues maintain subject Net gateways? How many liaise directly with user clientèle and assess services? How are values measured in terms of new products, in terms of user satisfaction, organizational co-operative efficiencies? What will clients in future require for their own desktop needs and what will the consequences be?

The implications and challenges for collection managers and technical services librarians are immense. No longer are the sacred cows of traditional librarianship permissible – for example, print storage or acquisition without evolution and evaluation. Collection managers have to evaluate complex issues of electronic licences, digital archiving and site compatibility for access to a variety of electronic files. There is no point in gaining access to full text electronic files if a significant intranet is not available in the organization nor adequate linking maintained.

DELIVERY ISSUES

The fax machine was very slow to take off in the 1970s, and only by the end of the 1980s did its use become relatively cheap and ubiquitous. Will fax become simply a subsidiary part of the PC? Certainly delivery mechanisms will spin off screen access facilities in a variety of forms. Collection managers will need therefore to be involved in a number of wider network dimensions.

357

If paper costs continue to rise then handheld digital devices with variable typefaces may well evolve more rapidly. It was fascinating that when the digitized serial project JSTOR began its public release in the USA in May 1997, the one problem that the developers had largely overlooked was the diversity of print outlets across some two hundred universities across the USA. How to retrieve and store information is thus as important as how to initially access it.

The invitation-only Mellon Conference on *Scholarly communication and technology* (papers available at <http://arl.cni.org/scomm/scat/index.html>) held at Emory University in Atlanta in April 1997, which this author attended, revealed the difficulties of the major content providers and the diverse cost models therein. Many of the skills required for a Net access environment can be provided by those not involved in the traditional librarianship or information sector. This should not be seen as a threat, as many do in an increasingly insecure job environment, but as a new window of opportunity as clients access information directly themselves. Facilitation of access will be just as important as the physical purchases of the past.

In this context Johanson, Schauder and Lim (1997) have written in the electronic-only *Australian humanities review*:

Many humanities scholars have stood by the centrality of fixed, canonical texts; part of the authority of texts has derived from their longevity in print form, and their survival in large publicly-accessible libraries. Undoubtedly some information technologies radically threaten the sanctity of traditional text, causing some concern. At the same time, many of the key texts are being reproduced (in facsimile) and disseminated more widely on computer networks than they have ever been. Generally what causes concern is that texts are no longer fixed in printer's ink on tangible paper, and that they are not presented with all the texture of their original physical embodiment, but in fact are no more than a string of bits, volatile, easily-altered, and infinitely-copyable on screen, and all at a keystroke.

358

The chaos apparent at times in the new electronic forms of sources is paralleled by the intellectual process of deconstruction of the canons themselves. This intellectual reaction requires still an intimate understanding of the contexts of textual creation. Whether or not a humanities scholar today uses primary, traditional texts, all humanities scholars need large collections of symbolic artifacts in order to function. There is a tradition of textual referral, of checking back to prior knowledge, accepted wisdom, the key writings or icons of proponents of influential ideas. Summaries of texts are insufficient for the humanities scholar: the full text is revered in that it may contain hidden meanings for future generations of scholars to recover.

This article, while short, is both stimulating and an attempt to reconcile the print and digital mediums. The fact that this author printed it out to read is indicative of trends. The fact that the article also has links to relevant electronic humanities sites is a microcosm of the print/electronic environment.

ELECTRONIC ACCESS

Mowat (1997), the Librarian of Edinburgh University, has written as follows in a future 'retrospective' on the fate of serials:

by the end of the first decade of the new century the last of those academics appointed during the sixties had finally retired... The increasing emphasis placed by university management on meeting standards of performance in technological as well as pedagogical expertise had already weeded out most of those who were totally unreconstructed. With widespread familiarity with new technology the reluctance to accord the same value to electronic information as to traditionally printed information had gone. This was helped by developments in the handling of networked information itself.

359

What is required for future access in institutional terms, in no particular order, are customized slices of information at lower prices, individual customization of services, co-operative mechanisms and faster decision-making. The issue whether to collect or to access data is an increasingly important and contentious one. In the research academic community the general dependence on print bears little relevance to usage but generations of scholars brought up before the Net have been reluctant to move to on-demand access.

It is well understood that monographs at the present time are unwieldy on the Net yet increasingly expensive for university presses to produce. Scholarly communication patterns will need to implement developments whereby books and chapters are available online with hypertext references and links, but with an easily available network print access outlet at reasonable cost and with appropriate copyright protection.

The method of delivery can also be diverse – by a variety of ftp (file transfer protocol) methods, by e-mail, by fax or by post. Open platform technology is essential. In terms of pricing we need to move to the 'Millicent' approach, that is, by pricing articles relatively low so that they get high use and thus high turnover using digital cash transactions. By pricing articles available electronically so highly that no-one uses them is to replicate the high-cost print serial scenario. In the bigger picture the links between the current different providers for example of ILMSs (Integrated Library Management Systems) with Webpacs, database providers, citation indexes, software agents and delivery mechanisms will all blur; see for example chapter 14.

What is required is a global one-stop shop. At the time of writing, (early 1998) the user has often to find out the publisher of electronic information rather than the title of a journal, for example, and to know by what licence or arrangement articles are to be accessed. *Science* is even basing, at the time of writing, its 1998 offerings to institutions on how many public access terminals are available to access the source. A bizarre concept!

Some publishers are offering individuals of a professional society access to online journals for as low as $25 per annum yet forcing institutions to pay exorbitantly high rates for the same access. How long will it be before institutions refuse to subscribe and tell individuals and the publishers to get on with it? Academics from professional societies won't see any need to change habits if costs are borne by a library and they get low personal cost access to data.

Most commercial publishers at the present time do not know how to collectively market their scientific publications, let alone price them. Many simply replicate their print costs or add an additional 10 to 15 per cent for electronic access. It is inevitable that the global academic communities (if they can get their collective act together – no easy matter) will eventually organize themselves to provide the refereeing and editorial services required for scholarly authentication. They will then make the texts available to non-commercial Net publishers or those publishers who have traditionally worked with the scholarly community but not derived excessive profits from the process.

A number of universities have claimed critical success in mass cancellations of journals and instead rely on document supply on-demand via firms such as *Uncover*. Such 'success' should be qualified until true electronic delivery is available on a desktop by the Net or e-mail attachments. *Uncover* requires the user to go through several processes of access and varying copyright fees which is often a disincentive to use. It's not surprising that access levels decline in comparison with the print subscriptions. *Uncover* trials in Australia, such as at the University of Western Australia and the University of Central Queensland in 1995/96 were not spectacularly successful and, in the case of the latter, direct ordering using library funds by academics has been terminated. Real online access to all the world's information will however increase demand for material.

The cost of scientific publications in the commercial arena continues to rise inexorably. The cost of information and indeed higher education needs to be addressed as the publishing cycle continues upwards while governments wish to extend education but are not willing to invest more funds per student.

DILEMMAS OF ELECTRONIC PUBLISHING

Various vendors now offer the same publisher's material. Okerson (1996), Deputy Librarian of Yale, in a speech given at the 1996 IFLA Conference in Beijing, indicated how universities prefer to buy information delivered through widely accepted non-proprietary formats and standard protocols so that this information can easily be accessible through a common front end for users. It is expensive and inefficient to deal with dozens of incompatible formats and services.

In Australia, users are offered a number of consortia deals each of which is different from the other in pricing structures and availability. Unless there is a full text link to the catalogue entry (and some universities are unwilling to provide links on a single year basis) then the user has to remember, as mentioned earlier, who is the publisher of each journal and has to go to a generic Web site. Some vendors provide customization by subject, others don't. Some are linked to document supply agencies, others aren't. The mechanisms of dealing with a number of diverse publishers have slowed down projects like Blackwell's Electronic Navigator as they attempt to ensure that a critical amount of material is uploaded.

Intelligent agents in many areas will replace intelligent librarians. As users can delineate their requirements in terms of access to 'x' or 'y' topics in their specialities then commercial and non-commercial providers will increasingly provide access profiles on a daily or weekly basis. Material inside that profile delivered by the agents will either be free, available under an institutional site licence, or at a price as the user pays to open the envelope of information. Resource discovery is thus increasingly a global activity with the focus of information search being in ever-expanding circles rather than focusing inwards back to a local print library as has been the situation in the past. Who provides the 'intelligence' in the searching is the key factor in the future digital library environment. Are libraries and librarians going to be the agents of information selection?

In future, indexing services will be less and less popular unless they are linked to full text sources, either of the original creator

362

direct, or by document access. Traditional catalogues are equally endangered unless seen as multi-source entry points to full texts. Why spend resources in future simply outlining the outside physical characteristics of a book item when it is the 'inside' text which is important? Is it more important to provide access to the material online than in a physical repository where use may be restricted to once a decade?

This is not to decry the need for 'print stack museums' or traditional libraries. Harold Billings, Director of Libraries at the University of Texas at Austin, described at the Chadwyck-Healey American Advisory Board Meeting in San Francisco in July 1997 the impact of a section of the University of Texas philosophy book stock, hardly used since 1931, but which was now vital to a change of fashion in one particular mode of philosophical inquiry. This writer unearthed in 1971 a collection of Mexican Independence pamphlets in the Bodleian Library, Oxford which had been uncatalogued and unused since their purchase from Henry Stevens of Vermont in the second half of the nineteenth century. This turned out to be one of the major collections of such pamphlets in the world. We need properly supported physical repositories with all the costs involved recognized by outside researchers, even if they are utilized in the future as perhaps manuscript collections are today. In this context there is always going to be a struggle between those who see a library as a place with resources that can be used now, and those who see it as a museum for preservation for future generations.

The majority view on resource access will always win out on campus because formula allocations will reflect the use or number criteria, but there has to be a system in place to accommodate the little-used material in a collaborative local, national or global framework. The relative failure of Australia's Distributed National Collection policy during the 1990s could partly be attributed perhaps to the perceived ownership of the concept by the National Library of Australia (to whom academic input is relatively limited) and to the fact that librarians involved in subject schemes believed that rationalization of resources could take place without involving the relevant academics. 'Older' collection managers may no longer *363* inhabit the real world as users in future will, to a large extent, determine the overall shape of the acquisition game.

National consortia already exist in the UK, Australia and New Zealand while in the USA many states such as Ohio, Georgia and California have state-wide initiatives on behalf of their population. Consortia deals are currently the flavour of the month in the USA so much so that there is now a 'Consortia of Consortia' group. Such groups, while extremely laudable in terms of bringing down costs, are often time-consuming to co-ordinate and it is difficult to keep track of the various options being offered to institutions who are part of several consortia. As indicated in the author's 1997 CAUSE Australasia keynote speech (Steele, 1997), mirror sites, caching, competitive price structures, consortia deals are all part of the infrastructure which has to meld with content provision, software gateways and intelligent agents.

COPYRIGHT

One of the major areas which will need global resolution is copyright and this is, of course, covered in chapter 8. Electronic access has so far produced even more restrictive action by many publishers through extreme licensing arrangements than has been the case for print. The example of *Science* magazine cited earlier is representative of the complexities that have entered the access and licensing scene.

Goldstein (Professor of Stanford University Law School) titled his 1997 book *Copyright's highway: from Gutenberg to the celestial jukebox*. He uses the term 'celestial jukebox' to incorporate a console/terminal which allows access to online text, music and video. In such a multimedia environment the nature of copyright, for example in interactive visual images, becomes more complicated but the concept of 'fair use' in a university environment is one which is in need of universal protection. The experiments with electronic reserves, for example at Monash and Loughborough Universities, have revealed the difficulties in gaining site provisions from individual publishers for permission to
scan articles into these collections.

OUTSOURCING AND STAFFING

Outsourcing is back in favour in the late 1990s. Technical services are the prime area for outsourcing (Hirshon and Winters, 1997) but collection access profiles and electronic reference services seem ripe for others to come in. Providing data and services was part and parcel of the trade of the major suppliers in the 1960s but this receded as OCLC (Online Computer Library Center), RLG (Research Libraries Group) and similar groupings took over such roles. The movement into the digital library environment coupled with significant budget cuts led to a re-investigation and popularity of outsourcing. Griffith and Queensland University of Technology Libraries have both signed outsourcing deals with Blackwells (UK) in 1996 and 1997 respectively. What is the role of the local library if print approval plans coupled with on-site delivery of supporting infrastructure is provided by a commercial vendor? The impact on staff and job security is obviously important, but the needs of the user and the budget of the institution have also to be included in the initial debate.

Many organizations are still driven by past traditions of collection service and access. Staff flexibility and risk-taking are essential. While total commitment to a strategic plan is essential on the one hand to ensure success, on the other hand a desire to seek total allegiance and/or collegiality can lead to conservatism and slowness in decision-taking. Just as organizations need to establish niche markets, so institutional libraries will need to refocus into groups which meet the needs of their specific clients. Librarians must recognize that change is continuous, change can be disconcerting and is certainly transformational. Library and other knowledge workers in traditional settings cannot be shackled by the historical ideologies of the profession. Matson and Bonski (1997) have indicated the need for information partnerships in the infrastructure for digital libraries. These would include domain experts, information technology providers and librarians.

The necessary skills base can be found in a variety of IT professions. Anderson (1997) sees the fundamentals in re-engineering as organizational alignment, vision and knowledge *365* work and these must be continually placed within the goals of the parent organization. Access to information will be by the individual at home or in business at the terminal screen and will be permanent or temporary depending on the mode of access. 'Look and see' will be followed by either 'pay and get' or 'public good free access'. Accountability and flexibility in information provision will need to be juxtaposed with new paradigms of information access and delivery.

The 1996 *Australian National University Library Review* recommended the establishment of subject and support clusters which has led to devolved budgets (including personnel, access and information votes) with specific client foci. This should allow flexibility and diversity in the management of and access to information, both print and electronic. There is still a need for 'generic' overlays, which cover databases on a campus-wide basis such as JSTOR and Reuters, but this process allows vastly different approaches to, say, the acquisition of Chinese vernacular material or slices of electronic science material.

New strategic alliances will need to be formed. The Australian National University at the time of writing has become part of the Pacific Rim Digital Library Alliance (PRDLA), which includes major university libraries from USA, China, Japan, Korea, Singapore and Taiwan. Initial projects of PRDLA will focus on digitization of texts of Pacific exploration and Chinese serials access via the Internet.

CONCLUSION

Looking far into the future is a dangerous game and the analysis of the 'retrohistory' of librarianship is both a fascinating and a salutary one. This writer undertook one such retrospective and prospective view for cataloguing in the 1980s (Steele, 1985). Recently Professor Gregory Benford has updated Isaac Asimov's *Foundation* series. Some of Asimov's original technology background looks pretty woeful even by today's standards, let alone the far future, for example in terms of his inter-library loan delivery predictions. Lyman (1997) has succinctly envisaged some

possible future scenarios for libraries ranging from the

privatization of knowledge (the reader is conceived of as a consumer not a citizen) to new forms of cyberian communities. New 'public places' may well emerge in an information-rich society which have far wider dimensions than our present print environment allows.

REFERENCES

Anderson, G. (1997), Re-engineering the academic library. In *Towards a worldwide library: a ten year forecast*, edited by A. H. Helal and J. W. Weiss. Essen: Universitatsbibliothek, pp. 115–135.

Brin, D. (1991), *Earth*. New York: Bantam, pp. 284–5.

Castells, M. (1996), *The rise of the network society*. Oxford: Blackwell.

Dowler, L. ed. (1997), *Gateways to knowledge. The role of academic libraries in teaching, learning and research*. Cambridge: MIT Press.

Duranceau, E. (1997), Beyond print: revisioning serials acquisitions for the digital age. <http://web.mit.edu/waynej/www/duranceau.htm>.

Ferguson, C. D. and Burge, C. A. (1997), The shape of services to come: value-based reference services for the largely digital library. *College and research libraries*, May, p. 252.

Gates, W. (1997), Keynote address to Special Libraries Association quoted in *Advanced technology libraries*, July, pp. 1, 4–6.

Goldstein, P. (1997), *Copyright's highway: from Gutenberg to the celestial jukebox*. New York: Hill and Wang.

Gregg, J. (1997), There's one sure thing about paradigms – shift happens. *Educom review*, (July/Aug), p. 10.

Hirshon, A. and Winters, B. (1997), *Outsourcing library technical services*. New York: Neil Schuman.

Johanson, G., Schauder, D. and Lim, E. (1997), The virtual library and the humanities. *Australian humanities review*. <http://www.lib.latrobe.edu.au/AHR/>.

Lesk, M. (1997), Digital libraries: a unifying or distributing force? *Scholarly communication and technology*, Mellon Conference. Papers available at <http://arl.cni.org/scomm/scat/index.html>.

Lyman, P. (1996), What is a digital library? *Daedalus*, (December), pp. 1–33.

Lyman, P. (1997), The Midas crisis. *College and research library news*, July/August, pp. 467–469, 499.

Lynch, C. (1997), Reflections on our future. *Bulletin of the American Society for Information Science,* December 1996–January 1997, pp. 21–22.

Maloney, S. (1997), Computers in libraries 97: looking for quality. *College and research library news*, June, p. 408.

Manguel, A. (1997), How those plastic stones speak! *Times literary supplement*, 4 July, p. 8.

Matson, L. and Bonski, D. (1997), Do digital libraries need librarians? An experiential dialog. *Online*, (November). <http://www.onlineinc.com/onlinemag/NovOL97/matson11.html>.

McLean, N. (1997), Global access to scholarly information: the quest for sustainable solutions (available from mclean@library.mq.edu.au).

Mowat, I. (1997), Back to the future: a history of serials 1997–2017. *Serials*, vol. 10, no. 2, p. 155.

Odlyzko, A. (1997), The slow evolution of electronic publishing (available from amo@research.alt.com).

Okerson, A. (1996), Some economic challenges in building electronic libraries. Paper presented to the *1996 IFLA Conference, Acquisitions and Collections Development Sector* <http:www.library.yale.edu/~okerson/alo.html>.

Steele, C. (1985), Managing cataloguers without catalogues or catalogues without cataloguers: a view from the twenty-first century. In *Cataloguing Australia*, December, pp. 102–114.

Steele, C. (1997), Digital dilemmas. In *Information technology – the enabler. CAUSE in Australasia 97. Proceedings.* Melbourne: CAUSE. p. 469.

Tapscott, D. (1997), *The rise of the net generation – growing up digital.* NY: McGraw Hill. p. 256.

Turkle, S. (1995), *Life on the screen: identity in the age of the Internet.* New York: Simon and Schuster.

Directory of organizations

American Library Association
50 East Huron Street
Chicago, IL 60611, USA

+1 312 944 6780
http://www.ala.org

American Society for Information Science
8720 Georgia Avenue, Suite 501
Silver Springs, MD 20910, USA

+1 202 4621000
+1 202 4627494 Fax
http://www.asis.org

ASLIB (The Association for Information Management)
Staple Hall
Stone House Court
London EC3A 7PB, UK

+44 171 903 0000
+44 171 903 0011 Fax
http://www.aslib.co.uk

Association of British Chambers of Commerce
212a Shaftesbury Avenue
London WC2H 8EW
UK

+44 171 240 5831/6

Association of London Chief Librarians (ALCL)

http://www.croydon.gov.uk/cr-alcl.htm

Australian Council of Libraries and Information Services (ACLIS)
c/o National Library of Australia
Canberra
ACT 2600
Australia

Australian Library and Information Association (ALIA)
P O Box E441
Queen Victoria Terrace
ACT 2600
Australia

BAILER (British Association for Information and Library Education
and Research)
CIS,
Queen Margaret College
Clerwood Terrace
Edinburgh EH12 8TS
UK

+44 131 317 3511
+44 131 316 4165 Fax
bruce.thomson@mail.qmced.ac.uk
http://epip.lut.ac.uk:80/bailer/directry.htm

BIDS (Bath Information and Data Services)
University of Bath
Claverton Down
Bath BA2 7AY, UK

+44 1225 826215
+44 1225 826176 Fax
http://www.bids.ac.uk

Book Industry Communication (BIC)
39/41 North Road
London N7 9DP, UK

+44 171 607 0021
+44 171 607 0415 Fax

British Association of Picture Libraries and Agencies (BAPLA)
13 Woodberry Crescent
London N10 1PJ, UK

+44 181 444 7913
+44 181 883 9215 Fax

British Computer Society
Anacomp Ltd
New Lodge Drift Road
Windsor
Berks SL4 4PQ, UK

http://www.bcs.org.uk

British Library:
St. Pancras
96 Euston Road
London NW1 2DB, UK

+44 171 412 7111
+44 171 412 7268 Fax
http://www.bl.uk

The British Library PORTICO information service is at:
http://portico.bl.uk

Document Supply Centre
Boston Spa
Wetherby
West Yorkshire LS23 7BQ

+44 1937 546000
+44 1937 546333 Fax

National Bibliographic Service
Boston Spa
Wetherby
West Yorkshire LS23 7BQ

+44 1937 546251
+44 1937 546586 Fax

Research and Innovation Centre
2 Sheraton Street
London W1V 4BH

+44 171 323 7060
+44 171 323 7251 Fax

Science Reference and Information Service
25 Southampton Buildings
London WC2A 1AW

+44 171 323 7494/7496
+44 171 323 7495 Fax

British Records Association
The Charterhouse
London EC1M 6AE
UK

+44 171 253 0436

British Standards Institution
389 Chiswick High Road
London W4 4AL
UK

+44 171 629 9000

BUBL Information Service
Anderson Library
Strathclyde University
101 St. James Road
Glasgow G4 0NS
UK

+44 141 548 4752
http://www.bubl.ac.uk

Business Archives Council
185 Tower Bridge Street
London SE1 2UF
UK

+44 171 407 6110

Business Link National Site

http://www.businesslink.co.uk

Canadian Library Association
200 Elgin Street, Suite 602
Ottawa
Ontario K2P 1L5
Canada

+1 613 2329625
+1 613 5639895 Fax

CAUSE
The Association for Managing and Using Information Resources in
Higher Education
4840 Pearl East Circle, Suite 302E
Boulder
CO 80301-6114, USA

+1 303 4494430
+1 303 440 0461 Fax
info@cause.org
http://www.cause.org

CD-ROM Standards and Practices Action Group (CD-ROM SPAG)

See now: Electronic Information Publishers Action Group

Charter Mark Office
Cabinet Office
Horse Guards Road
London SW1P 3AL, UK

+44 171 270 6343

CHEST (Combined Higher Education Software Team)
University of Bath
Claverton Down
Bath BA2 7AY, UK

http://www.chest.ac.uk

CIMTECH – Centre for Information Management Technology
University of Hertfordshire
College Lane
Hatfield AL10 9AB, UK

+44 1707 279691
+44 1707 272121 Fax
c.cimtech@herts.ac.uk

Coalition for Networked Information
157 New Hampshire Avenue, N.W.
Washington, D.C. 20036
USA

+1 202 232 2466
+1 202 462 7849 Fax
http://www.cni.org

Commission of the European Communities (CEC)
rue de la Loi 200
B-1049 Brussels
Belgium

ESPRIT (Directorate-General XIII-A)

+32 2 236 8003
+32 2 236 8597 Fax
http://www.cordis.lu/esprit/src

Information Society Project Office

+32 2 296 9206
+32 2 299 4170 Fax
http://www.ispo.cec.be

Commission of the European Communities (CEC)
Bâtiment Jean Monnet
Plateau du Kirchberg
L-2920 Luxembourg

CORDIS (EU R&D Information Service)

+352 4410 122240
+352 4410 122248 Fax
http://www.cordis.lu

INFO2000

http://www2.echo.lu/info2000

Libraries Programme (Directorate-General XIII-B)

+352 4301 2923
+352 4301 3535 Fax

Telematics Applications Programme

http://www.echo.lu/libraries/en/libraries.html

Commission on Preservation and Access
1400 16th Street NW, Suite 740
Washington, DC 20036-2217, USA

+1 202 939 3400
+1 202 939 3407 Fax

Consortium of Research Libraries (CURL)
Clare Jenkins, Executive Secretary
BLPES
10 Portugal Street
London WC2A 2HD, UK

+44 171 955 6314
+44 171 955 7454 fax
c.jenkins@lse.ac.uk
http://www.curl.ac.uk

Copyright Clearance Center (CCC)
222 Rosewood Drive, suite 910
Danvers
MA 01923, USA

Copyright Licensing Agency (CLA)
90 Tottenham Court Road
London W1P 9HE, UK

+44 171 437 5931
+44 171 436 3986

Council on Library Resources
1785 Massachusetts Avenue N.W.
Suite 313
Washington D.C. 20036-2117
USA

+1 202 483 7474
+1 202 483 6410 Fax

Data Protection Registry
Wycliffe House
Water Lane
Wilmslow SK9 5AF, UK

+44 1625 545700
http://www.open.gov.uk/dpr/dprhome.htm

Department of Culture, Media and Sport
Libraries and Information Division
2–4 Cockspur Street
London SW1Y 5DH, UK
+44 171 211 6000
+44 171 211 6210 Fax

Directory Publishers Association
93a Blenheim Crescent
London W11 2EQ
UK

+44 171 221 9089

ECHO (European Community Host Organization)
BP 2373
L-1023 Luxembourg

+352 3498 1200
+352 3498 1234 Fax
http://www.echo.lu

Electronic Commerce Association
Alexander House
High Street
Inkberrow
Worcester WR7 4DT
UK

+44 1386 793028
+44 1386 732268
http://www.ec-europe.de

Electronic Information Distributors Association (EIDA)
OCD, 33 rue Linne
Paris
75005 France

+33 1 44 08 78 30
+33 1 44 08 78 39 Fax
http://www.eida.ocd.fr

Electronic Information Publishers Action Group (eIP)
c/o EPS
104 St John Street
London EC1M 4EH
UK

+44 171 837 8901
emma@epsltd.demon.co.uk

European Bureau of Library, Information and Documentation
Associations (EBLIDA)
P O Box 93054
2509 AB The Hague
Netherlands

+31 70 3141780
+31 70 3141575 Fax

European Commission on Preservation and Access
Trippenhuis
Kloveniersburgwal 29
PO Box 19121
1000 GC Amsterdam, Netherlands

+31 20 5510 839
+31 20 6204 941 Fax
http://www.library.knaw.nl/epic/ecpatex/welcome.htm

European Foundation for Library Cooperation (EFLC)
BP 237
B-1040 Brussels, Belgium

+32 2 731 4772

European Information Industry Association (EIIA)
BP 262
L-2012 Luxembourg

+352 3498 1420
+352 3498 1234 Fax

European Information Researchers Network (EIRENE)
Instant Library Ltd
22 Frederick Street
Loughborough LG11 3BJ, UK

+44 1509 268292
+44 1509 232748
http://www.eirene.com

EUSIDIC (European Association of Information Services)
104b St John Street
London EC1M 4EH, UK

+44 171 336 7098
+44 171 336 7093 Fax
http://www.eusidic.org

FID (Fédération Internationale d'Information et de Documentation)
P O Box 90402
2509 LK The Hague
Netherlands

+31 70 3140671
+31 70 3140667 Fax

Group on Electronic Document Interchange (GEDI)
S. Koopman
PICA
P O Box 876
2300 AW Leiden
Netherlands

+31 71 257257
+31 71 223119 Fax

Institute of Information Scientists
44–45 Museum Street
London WC1A 1LY
UK

+44 171 831 8003
+44 171 430 1270 Fax
http://www.iis.org.uk

Institute of Management
Cottingham Road
Corby NN17 1TT, UK

+44 1536 204222

Institute of Personnel and Development
Camp Road
London SW19 4UX, UK

+44 181 263 3237

International Federation of Library Associations and Institutions
P O Box 95 312
2509 The Hague
Netherlands

+31 70 3140884
+31 70 3834827 Fax

International Forum on Open Bibliographic Systems (IFOBS)
National Library of Canada
395 Wellington Street
Ottawa
Ontario K1A 0N4
Canada

+1 819 994 6830
+1 819 994 6835 Fax

International Information Management Congress (IMC)
1650 38th Street Suite 205W
Boulder
CO 80301
USA

+1 303 440 7085
+1 303 440 7234 Fax

International Telecommunications Union (ITU)
Place des Nations
CH-1211 Geneva 20
Switzerland

+41 22 730 5111
+41 22 733 7256 Fax
http://www.itu.int

Internet Society

+1 703 648 9888
http://www.isoc.org

Investors in People UK
4th floor
7–10 Chandos Street
London W1M 9DE, UK

+44 171 467 1900

JANET User Group for Libraries (JUGL)
http://www.bubl.ac.uk/org/jugl/

Joint Information Systems Committee (JISC)
Northaven House
Coldharbour Lane
Bristol BS16 1QD, UK

+44 117 931 7403
+44 117 931 7255 Fax
jisc@jisc.ac.uk
http://www.jisc.ac.uk

LASER
Gun Court
70 Wapping Lane
London E1 9RL
UK

+44 171 702 2020
+44 171 702 2019 Fax
http://www.viscount.org.uk/laser

Library Association
7 Ridgmount Street
London WC1E 7AE, UK

+44 171 636 7543
+44 171 436 7218 Fax
http://www.la.hq.org.uk

Library and Information Commission
2 Sheraton Street
London W1V 4BH, UK

http://lirn.viscount.org.uk/earl/orgs/lic.htm

Library and Information Statistics Unit
Loughborough University
Loughborough
Leicestershire LE11 3TU, UK

+44 1509 22307
+44 1509 223053 Fax

Library Information Technology Centre
South Bank Technopark
90 London Road
London SE1 6LN, UK

+44 171 815 7872
+44 171 815 6699 Fax
http://www.sbu.ac.uk:80/~litc

LINC (Library and Information Cooperation Council)
Hampshire County Libraries
81 North Walls
Winchester SO23 8BY, UK

+44 1962 846109
LIBSPT@hants.gov.uk

LIRG (Library and Information Research Group)
Library
Goldsmiths College
New Cross
London SE14 6NW
UK

+44 181 692 7171 x2172
+44 181 692 9190 Fax

MIDAS-NET (Multimedia Information, Demonstration and Support Network)

+44 181 977 7670
+44 181 943 3377 Fax
URL: http://www2.echo.lu/info2000/midas/home.html

National Preservation Office
See British Library

+44 171 412 7725
vanessa.marshall@bl.uk

National Training Awards
Room W825
Moorfoot
Sheffield S1 4PQ
UK

+44 114 259 3419

New Zealand Library Association
20 Brandon Street
P O Box 12-1212
Wellington 1
New Zealand

+64 4 735834

NFAIS (National Federation of Abstracting and Indexing Services)
1429 Walnut Street
Philadelphia
PA 19102
USA

+1 215 563 2406
http://www.pa.tulsa.edu/nfais.html

NISS (National Information Services and Systems)
University of Bath
Claverton Down
Bath BA2 7AY
UK

+44 1225 826063
+44 1225 826177 Fax
niss@niss.ac.uk
http://www.niss.ac.uk

NTIS (National Technical Information Service)
5285 Port Royal Road
Springfield VA 22161
USA

+1 703 487 4650
+1 703 487 4134 Fax
http://www.ntis.gov

Project EARL
Gun Court
70 Wapping Lane
London E1 9RL
UK

http://www.earl.org.uk

Publishers' Association (UK)
19 Bedford Square
London WC1B 3HJ, UK

+44 171 580 6321
+44 171 636 5375 Fax

Records Management Society
6 Sheraton Drive
High Wycombe
Bucks HP13 6DE, UK

+44 1494 525040
+44 1494 465488 Fax

Research Libraries Group, Inc.
1200 Villa Street
Mountain View
CA 94041-1100, USA

+1 415 962 9951
+1 415 964 0943 Fax
http://www.rlg.org

SCONUL (Standing Conference on National and University Libraries)
102 Euston Road
London NW1 2HA, UK
+44 171 387 0317
+44 171 383 3197 Fax

Scottish Library and Information Council (SLIC)
74 Victoria Crescent Road
Glasgow G12 9JN, UK

+44 141 357 5004
+44 141 357 5006 Fax
http://www.almac.co.uk/business_park/slainte/index.html

Special Libraries Association
1700 18th Street NW
Washington DC 20009-2508
USA

+1 202 234 4700
+1 202 265 9317 Fax
http://www.sla.org

UK Coalition for Public Information
c/o Institute of Information Scientists [See above]

UK Internet User Group
Informed Business Services
41–47 Old Street
London EC1V 9HX, UK

+44 171 608 0608
+44 171 282 1999 Fax
http://www.ukiug.org

UK Office for Library and Information Networking (UKOLN)
University of Bath
Bath BA2 7AY
UK

+44 1225 826580
+44 1225 826229 Fax
http://ukoln.bath.ac.uk

UK Online User Group (UKOLUG)
The Old Chapel
Walden
West Burton
Leyburn DL8 4LE, UK

+44 1969 663749 tel/fax
http://www.ukolug.demon.co.uk

UK Serials Group
114 Woodstock Road
Witney
Oxford OX8 6DY
UK

+44 1993 703446
+44 1993 778879 Fax

UNESCO
7 Place de Fontenoy
75700 Paris
France

+33 1 45 68 45 00
+33 1 43 06 16 40 Fax

United Kingdom Education and Research Networking Association
(UKERNA)
c/o Rutherford Appleton Laboratory
Building R31
Chilton, Didcot
Oxford OX11 0QX
UK

+44 1235 445724
+44 1235 446251 Fax

World Intellectual Property Organisation (WIPO)
34 chemin des Colombettes
CH-1211 Geneva 20
Switzerland

Glossary

Added value. Extra features added to raw data to make it more appealing to the customer; also subtracted features, for example data with duplicates removed.

Agents. Software programs that can be customized by the user to perform specific tasks; most commonly, to retrieve certain types of information.

Alpha test. The first round of testing operations for new software.

ANR. Access to Networked Resources, a programme line of eLib with particular interest in the issues surrounding the creation of subject gateways to networked resources.

Applet. A small Java program that can be included on a Web page. When the page is viewed via a Java-compatible browser, the applet's code is transferred to the user's system and the program is run. Used to enhance Web pages with special effects or greater interactivity.

Architecture. The physical design and construction of a computer.

Artificial intelligence. A system which models or mimics aspects of human intelligence. The concept is embodied in hardware and software to make them more intuitive to the user.

ASCII. American Standard Code for Information Interchange. Created in 1968, this was for many years the standard code for transferring data between different software products.

Backup. Copying data from a file into another location for security purposes; for example copying files from a PC onto a floppy disk.

Bandwidth. The amount of information (measured in bits per second) that can be carried by a network.

Beta test. Testing software by releasing it to a small, selected group of users to reveal problems that were not apparent to developers.

Bits. The smallest unit into which data can be broken up and shipped around a computer. Measures such as 16-bit and 32-bit state how many bits are moved at one time: the higher the number, the more bits are moved and the faster the operation is performed.

Bps. Bits per second – the speed at which the data is transmitted in a network.

Broadband. A network with the capacity to transmit high volumes of information at high speed.

Browser. Software needed to retrieve text, images and other media from the World Wide Web.

BUBL. Bulletin Board for Libraries; an important network gateway for the library and information community.

Bugs. Faults in software which prevent it functioning properly.

Byte. Digitally, the space taken up on a computer by one letter or character; formed of eight 'bits'. A kilobyte is 1,000 bytes; a megabyte is 1,000,000 bytes; a gigabyte is a thousand million bytes.

CD drive. Peripheral used for playing CD-ROMs.

CD-ROM. Compact Disk-Read Only Memory. A storage device, identical in appearance to a music CD, but containing text, graphics, sound, video, or a mixture of these. The standard capacity is currently 650Mb, but larger capacities are in development. The current standard is sufficient to store 700,000 A4 pages of text.

CGI. Common Gateway Interface: the programming that makes it possible for users to interact with World Wide Web pages; for example, searching databases and retrieving specific information.

Client. Computer used to view the results of another computer's work. See also Server.

Client/server. See Client, Server.

Clump. An aggregation of catalogues, a term introduced in the UK at the 3rd MODELS Workshop in 1996. The clump may be 'physical' – in traditional terminology a union catalogue – or it may be 'virtual', being created at the time of searching from, for example, the catalogues of libraries having related subject collections, being in the same geographical area, or serving similar types of user.

Configuration. The way in which a computer or network is set up to operate. When successful, the system is referred to as being correctly configured. Correct configuration can be a time-consuming and frustrating business, but worth the effort in terms of increased efficiency and speed of the system.

Conflict. Disparities that may occur between different software packages, especially when they have been designed by different companies. The effect will be to prevent the computer operating properly, and may cause it to fail completely.

Conservation. Specific treatments and techniques applied in protecting library and archive materials from deterioration, and which involve intervention with the objects themselves.

Cookie. File left by some browsers on the hard disk of the user's computer after a visit to a Web site; the next time the site is visited, the owners already have user identification data.

CWIS. Campus Wide Information Service/System; co-ordinated network for general purpose use, usually in an academic context.

Cyberspace. 'Where a telephone conversation takes place.' Imaginary environment inside a computer or computer network in which things appear to happen.

Data warehouse. A complete historical database of an organization's business; costly and complex to create and maintain.

Database. A file of retrievable information, stored electronically.

Deacidification. General term for a variety of processes which remove or neutralize the acid present in paper documents. *391*

Digital library. Expression for a library or information service based on the electronic storage, handling, and transmission of information, and network access for users.

Digital Object Identifier (DOI). Internet-based technology which is set to become part of the infrastructure of electronic publishing; a unique number is assigned to specific published content, and such numbers are used by automated mechanisms to manage integrity, authenticity, and copyright. The system will cover books, journals, audio, video and software.

Digitization. Conversion into an electronic format which can be easily compressed and transmitted at high speed internationally using fibre optic cable and satellite systems.

Distributed environment. Networked computing system in which processing is carried out at various locations, not at a central hub.

Dublin Core. Fully, the Dublin Core Metadata Element Set, thirteen (latterly fifteen) metadata elements agreed at the 1995 Online Computer Library Center (OCLC) and National Center for Supercomputing Applications (NCSA) Metadata Workshop as key descriptors for networked resources.

Dumb terminal. A computer terminal which cannot operate unless it is connected to a server; it operates by using software stored on the network server.

DVD. Digital Versatile (or Video) Disc. Next step up from CD-ROM: a disc played in much the same manner, but holding over 4 gigabytes of data.

EDI. Electronic Data Interchange. The exchange of commercial information in digital form, for example between supplier and customer, without human intervention.

E-journals. Journals published in an electronic format; they may be delivered over a network or as a physical object, for example a CD-ROM.

E-mail. Electronic mail , a system of sending messages between computers, whether in-house or via the Internet.

Electronic commerce. Similar to EDI, but covering additionally processes such as ordering, invoicing, electronic cash payments over the Internet.

Electronic copyright.   The application of the copyright process to content published in electronic formats.

Electronic library.   A library or information service that uses electronic methods for the storage, handling, and transmission of information, and which provides network access to users.

Electronic publishing.   The publication and dissemination of information by electronic means.

eLib.   The Electronic Libraries Programme of UK Higher Education, established by JISC with a budget of £15 million over 3 years to fund projects in a variety of programme areas. The main aim of the eLib programme, through its projects, is to engage the Higher Education community in developing and shaping the implementation of the electronic library.

Encryption.   Means of encoding messages and data files to prevent unauthorized access to them.

End-user.   The individual who actually uses an electronic service or item of software.

Extranet.   Business-to-business links using Internet technology; an extension of the intranet, but with various controls on access to protect sensitive areas of the network.

FAQ.   Frequently Asked Questions. Describes points brought together in a document on the Internet to avoid repetition, for example in the activity of a newsgroup.

Fax/modem.   Peripheral giving access to telecommunications network. It can be used to send faxes to remote fax machines, or to other computers, and also to access the Internet and other online hosts using the correct software.

FIGIT.   Follett Implementation Group on Information Technology whose projects were then badged under the eLib name; follow-up to the Follett Report.

File.   Sections of storage into which data held on a computer is divided. In use, this mimics compartments in a filing cabinet.

Firewall.   Security software designed to prevent unauthorized access to computer systems.

Flaming.   Public criticism on the Internet of a user thought to have behaved in an unacceptable manner by sending junk e-mail.

Follett Report. The (UK) *Joint Funding Councils' Libraries Review Group Report* [chaired by Sir Brian Follett] which in 1993 made far-reaching recommendations on the electronic future of academic libraries.

Freeze drying. A method of drying paper documents damaged by water; materials are held in a vacuum at a temperature below freezing point, and as the temperature is raised the ice changes to vapour without passing through a liquid stage.

FTP. File Transfer Protocol: a method of copying files from or to a remote computer.

Fuzzy logic. Component of artificial intelligence; computers think in extremes – yes/no, black/white, hot/cold – fuzzy logic tells them that warm is between hot and cold.

Gatekeeper. One role of a publisher may be interpreted as determining whether or not a work is 'worth' publishing.

Gateway. A site or system of which the primary function is to provide access to other sites or systems.

Gigabyte. See Byte

Groupware. Software used on a LAN to enable teams or entire offices to communicate with each other and work on the same documents concurrently. Lotus Notes is a major example of groupware, and widely used. It also enables the setting up of information services such as tailored news services – a feed from an online host distributed automatically around the LAN.

GUI. Graphical User Interface; giving instructions to a computer by manipulating images on the screen rather than typing in text.

Hacker. Unauthorized user who tries to get into computer files by illegal means.

Hits. When searching a database, the number of instances that match the search criteria. In World Wide Web terms, the number of times a server is asked for information. Often erroneously used to describe the number of visitors to a Web site: however, one visit to a Web page with 10 graphics on it will be recorded as 10 hits, since the server will be asked for 10 different things.

Home page. The first page of a Web site which introduces an organization to the searcher or provides information about the extent of non-corporate pages.

Hot links. Cross reference facility that allows the searcher to jump between Web pages by pointing and clicking on specific words, often underlined and in a different colour from the rest of the text. Using HTML allows the author of the pages to insert hot links.

HTML. Hypertext Mark-up Language – the means used to write Web pages.

HTTP. HyperText Transfer Protocol: the underlying protocol that makes the World Wide Web work by governing the transfer of text and graphics.

Icon. An on-screen symbol indicating instructions or access points to programs or data.

Information management (IM). The acquisition, storage, organization, management, effective use, and communication of the information and knowledge resources of an organization, in support of corporate goals or institutional principles.

Information provider. The individual or organization responsible for preparing the information content of a database, directory, or other source item.

Information society. The concept that all aspects of life are becoming dependent on electronic access to information; there are social, economic and political considerations, as well as technological concerns.

Intelligent agent. An Internet utility that learns from a user's responses with the intention of providing more focused search results.

Interactivity. The two-way exchange of data and information between computer and user.

Internet. The global network, currently estimated to have fifty million users, which links computers to each other all over the world.

Intranet. An in-house network which uses web browsers originally developed for the Internet in order to allow easy searching and access by users.

Intuitive searching. Retrieving information from databases using menus or plain English as opposed to Boolean logic or other less flexible means.

IP address. Physical address of a file on the Internet; what a URL refers to.

ISDN. Integrated Services Digital Network; like a normal telephone line but using digital signals with a transmission speed roughly five times faster than a standard telephone line.

ISP. Internet Service Provider. See Internet, Service provider.

JANET. Joint Academic NETwork – one of the earliest forms of the Internet, limited still to the UK academic community, but now also linked to the Internet itself. It was originally set up as a means of communicating research between academics. SuperJANET is a high speed broadband version of the network.

Java. A programming language developed by Sun Microsystems that makes the World Wide Web more interactive, adding animation, scrolling messages, sounds. See also Applet.

JISC. Joint Information Systems Committee. Funded by the Scottish Higher Education Funding Council, the Higher Education Funding Council for England, the Higher Education Funding Council for Wales and the Department of Education Northern Ireland, the mission of the JISC is 'to stimulate and enable the cost effective exploitation of information systems and to provide a high quality national network infrastructure for the UK higher education and research councils communities'.

JPEG. Image encoding format developed by the Joint Photographic Experts Group, also known as JPG; one of the *de facto* image standards for the World Wide Web.

Jukebox. Several CD-drives stacked and connected together. Some jukeboxes may have up to fifty different drives, capable of being accessed by many people at the same time via a network.

Kilobyte. See Byte

Knowledge management. Building on to Information Management, to provide an active record of all organizational data, processes, and personnel knowledge so that these can be shared by all in the organization to achieve greater efficiency.

Legacy systems. Software application programs that have been in use for a long time, and have become technologically outdated. They can be difficult to merge into more recent programs, and expensive to replace.

Local Area Network (LAN). A network operating within a restricted geographical area.

Megabyte. See Byte

Metadata. Data describing a resource, or data about data; a MARC record is metadata, describing a book or other item through pre-defined elements or attributes. The expansion of electronic resources on the Internet has necessitated a consideration of metadata to assist in resource discovery and one method suggested is Dublin Core.

Metropolitan Area Network (MAN). Extension of a LAN to cover a wider range of providers and users in a community area; implies that public access should be available in addition to institutional or corporate use.

MIA. MODELS Information Architecture, a proposal arising from the sixth MODELS Workshop in 1998 for a software broker that uses Z39.50 to provide large-scale access to distributed information resources: catalogues; clumps; CD-ROMs; electronic documents; Web indexes and gateways.

MODELS. MOving to Distributed Environments for Library Services, a UKOLN initiative supported by the Electronic Libraries Programme and the British Library Research and Innovation Centre and motivated by the recognized need to develop an applications framework to manage the rapidly multiplying range of distributed heterogeneous information resources and services being offered to libraries and their users; a number of MODELS Workshops have been organized to discuss these issues with leading players.

Modem. The telecoms connection between a PC and the Internet Service Provider. A modem may be internal (a card which slots inside the PC) or external (a box that sits on top of it.) Normal telephone leads and jackpoints are used to effect the physical connection.

Multicasting. A developing Internet system by which the same information is delivered to many users simultaneously, thus speeding data access.

Multimedia. The use of multiple forms of media in one product; for example the combination of text with sound and video. *397*

Navigation.   Finding one's way around the World Wide Web which can include using hot links or search engines.

Network.   Linking computers together, thus enabling the sending of files and e-mail between them. See also Extranet, Internet, Intranet, Local Area Network, Metropolitan Area Network, Wide Area Network.

Network computer.   A screen-and-keyboard combination which is connected across the Internet to a larger computer where all the applications are installed. See also Thin client.

Newsgroups.   Discussion groups operating on the Internet.

NEWSPLAN.   UK-based programme seeking to preserve local newspapers held in libraries and archives throughout the country.

Objects.   Modular software units which contain data; they model real-life entities such as 'customer' or 'account' and relate to each other as their real-life prototypes would do. Useful and cost saving in construction of an information system to model a commercial organization, as they can be re-used and can be related in new ways without extensive programming.

On-demand publishing.   Publishing system based on electronic archives; produces materials and documents as and when they are required by users.

Online host.   Organization providing access to databases licensed from other providers; typically, the user is given a user ID and a password in exchange for paying a subscription or a time-based fee.

OPAC.   Online Public Access Catalogue.

Open systems.   Computers which conform to recognized international standards, allowing different types of hardware and software to work together.

Optical fibre cable.   Thin strands of glass or other transparent material manufactured into high-capacity cable for carrying data via light beams.

Outsourcing.   Using an outside agency to provide services previously provided in-house.

Password.   A security method requiring a user to enter a confidential code to gain access to a computer or file.

Pay-as-you-go. Method of charging for use by an online host; charges are usually per minute, with a minimum quarterly or monthly amount payable.

PC. Personal Computer; originally this referred to the IBM machine only, but it has now become common usage to mean any small desktop computer.

Peripheral. Any piece of hardware which can be added on to a computer, such as CD drives, fax/modems and modems, scanners, and printers.

Piracy. Unauthorized copying and/or resale of products.

Platform. A computer hardware system, usually including the operating system.

Posting. Sending a message to a public online area.

Preservation. The managerial and financial considerations involved in ensuring the long-term physical safety of library and archive materials and their information content.

Protection. See Security.

Protocol. An agreed way of doing things; protocols are important for the Internet as two computers cannot communicate until they have established an agreed method by which to do so.

Push. A solution to the problem of information overload; rather than the user searching the whole of the Internet or World Wide Web, news and other information that might be of interest are fed – or pushed – to the user.

Query by image content (QBIC). Strategy for retrieval from a database of visual images; interrogation is based on content features such as colour, shape and size.

RAM. Random Access Memory; the computer memory facility in which stored data can be accessed at any point without delay, regardless of position.

Real time. Telecommunications link taking place 'live'.

Relative humidity. The percentage of the quantity of water in a volume of air, in relation to the maximum quantity it can hold at a given temperature.

ROADS. An eLib ANR project which created generic, highly configurable 'toolkit' software from which subject-based Internet directory services can be readily constructed.

Robot.   Software that traverses the World Wide Web following links between pages and copying relevant information to create indexes searchable via Internet search engines.

Scanner.   Computer peripheral used to copy a document or graphic into a computer system.

Search engine.   Either software produced by a CD-ROM publisher which searches their disc, or a World Wide Web browser that searches for information on requested topics.

Security.   Systems of protection that prevent unauthorized access to a network or to specific files.

Server.   A computer which performs a specific function, such as running the software for a network; many client computers may be based around one server.

Service provider.   An organization that provides information and other services to subscribers, maybe online or via the Internet. Also known as Internet Service Provider.

SGML.   Standard Generalized Markup Language; defines the structure of a document, marking where each element (such as a new paragraph, different levels of heading) begins and ends. HTML is a subset of SGML.

Shareware.   Software protected by copyright but distributed for a minimal fee.

SMTP.   Simple Mail Transfer Protocol: the standard that defines the format of electronic mail messages for delivery over the Internet.

SOHO.   Small Office, Home Office – a typical teleworking environment. A SOHO person may be self-employed, or working for an organization.

Spam.   Unsolicited e-mail.

Stand-alone.   Computer which operates in isolation and is not attached to a network; it has its own software and operating system and does not share applications with other computers.

SuperJANET.   A high speed broadband network, part of JANET.

Surf.   The verb used by enthusiasts to describe the experience of navigating through the World Wide Web using a browser.

TCP/IP.   The protocol by which devices on the Internet communicate. Other higher level protocols such as HTTP, SMTP and FTP cannot operate unless a lower level of TCP/IP connection has first been established.

Teleconferencing.   Networked collaboration between colleagues accessing a central database and communicating in real time using text messages, voice and video. Users may share a joint view of a piece of work on screen.

Teleworking.   Working from home – rather than commuting to an office – using phone, fax, e-mail and other telecommunications links. Cost and time saving to employee and employer, but social isolation is seen as a disadvantage.

Tendering.   The competitive process of contracting out services; potential suppliers make bids (tenders) in competition with others to provide services.

Thin client.   An extension of the client/server principle as applied to network computers. Operating system, data and applications are kept on the server: the client is reduced to being nothing but a screen and a keyboard for interaction with the system.

Tiff.   Tagged Image File Format: one of the industry standards for image file formats, especially useful for high-resolution images as it can store literally millions of colours.

UNIverse.   Project funded for 30 months from October 1996 by the European Commission under the Telematics for Libraries 4th Framework Programme to create a pan-European virtual union catalogue of 50 libraries using Z39.50 technology.

URC.   Uniform Resource Characteristics; additional information beyond name and location which describes a digital object; examples might be ownership of intellectual property rights, or cost.

URL.   Uniform Resource Locator; the address of a Web site.

URN.   Uniform Resource Name; a name applied uniquely and permanently to a distinct object and designating it independently of its particular location on the World Wide Web.

Usenet.   Large network of public discussion groups on the Internet.

Vacuum drying.   Method of drying paper materials damaged by water, by placing them in a vacuum at a temperature above freezing; the water evaporates.

401

VAN. Value Added Network. The services of a network provider who does not simply carry messages but adds extra services such as payment facilities or other EDI features.

Verification. The process of checking authenticity, maybe of a user password to a network.

Video conferencing. Holding conferences and meetings between people on separate sites using special video equipment attached to computers with modems. The facility is still relatively new and not yet completely reliable, but has great potential.

Virtual libraries. Provision to users of library and information services by electronic means; if all items can be stored and delivered over a network, then the actual physical library is unnecessary, though this is unlikely to happen for some time.

Virtual Reality. Method of simulating a three-dimensional environment on a computer screen. Generally possible to 'walk' around it and manipulate 'objects'. Can be used for training, or for planning new buildings, or as a means of interfacing with the computer.

Virus. Computer programs that have the ability to replicate and infect other programs; they vary in the amount of damage they can cause.

Voice mail. Storage of voice messages for retrieval by the addressee; similar to e-mail, as the messages are stored digitally and only reconstituted when the addressee accesses the system to collect mail.

VRML. Virtual Reality Modelling Language: a language that brings together virtual reality and the World Wide Web by enabling virtual reality environments to be linked together in the same way as Web pages.

Web browser. Software which allows the user to search the World Wide Web and to display the results.

Web page. A single document on the World Wide Web.

Web site. A collection of Web pages about a particular organization, group or individual.

Webmaster. Controller of a site or a collection of pages on the World Wide Web.

402 **Webpac.** An OPAC accessed via a Web browser.

Wide area network (WAN). A network that operates over a geographically dispersed area – maybe internationally.

World Wide Web (WWW). Vast and rapidly growing collection of documents and media materials available via the Internet characterized by its use of hypertext links and accessibility across platforms.

Z39.50. Standard for the request and transmission of bibliographic and related data; as a retrieval protocol it allows client applications to query databases on remote servers, to retrieve results, and to carry out some other retrieval-related functions.

Index

Gower Handbook of Internal Communication

Edited by Eileen Scholes

Employee commitment can mean the difference between success and disaster. So internal communication is now a key issue for senior management. This *Gower Handbook* recognises IC's emergence as a new management discipline. It is aimed both at the generalist manager who needs to come to terms with the theoretical and technical aspects of internal communication, and the media specialist now seeking wider management skills and perspectives.

Early chapters examine changes in IC's strategic context. These include organizations' increasing need for innovation and flexibility; the disappearance of 'loyalty' among employees; growing recognition of the importance of corporate 'brand' and how to sustain it; and the effects on traditional work and management patterns of new computer networks. Step-by-step guides introduce the reader to creating IC strategies and to carrying out research and measurement. Over 45 communication techniques, from team meetings to web sites, are evaluated for use in differing circumstances. The *Handbook* also looks at how to set about developing good communicators; and finally presents 16 practical case studies in key application areas. Organizations featured are all leaders in their field, among them Andersen Consulting, The Body Shop, BP Chemicals, IBM, The Boots Company, Glaxo Operations, Rover, SmithKline Beecham, WH Smith and Unigate Dairies.

Eileen Scholes and her team have compiled what is probably the most comprehensive - and is certainly the most authoritative - guide available to the principles and practice of internal communication.

Gower

The Gower Handbook of Management

Fourth Edition

Edited by Dennis Lock

'If you have only one management book on your shelf, this must be the one.'

Dennis Lock recalls launching the first edition in 1983 with this aim in mind. It has remained the guiding principle behind subsequent editions, and today *The Gower Handbook of Management* is widely regarded as a manager's bible: an authoritative, gimmick-free and practical guide to best practice in management. By covering the broadest possible range of subjects, the book replicates in book form a forum in which managers can meet experts from a range of professional disciplines.

The new edition features:

- 65 expert contributors - many of them practising managers and all of them recognized authorities in their field
- many new contributors: over 1/3 are new to this edition
- 72 chapters, of which half are completely new
- 20 chapters on subjects new to this edition
- a brand new design and larger format.

The Gower Handbook of Management has received many plaudits during its distinguished career, summed up in the following review from *Director*:

'... packed with information which can be used either as a reference work on a specific problem or as a guide to an entire operation. In a short review one can touch only lightly on the richness and excellence of this book, which well deserves a place on any executive bookshelf'.

Gower

Gower Handbook of Management Skills

Third Edition

Edited by Dorothy M Stewart

'This is the book I wish I'd had in my desk drawer when I was first a manager. When you need the information, you'll find a chapter to help: no fancy models or useless theories. This is a practical book for real managers, aimed at helping you manage more effectively in the real world of business today. You'll find enough background information, but no overwhelming detail. This is material you can trust. It is tried and tested.'

So writes Dorothy Stewart, describing in the Preface the unifying theme behind the Third Edition of this bestselling *Handbook*. This puts at your disposal the expertise of 25 specialists, each a recognized authority in their particular field. Together, this adds up to an impressive 'one stop library' for the manager determined to make a mark.

Chapters are organized within three parts: Managing Yourself, Managing Other People, and Managing the Business. Part I deals with personal skills and includes chapters on self-development and information technology. Part II covers people skills such as listening, influencing and communication. Part III looks at finance, project management, decision-making, negotiating and creativity. A total of 12 chapters are completely new, and the rest have been rigorously updated to fully reflect the rapidly changing world in which we work.

Each chapter focuses on detailed practical guidance, and ends with a checklist of key points and suggestions for further reading.

Gower

Managing Information Services

An Integrated Approach

Jo Bryson

This comprehensive handbook covers key management issues and explains the principles which will guide information professionals through the maze of common problems. To reflect the increasing integration of library, information centre, records, Information Technology and telecommunications management, the book takes an integrated approach to managing the modern information centre where first class customer service, high productivity and focusing on competitive advantage are essential.

Managing Information Services is based on Jo Bryson's influential textbook *Effective Library and Information Centre Management*, which was always valued by professionals as well as students. It covers a full range of management topics, from strategic, technology and human resources planning, to leadership, change management, team building, and conflict and stress management. It also includes sections on:

- service delivery (quality control, client focus, outsourcing, performance measurement)
- risk management (business continuity, return on investment, information security)
- managing corporate information and communication, the information lifecycle.

Information managers who want to not just manage but get results and help their staff perform should keep this book by their side.

Gower